SHADOW AND SHELTER

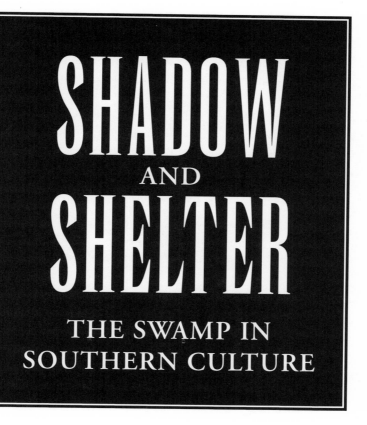

SHADOW
AND
SHELTER

THE SWAMP IN
SOUTHERN CULTURE

Anthony Wilson

UNIVERSITY PRESS OF MISSISSIPPI • JACKSON

www.upress.state.ms.us

The University Press of Mississippi is a member of
the Association of American University Presses.

Parts of the chapter "The Swamp in the Twentieth-Century South" have been previously
published as "The Music of God, Man, and Beast: Spirituality and Modernity in *Jonah's
Gourd Vine*," *Southern Literary Journal* 35.2 (Spring 2003): 64–78. Copyright © 2003 by the
Southern Literary Journal and the University of North Carolina at Chapel Hill Department
of English. Reprinted with permission.

First edition 2006

∞

Library of Congress Cataloging-in-Publication Data

Wilson, Anthony, 1975–
    Shadow and shelter : the swamp in southern culture / Anthony
Wilson.— 1st ed.
        p. cm.
    Includes bibliographical references and index.
    ISBN 1-57806-804-5 (cloth : alk. paper) 1. Southern States—Civilization.
2. Group identity—Southern States. 3. Swamps—Social aspects—Southern
States. 4. Swamps in literature. 5. Southern States—In literature.
6. American literature—Southern States—History and criticism.
7. Swamps—Southern States—History. 8. Swamp ecology—Southern
States. 9. Southern States—Environmental conditions. I. Title.
    F209.W55   2006
    975—dc22   2005011648

British Library Cataloging-in-Publication Data available

CONTENTS

Acknowledgments

VII

Introduction

IX

The Swamp and Antebellum Southern Identity

3

The Southern Swamp in the Civil War, Reconstruction, and Beyond

62

The Swamp in the Twentieth-Century South

104

The Swamp in the Postmodern South
Conservation, Simulation, and Commodification

163

Bibliography

194

Index

205

ACKNOWLEDGMENTS

This book would not have been possible without the patience, generosity, and assistance of many people. I thank Michael Kreyling, who has shepherded this project since the dissertation stage, and whose advice and encouragement led me into the swamp and helped me find my way out again. I thank Sam Girgus for his fresh perspective and expertise, Marcia Gaudet for her insight and her willingness to help above and beyond the call of duty, Mark Schoenfield, for his dedicated and perceptive readings and illuminating commentary, and Don Doyle for his help and support. I also thank Nancy Walker, a friend and mentor whose passing was a profound loss on so many levels. Thanks are also due to John Lowe, a good friend and true colleague, who advised me in the early stages and has encouraged me throughout the process, and to Seetha Srinivasan, director of the University Press of Mississippi, who recognized potential in this project in its very early stages, and who has been patient, supportive, and extraordinarily helpful throughout my association with her.

I could not have completed this project without the love, support, and patience of my family. I thank my long-suffering wife, Jeanette Wilson, who helped me in more ways than she can know. I thank my brother, Dr. Matthew Wilson, for his advice and support. I thank my mother, Dr. Mary Ann Wilson, a brilliant teacher and distinguished scholar who inspired and guided me, and who waded through more drafts and revisions of various chapters than she would probably care to remember. And I thank my father, the late Dr. James D. Wilson, who is in many ways responsible for who I am and what I do.

INTRODUCTION

This book considers constructions of varied Southern identities through the twin lenses of ecological and literary history, centering on a feature of the landscape that has been linked profoundly and uniquely to the American South—the swamp. The swamp occupies an intriguingly complex and liminal space in the Southern and national imaginations and signifies powerfully across discourses of race, cultural and literal contagion, ethnography, and ecology. The mercurial trace that the swamp registers on Southern intellectual history continually inscribes themes of purity and adulteration played out in an array of political, cultural, and psychological contexts. The central paradox that I explore here focuses on the interplay of contradictory but equally prevailing tropes: first, the trope of the swamp as the always present but always denied underside of the myth of pastoral Eden that defined the antebellum South and informs or colors general imaginative conceptions of the South even today; and second, the more recent figuration of the swamp as the last pure vestige of undominated but ever threatened Southern ecoculture, the last bulwark against Southern absorption into the undifferentiated and commodified mass of American culture. The Southern swamps have become shrinking havens for the vestiges of the very culture they once thwarted and frustrated. As the South comes to look more and more like the rest of America, colonized by the relentless progress of strip malls and suburban sprawl, Southern wooded wetlands have come to embody—for descendants of both the white mainstream culture that once sought to subjugate them and the subcultures that once lived among them—the last part of the South that will always be beyond cultural dominion, however illusory that understanding might be. This book maps the cultural shift that enabled this transition in understanding the Southern swamps—the move from a dominant narrative of "Southern identity" to a more pluralistic, less clearly essentializable understanding of Southernness.

Scholars of Southern culture have begun to isolate physical and culturally marked spaces within the formerly monolithic South. The recent Prentice Hall anthology edited by Edward Francisco, Robert Vaughan, and Linda Francisco, *The South in Perspective* (2000), for example, divides Southern texts by region, breaking down a monocultural vision of the South not only by race but by place. This move transcends the relatively clearly divisible subcategories of Appalachia and the Southwest to acknowledge subtler cultural divisions within the capital *S* South itself. Houston Baker and Dana Nelson, in listing their hopes for a new Southern studies, encourage this destabilization of monolithic conceptions of the South, and call for works that will "enable the process of imagining, articulating, and recognizing antiracist, antiregionalist spaces inside the nationalist machine of 'The South'" (234).

The Southern swamps, at times, are a literal fit for this description: through charting their evolution, we can gain a unique perspective on both the "machine"—the conscious project—of the South and on those elements within the South that resisted, revised, or rejected that project, often from the forbidding but sheltering bounds of the swamps. Despite this new focus on subversive space within the South itself, Southern studies has yet to engage the cultural significance of the swamps. Theorists who approach Southern culture from a literary standpoint, while they acknowledge the seeming ubiquity of swamps in Southern letters, tend to stop their analyses—to echo the title of Louis Rubin's classic study of Southern literature—at the edge of the swamp. The works that I have found most helpful in researching the swamp and Southern culture, such as Ann Vileisis's *Discovering the Unknown Landscape: A History of America's Wetlands* (1997) and Jack Kirby's *Poquosin: A Study of Rural Landscape and Society* (1995), come from other disciplines, primarily ecological history. Southern studies has been content to leave the swamps as nether realms of occult and tropic mystery: these spaces have yet to be adequately historicized in the context of an evolving Southern culture or cultures.

Despite its focus on the relationship between landscape and identity, this book is less an overview of how the Southern swamp landscape shaped an overarching sense of cultural and literary identity than an examination of the ways in which the swamp undermined the conscious project of mainstream white Southern self-creation. In this sense, I adopt an ecocritical methodology in considering the natural world as not only shaped and constructed by, but also influencing, human cultures. Thus, I follow Stephen Adams's stated aims, in his 2001 book *The Best and Worst Country in the World: Perspectives on the Early Virginia Landscape*, to "[study] human culture as both a product of and process within the evolution of ecosystems" and to "[study] the environment through its cultural representations—the ways in which place shapes and is shaped by culture" (9). The South, as political fact and as ideological construct, has been perhaps the clearest geographically and culturally marked obstacle to any totalizing narrative of American history. It has become a truism in Southern literary and cultural criticism to describe Southern identity as less a self-evident fact than a kind of collective project, a conscious construction often in strict defiance of objective fact or historical reality: critics such as Daniel Singal in *The War Within* (1982), Richard Gray in *Writing the South: Ideas of an American Region* (1996), Lewis Simpson in *The Dispossessed Garden* (1975), and Michael Kreyling in *Inventing Southern Literature* (1997), among many others, attest to and examine the quasi-literary creation of Southern identity in their work. This book is a study of a consciously and painstakingly created "mind" and of a real and figurative obstacle to that creation. The unique qualities of both the project of defining Southern identity and of the ever-present swamp engage one another in a unique dialectic of mastery and subversion, of culturewide efforts at self-definition and codification of idealized Southernness and the ubiquitous landscape feature that became their nemesis.

Within this abstracted Southern culture, swamps remain tangible, physical spaces rather than simply collections of tropes. As Simon Schama, Donna Haraway, and others have claimed in a variety of ways, landscape is always, at least in part, a creation of culture—but the range and limits of that cultural creation are what interest the ecocritic. For W. G. T. Mitchell, in his 2002 book *Landscape and Power*, landscape becomes less a descriptive term than an act of creation: "[L]andscape doesn't merely signify or symbolize power relations; it is an instrument of cultural power, perhaps even an agent of power that is (or frequently represents itself as) independent of human intentions" (2). Perceiving the swamps as pure ideas rather than as dialogic participants in cultural definition risks occluding their significance in the formation and evolution of multiple Southern cultures, both within and without the project of "writing the South." Previous, less culturally focused studies of swamps and wetlands from the perspective of literary and cultural criticism have tended to emphasize the swamp's tropic significance while downplaying its status as physical reality. David Miller, in *Dark Eden: The Swamp in Nineteenth-Century American Culture* (1989), approaches the swamp from a primarily aesthetic perspective: he examines the image of the swamp "as perceived in contemporary descriptions and representations, in relation to the prevailing epistemological and aesthetic criteria, in order to show how it came to challenge the Romantic-realist iconography" (4). While Miller's book achieves its stated goal admirably, his conclusion that the swamp "as a particular landscape with established iconographic features is eventually subsumed by more abstract and general categories such as 'the material,' 'the primitive,' or 'the feminist' " and his statement that by the close of the nineteenth century "it is as if having undermined its inherited cultural norms, it is ready to be discarded" (16) are inadequate for describing the evolving dialectic of the swamp and constructions of specifically Southern identity. Rod Giblett's abstract claim in *Postmodern Wetlands* (1996) that "the wetland is a place to celebrate the ambivalence and fluidity of the postmodern . . . the wetland is the polysemic postmodern place par excellence, the place of multiple meanings where sense slips and slides never fixing on a point or a definition" (20) is equally inadequate. In the South, wetlands are and always have been, for all their shifts in tropic and iconographic significance, a tangible reality. The specter of their loss has profoundly shaped Southern cultural traditions.

For Southerners, the swamp was foremost a physical fact. Giblett's claim that "rather than fascination, horror has been the typical patriarchal response to wetlands which have been seen as infested with malaria, miasma, and melancholia" (4) reduces fears of disease to mere responses to trope, equates malaria with melancholia, and risks losing sight of the grim realities of the swamp. Although we now know that malaria comes from mosquitoes rather than from the literal exhalations of the swamp, the disease-bearing insects congregated in swampy areas and semitropical climes, so that nice distinction meant little to those who fell prey to the disease. Diseases that thrived in swamps took a genuine toll on the South: Edmund Ruffin, a figure who will be discussed here at length, lost his family to malaria. Further, reducing the fear of swamp diseases to a "strong association in patriarchal and filiarchal western culture between the nether regions of the body and the nether lands of the physical and metaphysical wetlandscape" (127), as Giblett does, overlooks the legions of slave laborers who died in swamps, whether in trying to escape from plantations or trying to clear the Great Dismal Swamp for George Washington's Great Dismal Swamp Company. In the antebellum North, where abolitionists applied disparaging images of swamps they had often never seen to describe the moral decadence of the entire South, the swamp's significance may have been confined to the abstract and theoretical. In the South, though, the swamp remained more than anything else a physical reminder of the barrier between the actual and the ideal, an obstacle to the creation of an idealized agrarian society.

The term *swamp* defies easy categorization. The *Oxford English Dictionary* attests to both the vagueness and ephemerality of the original definition: it defines a swamp as "A tract of low-lying ground in which water collects; a piece of wet spongy ground; a marsh or bog. Orig. and in early use only in the N. American colonies, where it denoted a tract of rich soil having a growth of trees and other vegetation, but too moist for cultivation." The *OED* not only posits *swamp* as synonymous with "marsh" or "bog" but also specifies its origins as describing land "too moist for cultivation." In this sense, as contemporary technologies have made clearance and cultivation of virtually any nondesert land practicable, swamps as originally described may no longer exist. More scientific definitions are almost equally vague: as John V. Dennis acknowledges in his 1988 study *The Great Cypress Swamps*, "*Swamp* is a word that resists precise definition. Sometimes defined as a tree-studded wetland and other times as a tract of wet, spongy land saturated and often partially or intermittently covered with water, a swamp is not always easily separated from a marsh. . . . [S]o long as wet, wooded areas exceed the acreage of open areas, the term *swamp* for the whole seems appropriate" (1). The distribution of swamps in America provides a telling perspective on how swamps became linked to the South in the American imagination. As Vileisis tells us, the South houses the greatest concentration of wetlands in America. A study of the distribution of colonial-era wetlands, circa 1780, reveals that Louisiana and Florida fall into the highest category of concentration, with 50 to 55 percent of their total land mass composed of wetlands; Mississippi and the Carolinas fall into the second tier, with between 25 to 50 percent, and Georgia and Alabama both have between 12 and 25 percent total wetland composition. Though wetlands are hardly restricted to the American South, a general and gradual gradation in the type of wetland one encounters occurs as one moves farther South: golden marshes become dense swamps as the wetlands become progressively wooded. Midwestern wetlands consist primarily of prairie potholes and peat bogs, while New England's wetlands were largely arable marshes (Vileisis 30–32).

European settlers regarded the Southern swamps and the New England coastal marshes very differently, and their responses were value laden from the beginning. As Vileisis explains, "To European settlers, the coastal marsh landscape appeared pastoral and less threatening than dense forests. . . . While the abundant grasses and sedges of coastal and riparian marshes presented colonists with familiar pastoral landscapes, the swamps they found in the interior had an entangled, foreboding appearance" (32). While the unthreatening expanse of golden marshes that comprised New England's wetlands was easily reconciled with a pastoral vision, the Puritan settlers quickly passed judgment upon the dark and dense swamps. The foundational rhetoric of the "City on a Hill" initially cast topography itself in moralistic terms, and the dark, forbidding lowland swamps fit neatly into a moralized American geography.

Traditionally, the term *swamp* has been more useful as an evaluative description of land that resists reclamation for agricultural or development purposes than a clear scientific designation; the swamp is typically defined as an area outside civilization whose geographical features—notably its treacherous mix of water and earth—render it resistant to colonization or agriculture. While the common shorthand definition of a swamp, according to Dennis, is a wooded wetland, the term carries far more traditional, trope-laden significance than a scientific definition admits. As Vileisis points out, the term itself was initiated with Puritan settlers who had no real context for the dark, wooded swamps they encountered: "English-speaking settlers had no readymade word for these places because the forested wetlands of England had long been eliminated" (33). The term *swamp* was their creation. Despite the practical unfamiliarity of the swamps to European settlers, there is, as Giblett explains, a centuries-old tradition in European literature of literally demonizing the swamp. Both Dante and Milton link the swamp to physical visions of the underworld, "Dante by figuring one circle of hell as a slimy stygian marsh, and Milton by troping Satan as a monstrous swamp serpent who is generated out of the slime of hell" (5). In *Pilgrim's Progress*, a staple of the colonial library, John Bunyan claims that "[t]his *miry slow*, is such a place as cannot be mended: it is the descent whither the scum and filth that attends conviction for sin doth continually run, and therefore it is called the *Slow of Dispond*" (15). The metaphorical language of European literary tradition found, in the shadowy Southern swamps, a more apt physical analog and embodiment than it did in the golden coastal marshes of New England.

Further, swamps are stigmatized by their practical resistance to classification according to ownership. As Vileisis points out, "Traditionally, land has been considered as private property and water as public property—because wetlands are not only land but land *and* water, regarding them simply as real property with no other consideration has been a fundamental error in paradigm" (5–6). The swamps' essential resistance to culturally viable classification was compounded by the nature of their earliest denizens. The practical presence of Native Americans in the swamps only underscored their wicked association for Europeans who viewed the Indian as the embodiment of savagery: "Because Puritans associated Indians with the evil, the sinful, they attributed Indians' familiarity with swamps as a sign that the landscape itself was evil" (Vileisis 34). Demonized in figures and intractable in practice, swamps have represented a challenge to imposed order since well before the colonization of America.

And yet, the very qualities of alienation from societal order and of ideological rejection in intellectual and literary tradition held a profound appeal for American writers and thinkers outside the South, who elevated the swamps for the characteristics that led most to shun them. Thoreau, for example, said that "[w]hen I would recreate myself, I seek the darkest wood, the thickest and most interminable and, to the citizen, most dismal swamp. I enter a swamp as a sacred place, a *sanctum sanctorum*. There is the strength, the marrow of Nature." Walt Whitman, too, extolled the charms of the specifically Southern swamps before the Civil War in his poem "O Magnet South" (1860): "O the strange fascination of these half-known half-impassable/swamps, infested by reptiles, resounding with the bellow/of the alligator, the sad noise of the rattlesnake" (lines 34–36).

More than any scientific definition, the swamp's overwhelming burden of tropes has come to constitute its identity. In fact, as Vileisis recounts, the fledgling environmentalist movement in the mid-twentieth century recognized the need for new nomenclature in arguing for wetland preservation: "In the 1950s, ecologists coined the term *wetland* to replace the imprecise and value-laden *swamp*" (7).

While the swamp's tropic significance came to define it for much of the nation, for the South its physical presence as obstacle to agriculture and shelter for the dispossessed keeps its significance grounded in tangible reality. The swamp carried both a promise of freedom for escaped slaves, and a threat to social order for the plantation aristocracy. Reducing the swamp to tropes and abstractions ignores the specificity and variety of Southern cultural experiences: the swamp retains significance not only for those who dwelt (and still dwell, in the case of a few remaining communities in Southern Louisiana and other places) within it but also as a locus of alternative memory, independent of the white patriarchal master narrative. In this sense, the swamps represent what Baker and Nelson would call "antiracist, antiregionalist spaces inside the nationalist machine of 'The South'" (234): physical obstacles to the ideological project of Southern cultural creation.

As important as such a practical consideration of the Southern swamp is, it carries with it a host of difficulties, most of which result directly from the cultural remove of the swamps themselves. The demographics of the Southern swamps represent a particularly thorny problem. There is ample evidence that indigenous peoples lived and thrived in the Southern swamps. Adams gives a detailed account of how the Hopi and Powhatan Indians, among others, built thriving cultures in woodland and swamp areas of Virginia for thousands of years (from ca. 1500 B.C.) before their first contact with European settlers (29–32). Further, as Vileisis points out, "Native Americans hunted, fished, and gathered but also farmed small plots to supplement their food supplies. . . . Archaeological evidence suggests that Indians grew corn even in protected clearings within heavily forested swamps" (17). Despite the swamps' obvious bounty, European settlers even in the swampiest areas generally avoided them. Planters who could cleared as much swampland as possible, thus transforming swampland into farmland. Those without the means to clear and farm swampland were driven further into the swamps as land was cleared and claimed and thus vanished from the limited census data available. Carl Brasseaux, in his 1992 book *Acadian to Cajun: Transformation of a People, 1803–1877*, advises that "[t]he population, slave, and agricultural schedules of Louisiana's nineteenth-century census reports must be approached warily because local census takers, often political hacks, were notoriously careless. Individuals residing some distance from the main roads were routinely ignored" (xii). Similar problems confront any attempt to gain empirical data about swamp denizens through much of Southern history (and even today, in the ever smaller swamp communities in rural Louisiana): because swamps were by definition regions that had not been officially "settled" or colonized, their inhabitants were rarely officially recorded. As many were fugitives and virtually none conformed to the myth-making agenda of antebellum Southern society, this state of affairs was mutually beneficial to both Southern society and those who dwelt outside of it. Factual and practical accounts of the swamp before the twentieth century come, by and large, from those who explored or sought to drain or exploit them and thus tend to be the work of fascinated outsiders or outright adversaries.

The changing status of the swamp reflects a series of redefinitions of Southern culture, from the colonial era through reconstruction and modernity into the present. Neither sweeping formulations of the wilderness and the American imagination nor theoretical abstraction from historical fact can account for these shifts. The swamp's multivalent resistance to conventional narrative constructions of culture is the key reason for its significance to Southern studies.

The white, aristocratic South's powerful investment in quasi-literary self-creation places the swamp's significance in sharp relief. Since the time of William Byrd II, the figure generally portrayed as the prototypical Southern gentleman and one of the earliest white explorers of the Southern swamp, and arguably until after the Second World War, the Southern elite has attempted to define itself and its region according to a set of interdependent myths. The Cavalier ideal, the myth of racial purity, and the Cult of Southern Womanhood all emerged as a means of justifying the South to outside observers, first in a supercilious colonial-era Europe and subsequently in an equally disdainful North. At the heart of all these myths was a drive for cultural and social order, a codification of accepted Southern behavior that would become an obsessive project for defenders of the plantation aristocratic culture. Though the South and the swamp become clearly linked in discourses of separateness that originate in the North, the swamp remains a separate, intractable space within the South's own self-narrative. Because of the South's pragmatic origins as a culture built on the promise of agricultural profit rather than of religious freedom, Virginia, as the flagship of the Agrarian and potentially Arcadian South, conceived of its role with a mixture of pastoral idealism and acute commercial consciousness. The swamp, of course, runs counter to both—for the antebellum South, the swamp is from the beginning not only the antithesis of the pastoral ideal but a very real obstacle to commercial prosperity. Thus, even within the region that the North tends in later years to identify with the swamp, the swamp itself remains a space resistant to inclusion in a distinct Southern narrative of practical agrarian idealism.

As Southern culture evolves into the plantation system in the first half of the nineteenth century, the swamp becomes more clearly opposed, both figuratively and practically, to prevailing ideals of white Southern society, which emphasized racial and cultural purity and ironclad class distinctions. The swamp's status as haven for civilization's exiles gives its threatening significance for the white

South a new and more powerful dimension. Further, the swamps carried vastly different connotations for those who lived among them than they did for the landed gentry. The poorer farmers, Acadian trappers and fishermen, Native Americans, free mulattoes, and swamp Maroons, who have until fairly recently been as absent from our conceptions of Southern culture as they were from official census documents, often regarded swamps as shelter or livelihood. Even as the African-American literary and cultural conception of the antebellum South obviously runs sharply contrary to the prevailing privileged white narrative, the swamp itself signifies differently for groups not included in the idealized vision of Southern society. Though the swamp represented a mysterious and demonic realm for white Southerners, it was a forbidding but welcome place of escape for runaway slaves. The swamp, though still a place of fear and uncertainty, was also the source of livelihood for many Southerners, and became a home for the desperate and disenfranchised.

These initial understandings provide the foundation for the study of the evolving relationship between the swamp and Southern cultures (in pluralizing this term, I include cultures outside the dominant white aristocracy and significantly linked to the swamp, including Southern African American, Creole, Cajun, and Native American cultures) that this study charts. The work is divided chronologically into four major chapters, each considering a particular era in the South's relationship to its swamps.

The first chapter, which charts the relationship of the swamp to the creation of Southern identity from the colonial through the antebellum era, begins by theorizing in detail the ways in which the swamp proved profoundly inimical to the project of constructing Southern identity, using anthropologist Mary Douglas's theories of cultural purity and ambiguity to contextualize the swamp with reference to Singal, Bertram Wyatt-Brown, and others with ideas about the self-conscious creation of the mythical Cavalier South. I provide a history of white Southern perspectives on swamp dwellers, both racial others and white exiles from the "circle of Southern honor," that underscores the swamp's distance from dominant cultural ideals. The swamp, like the animal self always battled and denied by the cavalier, was in many ways the essence of the Southern problem: it had no place in the myth of self-creation that constituted the ideal South, and yet it was an utterly inalienable part of the South itself and therefore ingrained into Southern identity from the very beginning.

I begin by considering swamp discourses outside the Southern literary and philosophical mainstream: slave narratives such as Harriet Jacobs's, the frontier humor of Henry Clay Lewis, and critiques of Southern culture by women both within the South (Fanny Kemble) and without (Harriet Beecher Stowe). I then examine how key mainstream antebellum writers, thinkers, financiers, and scientists dealt with the swamp as trope, symbol, signifier, opportunity, and problem and how, even in the most archetypal Cavalier or plantation romances of William Gilmore Simms and John Pendleton Kennedy, the swamp consistently reemerges as an insurmountable obstacle. Beginning with William Byrd II, I examine early utilitarian efforts to chart, describe, and drain the swamps, as well as attempts to represent the swamps and their denizens. By contrast, I consider the perspective of William Bartram, naturalist and non-Southerner, in representing the Florida swamps and the Native American tribes he encounters, in an effort to characterize Byrd's perspective as a product of his status as self-conscious Southerner whose prosperity could depend on the tractability of the land he surveyed. The failed quest of George Washington's Great Dismal Swamp Company, who found their endeavor to drain the Great Dismal Swamp thwarted to such an extent that their only real profit came from the seemingly inexhaustible timber produced by their efforts to clear it, completes the consideration of the swamp in the pre-Victorian era. The white overseers who had financial interest in draining the swamp, and the slave laborers who found a curious freedom in the swamp despite deplorable labor conditions, saw it very differently. The ultimate image of the swamp that emerges from these three early encounters underscores Schama's statement that landscape is essentially an imaginative creation. Depending on the values one imports, the swamp's character changes drastically. As Bartram's work and, ironically, the history of the Great Dismal Swamp Company attest, the swamp can be a cornucopia if one does not seek to subjugate it. The effort to transform its natural state into the pastoral garden, however, transforms the swamp into an entity that is stubborn, deadly, and intractable. Approached with a romantic sense of nature as inherently benevolent, the swamp becomes a shady paradise. With the onset of the Cavalier tradition's drive to subdue the natural, particularly in the South, where, as Singal tells us, Victorian ideals were typically distilled into simplest terms, the swamp would remain as Byrd designated it—a moral and commercial enemy.

Edmund Ruffin and William Gilmore Simms represent transitional figures in defining the evolving literary and cultural relationship of the swamp to Southern identity. I refer to Ruffin and Simms as "transitional" each for different reasons. Although their careers and viewpoints were markedly different, each bridges a kind of gap in Southern understandings of the swamp with regard to identity. Moreover, each man's writings can be considered representative of a different pole in perceptions of the Southern swamp: Ruffin, the man of science, entered the swamp with an attitude of scientific and agricultural empiricism that remained largely uninflected by his passionate proslavery and pro-Southern views as they emerged in the 1850s, while Simms, though less politically passionate about the Southern system for which he had been elected de facto literary spokesperson, created a romantic vision of a swamp divorced from reality, a swamp that, for all its terrors, showed a peculiar obedience when confronted by the force of character that marked the archetypal gentleman cavalier. Considered together, Ruffin and Simms represent a transitional point in the evolution from physical to linguistic strategies of Southern approaches to the swamp's anomalous ambiguity.

Finally, the first chapter turns to John Pendleton Kennedy and Edgar Allan Poe, Southern cultural archetypes who are generally considered virtual opposites in their presentations of Southern pastoral. I compare *Swallow Barn* and "The Fall of the House of Usher" as final stages in the prewar South's attempts to reconcile the ambiguity of the swamp. After a general surrender in the endeavor to drain, clear, and farm the swamps—the effort to master and destroy them physically, according to Douglas's paradigm—the struggle to reconcile the swamp with the rigid, slow-evolving creation of Southern identity moved from the physical realm to the realm of language and ideology. Though Kennedy recognizes that the swamp is indomitable, he responds with an emphatic separation of the swamp from the plantation world: although the ruling class cannot control the swamp either physically or linguistically, they gain a kind of dominance by exiling it, quarantining its dangers in a designated space. Utterly beyond the gentleman's experience, the swamp can comfortably remain a place of mystery so long as its removal from the plantation life can be underscored. And yet, as Poe's chilling tale underscores, this ideological exile remained artificial and imperfect. Poe represents the swamp as permeating the very society that shunned it, reflecting society's internal corruption rather than generating its own. He ultimately renders it the symbolic vehicle of a self-destructively insular culture's own implosion.

Chapter 2 concerns the Southern swamp during the Civil War, through reconstruction, and on until the turn of the century. It examines the role of the swamps in war, considering newspaper articles, personal memoirs, and accounts of life in Andersonville, a hellish prison camp that sat on the edge of the swamp, and shows how practical wartime exigencies contributed to drastic reconceptions of the swamps by many of those who traditionally shunned them—notably Southern women like Eliza Andrews. The stigma that northern thinkers and writers had attached to the swamp before the war faded in favor of a new vogue for swamp tourism and aestheticization after the war. Made accessible by advances in transportation technology and free from the taint of Southern culture, the swamps became fascinating for visitors from the North. The section considers travel writing by Northerners surveying a defeated South, and describes the formation of an "aesthetic of ruin" that could only develop from the perspective of a victor surveying a defeated land. This aesthetic simultaneously praised and romanticized the swamps while denigrating the deplorable conditions of the Southern culture that surrounded them. The writers perceive, in both the swamp and in the defeated South, a beauty born of death and torpor, which stands in sharp relief to the otherwise rapidly progressing nation. Thus, the South remains linked with the swamp, but in a way that elevates decadence and defeat to a kind of paradoxical beauty.

In response to this aesthetic of ruin, a literature of reaction emerged in the South. The chapter tracks the exile of the swamp from Southern postwar literature in favor of mythic hagiographies of Confederate heroes and portraits of an idealized South free from the stigma of the trope-laden swamp: a backward-looking sanitation and idealization of Southern culture. I then turn to the work of Thomas Nelson Page, perhaps the most popular and influential Southern fiction writer of his era, and consider the peculiar representation of the swamp as exiled locus of Southern racial guilt in his oddly uncharacteristic ghost story, "No Haid Pawn."

From backward-looking idealizations, I turn to forward-looking representations of the swamps. I consider the work of George Washington Cable in representing New Orleans, the Southern city most literally and figuratively linked to the swamp and ironically the most urban and cosmopolitan Southern center. New Orleans, the cultural and economic center of Louisiana throughout the nineteenth century, distilled both the typically Southern and the subversive and exotic elements of the state. Characterized by strict social categories and lax moral codes, by jealously defended bloodlines and by the unique and vital cultural mix brought about by its status as the South's major port city, New Orleans, like the swamp itself, remained both inextricably part of the South and unassimilably alien to it. I examine Cable's appropriations of the swamp in "Jean-Ah Poquelin" and *The Grandissimes* to mount critiques of old New Orleans and, by extension, Southern, culture, particularly in the field of race relations. Though

Cable does not romanticize the swamp, he presents it, in these two works, as preferable to the decaying and degenerate society that lives at its borders.

Finally, I turn to Sidney Lanier, who, in contrast to Cable, seeks to separate the swamp entirely from culture. Lanier sees in the swamp a canvas of infinite imaginative possibilities, and in his prose and poetry celebrates them: his swamps are creations of the individual, rather than cultural, imagination. Lanier's imagining the swamps as spaces removed from cultural determination, separate from both trope-laden past and encroaching future, places him in the ecological tradition of nature writers like Thoreau and signifies a liberation of the swamps from the rote rhetorical categories of old: literary swamps of the modern era would reflect this new range of possibilities.

The modern era, a time of both rapid advancement and staunch reaction, found the South in transition. The third chapter begins by recounting a two-pronged threat to the Southern swamp, in both literal and figurative dimensions. The literal threat is the timber industry's rapid destruction of significant portions of the Southern wetlands in the early twentieth century; the figurative threat is the reactionary assault on ambiguity evinced on one hand by the resurgence of the Ku Klux Klan in the 1920s and the revival of religious fundamentalism and on the other by the conservative reaction of the Fugitive Agrarians to the dangers of industrialization. To critique both an oppressive or immoral past and an industrialized future, Southern writers who made the swamp central to their works exploited its status as removed from mainstream culture, as essentially and fundamentally liminal, and as physically endangered. While many of the most significant works that explore and make use of the swamp can be viewed as in part reactionary, critical of the industrialization sweeping the South even as the Agrarians were, a significant part of their reaction was directed at Southern culture itself—both at its complicity in its own perceived impending demise and at the values and social strictures that flawed the Old Southern traditions.

Voices that had formerly not engaged the swamp landscape outside of prescribed forms and tropes embraced the swamp as a place that encouraged and enabled new, more complex symbologies: African American, female, queer. Many of these voices understandably embraced the changes against which the South fought so stubbornly. Male authors who identified more fully but no longer unquestioningly with Southern culture and Southernness regarded the natural world and the aging systems that repudiated it, as well as the fading traditions that cherished it, with new eyes. Considering works by Zora Neale Hurston, Lillian Smith, and William Faulkner, as well as the birth of Southern environmentalism and ecological consciousness, I examine the ways in which the swamp's physical and tropological significance underwent sweeping revisions during the modern era: the swamp remained a space for those who did not fit the circle of honor, but it was no longer a hell of exile. It became a signifier of an alternative, more inclusive Southern culture, of an elemental but not fundamentalist sanctity, apart from the legacy of the Victorian South.

While she follows W. E. B. DuBois and Jean Toomer in redefining the swamp as a place of sanctity and race memory for Southern African Americans, Hurston is almost unique among the writers identified with the Harlem Renaissance in the ambivalence that she expresses in *Jonah's Gourd Vine* regarding the transformations that modernity brought to Southern African Americans. Positing the swamp as a transitional space of pure, natural communion, Hurston captures her protagonist John Pearson in a moment of cultural transformation. In her appreciation of the traditions and inherent spirituality embodied in the swamp, Hurston reclaims the fading region from the perspective of a Southern African American, ignoring its traditional status as a place of fear, danger, and exile.

Smith and Faulkner are the focus of the remainder of the third chapter. Each interrogates the idea of the swamp as a space of purity, of removal from social codes and societal guilt, with thematically similar but productively different results. Smith's *Strange Fruit* presents an unbalanced interracial relationship fueled by Tracy Deen's essentialist conception of Nonnie as a being of uncomplicated and elemental sexuality, as dark and alluring and free with her charms as the swamp to which she feels strangely connected. Faulkner's *Go Down, Moses* explores the possibility of the Mississippi bottomlands as a space removed from racial guilt, as the source of an alternative lineage, bloodline, and spirituality. Both authors ultimately undermine the idea of the swamp as escape from cultural codes and history; in so doing, Smith lodges a powerful social critique, and Faulkner paves the way for a postmodern deconstruction of swamp tropes.

My fourth chapter deals with the representations and realities of the swamp in what Ted Spivey calls the "restored South" in his book *Revival: Southern Writers and the Modern City* (1986): the South since 1945, "a region restored to the nation as a whole, no longer a region proud of its separateness" (7). The belated discovery that has occurred "only in the past thirty to forty years" (Vileisis 4) that wetlands are actually beneficial to the environment, in fact preventing the very problems of flooding and pollution they were once charged with causing, has led to an ironic drive to save them. As Vileisis points out, "by retarding runoff and allowing water to seep back into the ground, many wetlands have played a critical role in recharging the aquifers that people rely on for agricultural and domestic water supplies. . . . Wetlands have also preserved water quality by filtering excess nutrients and pollutants" (4). The discovery of the swamp's vanishing natural gifts has brought with it an awareness of the swamp's vanishing cultural legacy. In an era when the swamps have been essentially parceled off from the South as a whole, the few parts of the South whose local cultures have been built upon and still rely on the swamp, particularly Cajun communities in south Louisiana, face a seemingly inevitable cultural loss. Setting the stage with an overview of pop culture representations of the swamp in the late twentieth century, I move into a study of the film adaptation of Vereen Bell's 1942 novel *Swamp Water* and the images of Southern culture conveyed by the changes demanded by producer Daryl Zanuck. From here, I progress to a more culturally specific and contemporary analysis of the phenomenon of ecotourism and the specific subgenre of swamp tours in south Louisiana. I further explore the environmental movement's physical efforts to preserve the swamps in the latter part of the twentieth century. At a time when the swamps are vanishing, or, as Baudrillard would claim, have already been destroyed and replaced by simulacra by a number of disparate forces, I examine the continuing roles of the literal and figurative swamps in influencing what remains of a particularized facet of Southern identity.

In response to the postmodern conception of swamps as vanished and simulacral, I consider works by two contemporary authors—Louisiana writer Tim Gautreaux and Native American poet and novelist Linda Hogan—that consider the role of swamps and swamp-identified cultures in the contemporary world. Each of these authors sounds a cautious note of hope for the perpetuation both of the swamps and of the traditions they have fostered in cultures outside the mainstream white South and suggests that, however fragile they may be, the swamps remain significant, and even powerful, in postmodern society.

The ultimate goal of this work is to encourage a blending of ecocritical and cultural studies approaches in considering Southern culture and literature. In a work of this scope, it is impossible to be encyclopedic, and there are many areas of the literary, cultural, and historical swamps that remain to be explored. Hopefully, this book will contribute to a new and exciting area in Southern studies—one that sheds new light on the myths, cultures, and environmental history of the South, while in some way encouraging and fostering ecological consciousness about the natural and cultural importance of our rapidly vanishing wetlands.

SHADOW AND SHELTER

THE SWAMP AND ANTEBELLUM SOUTHERN IDENTITY

The swamp and the myth of the plantation South have always been at odds. For the Cavalier-era Southern mind, ideas of control, purity, and dominion over nature (both within and without) were essential; in both literature and in the real world, the swamp always defied those ideas. In his influential 1996 study *Landscape and Memory*, Simon Schama claims that "[b]efore it can ever be a repose for the senses, landscape is the work of the mind. Its scenery is built up as much from strata of memory as from layers of rock" (6–7). He prefaces his work, however, with an epigraph from an entry in Thoreau's journal on August 30, 1856, which iterates the same idea with a crucial difference: "It is vain to dream of a wildness distant from ourselves. There is none such. It is the bog in our brains and bowels, the primitive vigor of Nature in us, that inspires that dream" (qtd. in Schama 1). For Schama's sweeping study of the dialectical relationship between landscape and mind, the two above quotations work fairly unproblematically in concert. For the student of the Southern antebellum "mind," and I use that term fully cognizant both of its limitations and of its utility, the contrast between the two ways of describing the same essential phenomenon is clear: for the antebellum Southern aristocrat, a landscape as a work of the mind would be absolutely and categorically distinct from "the bog in our brains and bowels." The distinction, for the Cavalier-influenced Southern mind, would be as sharp as that between Jekyll and Hyde—one, an ideal of control; the second, a savage nightmare whose horror inheres in its essential inalienability.

3

The tension that arises between the two above quotations in the context of the Old South captures the aspect of the antebellum aristocratic Southern psyche most offended and frightened by the swamp and its factual and fictitious characteristics—and, not coincidentally, hints at why the swamp became, to a limited but significant degree, a haven for those outside what Bertram Wyatt-Brown has called "the circle of Southern honor." William Bedford Clark's portrait of the South in the American cultural imagination in his 1974 article "The Serpent of Lust in the Southern Garden" is significant in situating the swamp in relation to a dominant Southern myth of idyllic agrarianism. Clark claims that "[i]n the minds of many Americans, there are two Souths"; one is "an idyllic land of plenty . . . inhabited by a happy and hospitable people for whom life is pleasure and pleasure a way of life," the other, a "nightmare world of torrid and stifling heat in which uncontrollable passions and senseless acts of violence become the outward manifestations of a blighting inner corruption, a secret sin poisoning the very mainstreams of Southern life" (291). This nether South, quarantined by the ongoing project of retrospective Southern myth making, is indelibly linked to the swamp in the only problematically separable realms of Southern history and literature. Leslie Fiedler has described the subgenre that we now call "southern gothic" as a "series of bloody events, sexual by implication at least, played out . . . against a background of miasmal swamps, live oak, Spanish moss, and the decaying house" and evoking "the deepest guilts and fears of transplanted Europeans . . . in a community which remembers having sent its sons to die in a vain effort to sustain slavery" (294). The geographical feature of the Southern swamp has traditionally become host to the idealized and prosperous South's lurid underbelly. One intriguing commonality among recent studies of the central myths that structured antebellum Southern society is that they all seem to have rested on uniformly shaky ground. Lucinda MacKethan, among others, has argued that the image of the plantation South as Arcadian ideal is primarily a retrospective creation of writers from Reconstruction to the present (3). As soon as one looks closely at the institutions of the antebellum Southern planter class, the lines that seemed so sharp in defining Wyatt-Brown's circle of honor become blurred and treacherous—a fact that made the maintenance of those besieged lines all the more obsessively important to the Southern Cavalier gentleman. Further, the imperiled nature of those dividing lines underscores the idea of Southern culture as a conscious, partially literary creation. In his 1982 study *The War Within*, Daniel Singal reveals the fundamental defensiveness at the heart of the Southern Cavalier myth. At least as early as the era of William Byrd II, the Southern gentleman felt pressure to justify himself as such by the standards of Britain and, increasingly, of the rest of the colonies. Singal points out that the South's very landscape threatened its adherence to European ideals: because of the physical distances between plantations and homes in the South, and the general lack of central control or cultural cohesion, the South found itself at variance with the eighteenth-century ideal of a stable, cohesive community—"and as everyone knew, this sort of loose and open society, where each individual was free to pursue his own ambitions, was the perfect environment for the virus of human greed (along with the rest of man's worst instincts) to develop and thrive" (17).

The image of infection here—the idea of the South's geography as breeding ground for "the virus of human greed"—will become particularly important in specific relation to the Southern swamp. For now, though, it becomes an important rhetorical index for the drive to purity at the core of Southern Cavalier society. Singal describes the Southerners as "other Victorians" and seizes on certain aspects of the Victorian mind in a way that will be particularly important to our understanding of what the swamp will represent to the Southern mind. Culture, to the Victorians, existed "to refine, inspire, and 'elevate' an individual from the moral standpoint, raising him above the common herd. Those who possessed culture were thought to be 'civilized,' those who lacked it were 'savages.' . . . [T]he separation between the barbaric and the civilized, the animal and the human, became in fact the very bedrock assumption of their thought" (5). As Singal illustrates, *division* is crucial to Victorian values. Purity, both within, at the level of personal morality and without, at the level of class distinction, was the utmost goal. As Wyatt-Brown points out, those levels blurred in the South as the drive for purity became a fanatical dedication to preserving pure bloodlines: "Since the earliest times, honor was inseparable from hierarchy and entitlement, defense of family blood and community needs. All these exigencies required the rejection of the lowly, the alien, and the shamed. Such unhappy creatures belonged outside the circle of honor" (4). And yet, those unhappy creatures always seemed to threaten the borders of that circle. W. J. Cash's barbed and polemical *Mind of the South* (1941) reveals, if not the actual weakness of familial and honorable distinction, then a perception of that weakness, which would be just as painful to the honor-obsessed Southern mind: "[I]n any given region the great planter who lived on the fertile lands along the river, the farmer on the rolling lands behind him, and the cracker on the barrens back of both were as often as not kindred" (26). The preservation of honor and purity was an all-encompassing, if ultimately losing, battle. The Southern aristocracy came to view its lot as a perpetual fight against nature itself: against the uncivilized individualists who threatened to infect the delicate system with the virus of greed; against those of impure blood, lineage, or reputation who might also wear away at the bedrock of Southern society; and against moral infection, which had its roots within, in the carefully controlled but ever-present animal self.

The practical impossibility of such control was of little concern to the Southern gentleman, for reasons that Kenneth Greenberg makes clear in *Honor and Slavery* (1996). Greenberg points out that, on a fundamental level, "Southern men of honor were 'superficial.' They were concerned, to a degree we would consider unusual, with the surface of things—with the world of appearances" (3). The accusation of lying was of paramount significance among Southern gentlemen: "[T]he central insult that could turn a disagreement into a duel involved a direct or indirect attack on someone's word—the accusation that the man was a liar. To 'give someone the lie,' as it was called, had always been an insult of great consequence among men of honor" (8). In the South, " 'giving the lie' to someone meant announcing that his appearance differed from his true nature—proclaiming as false his projection of himself" (9). Honesty itself was less important than the social standing necessary to prevent being revealed as a liar. Greenberg recounts an anecdote about Jefferson Davis fleeing Union forces dressed as a woman; the real shame, he argues, lay not in Davis's disguise, but in its removal against his will: "The man of honor was the man who had the power to prevent his being unmasked. . . . A Southern gentleman could wear anything—even a dress or a lie—as long as he could prevent it from being removed" (25). Honesty matters less, Greenberg argues, than the ability to enforce one's own construction of one's self—to maintain the gentlemanly masquerade.

It is fitting, then, that the Southern aristocracy's primary defense against detractors was an elaborate and culturewide mask. In answer to the South's perceived shortcomings—the individualism and lack of cohesive control that threatened to render Southern society unfit by European and subsequently by American standards—came the Cavalier myth. As Singal puts it, "With his larger-than-life scale and his aura of romance, the Cavalier has in fact become the very symbol of the South, intimately bound up with the region's sense of identity, providing Southerners with their predominant source of common pride in the perpetual struggle with yankeedom" (11). The quintessence of Southern gentlemanly behavior, the cavalier became the defender of purity, the paragon of control and civilization: "[F]or the certifying mark of the Southern gentleman was his complete self-control. . . . [O]nly the cavalier possessed the heroic force of character which was required to hold back the restless flood of savagery that threatened to overflow the country" (18). He maintained moral, social, and sexual purity at all costs; he was master of his domain and, most importantly, master of himself.

If the Cavalier myth can be interpreted as a literary and linguistic attempt to control fundamentally uncontrollable forces, then the swamp emerges as its nemesis: the distillation of pure wildness, the uncontrollable element in the pastoral garden. Throughout the nineteenth century into the era of modernism, the swamp remains a separate, intractable space within the South's own self-narrative. In his 1980 study *The Brazen Face of History*, Lewis Simpson characterizes the antebellum mind of the South in a manner naturally at odds with the swamp. Long before the South emerged as a political obstacle to a totalizing American ideal, Simpson claims, the Southern mind developed an ideological conception of its place in the New World quite distinct from the Puritan theological understanding of America as the divinely endowed Garden of the World: "[B]y and large, the southern literary mind did not envision a coalescence of the Kingdom of God and the Garden of the World as a way of substituting for the loss of a revealed history. . . . [Virginia's] role in history was to propagate, not the gospel, but tobacco" (119). Virginia, flagship of the Agrarian, potentially Arcadian South, conceived of its role with a mixture of pastoral idealism and acute commercial consciousness. The swamp, of course, runs counter to both—for the antebellum South, the swamp is from the beginning not only the antithesis of the pastoral ideal, but a very real obstacle to commercial prosperity. Thus, even within the region that the North tends in later years to identify with the swamp, the swamp resists inclusion in a distinct Southern narrative of practical agrarian idealism. Identification of the South with the swamp has long been a sore point for the South's ideological defenders, and early Southern writers tended to de-emphasize swamps. Notably, Thomas Jefferson's otherwise encyclopedic *Notes on the State of Virginia* elides any direct reference to the vast swamps in the state's Tidewater region. The Great Dismal Swamp is mentioned not at all by name, and at one point he consciously minimizes the significance of data collected from the eastern part of the state, claiming in his discourse on climate that "Williamsburgh is much too near the South-eastern corner to give a fair idea of our general temperature" (83). A great part of the reason for Jefferson's omissions was a sense of defensiveness about the New World, which had been derided by European naturalists, particularly by a French scientist named Georges-Louis Leclerc, Comte de Buffon, who was "perhaps the most influential and widely known natural historian of the late eighteenth century" (Shuffleton xxii). De Buffon, in his *Histoire Naturelle, Generale et Particuliere*, argued that animals in America were smaller than those in the Old World, in large part because the new world was "filled with moist, unhealthy vapors, where 'everything languishes, decays, stifles'" (Shuffleton xxii). De Buffon even went so far as to claim that the stunted growth of animals was mirrored in the human inhabitants of such a climate, rendering them lazy and worthless. Clearly, in taking up the American case against this judgmental European account, Jefferson would not help his cause by lingering on the swamps; in fact, he takes pains to minimize their significance and even, when debating De Buffon directly, to call into doubt their status as a geographic feature unique to the New World: "I will not meet this hypothesis on its first doubtful ground, whether the climate of America be comparatively more humid? Because we are not furnished with observations sufficient to decide this question. . . . [T]ill it be decided, we are as free to deny, as others to affirm the fact" (48). Jefferson goes on to attest that a combination of heat and moisture are in fact key to animal health and points out that regardless, climate is subject to change through the intervention of cultivation and agriculture. Thus, Jefferson gives voice, indirectly, to the prevailing Southern strategy for dealing with swamps in the latter part of the eighteenth century—whatever problems they pose will be averted with the inevitable advance of agriculture. In the meantime, Jefferson rather selectively emphasizes medicinal springs when speaking about the wetland portions of the state and omits the Great Dismal Swamp from the bulk of his discourse. Thus, in one of the most famous early attempts to define America and the American South for a European audience, the swamp is conspicuously omitted from the narrative of self-creation.

Set apart from the civilized South for both practical and symbolic reasons, the swamp posed a problem for the categorical Southern mind due to its very ambiguity. First, defining a physical swamp is not always an easy matter: as Jack Kirby indicates in his 1995 study *Poquosin: A Study of Rural Landscape and Society*, all of Tidewater Virginia can be considered a kind of transitional swamp, troubling traditional English classification. Traditionally, the definition of a swamp precludes human development: as swampland is cleared and farmed, it ceases to be called swampland. Much of Washington, D.C., to choose only one particularly dramatic example out of many, stands on land that would initially be designated a swamp—few would use that term, at least in its literal sense, to describe it now. But alongside the difficulty in physically defining the swamp, and in demarcating its borders, comes a vivid consciousness of swamps as definite regions with a characteristic wildness, whether lauded for their beauty or feared for their dangers. Working against the tendency of Yankees and Europeans to characterize the South as a whole as a collection of settlements in a vast and backward swamp, identity-conscious Southerners undertook to resolve the ambiguity that threatened to blur the lines between their carefully cultivated civilization and the ubiquitous wilderness of the swampland at its edges. Even those wealthy planters who cultivated crops, like rice, that grew best in swampy or semiswampy environments often stayed clear of their farms for much of the year: as Dana Nelson recounts in *Principles and Privilege: Two Women's Lives on a Georgia Plantation* (1995), "Preferring the cultural benefits of city life and having associated what was actually malaria with the 'miasmatic air' of the warm, swampy coast, the planter elite argued that it was imperative to their lives and lifestyle to live inland" (xxi).

Mary Douglas' seminal anthropological work, *Purity and Danger: An Analysis of Concepts of Pollution and Taboo* (1966), is instructive in situating the swamp's figurative link to the ongoing project of Southern self-creation and in explaining the nature and origin of the physical swamp's link to the South's moral and cultural "underside." Describing the definition and function of pollution in a culture, Douglas argues: "Where there is dirt there is a system. Dirt is the by-product of a systematic ordering and classification of matter, in so far as ordering involves rejecting inappropriate elements. This idea of ordering takes us straight into the field of symbolism and promises a link-up with more obviously symbolic systems of purity. . . . In short, our pollution behavior is the reaction which condemns any object or idea likely to confuse or contradict cherished classifications" (35–36).

As we have seen, the swamp's very physical ambiguity, mirroring Douglas's example of treacle as "anomalous in the classification of liquids and solids, being in neither one nor the other set" (37), makes it fundamentally problematic to a system as obsessively devoted to order and classification as the antebellum South. A natural enemy to any Victorian, European, or Southern construction of "purity," the essence of the swamp's threat is, in a sense, its betweenness, its treacherous mixture of land and water that can give way at any moment beneath the unwary foot. This threat is compounded by its very atmosphere, the mysterious miasma—then thought to cause malaria by its very respiration—whose very name comes from the Greek *"to pollute or stain."* To the order-obsessed South, the ambiguous, ubiquitous swamp becomes abject: as Julia Kristeva, whose notion of the abject owes much to Mary Douglas's work, explains, "It is . . . not the lack of cleanliness or health that causes abjection but what disturbs identity, system, order. What does not respect borders, positions, rules. The in-between, the ambiguous, the composite" (3). For the antebellum South to maintain its meticulously constructed self-representation, this ambiguity had to be dealt with.

Douglas goes on to list four primary cultural means of dealing with troublesome ambiguity. The first, declaring them sufficiently rare that they do not pose a genuine threat to society's classifications, was a physical impossibility in the case of the ubiquitous Southern swamp. As Tynes Cowan has observed, "It seems that any plantation would have a swamp of some size within walking distance" (194). The other three strategies that Douglas describes all emerge, to some extent or another, at various points in the developing narrative of Southern culture's relationship to the swamp: attempting to physically control or destroy it—efforts that we will see suggested or employed in various ways as this chapter progresses; demanding its avoidance; and designating it as a source of danger—a strategy that might be extended to describe the tradition of cataloguing the swamp's real and romanticized dangers (Douglas 41). In a sense, the pattern that emerges in Southern attitudes toward, and representations of, the swamp before the Civil War can be characterized as another kind of "War Within"—a movement from one of Douglas's strategies to the next. Overall, a progression emerges from a series of attempts to dominate or destroy the swamp through physical or agricultural means to a linguistic method of coping with the swamp—a more profoundly literary, romantic, and essentially unreal mode of representation that attempted to place the swamp and its tropes in the domain of folklore, to render it a supernaturally wild place of devils and pestilence.

The swamp threatened subversion in its function as well as in its essence. In both history and fiction, the swamp embraces civilization's exiles, hiding the escaped slave, harboring the hunted Seminole, providing new community for the exiled Acadians, defending and nourishing those excluded from the Southern narrative. As such, its threatening significance for the white South takes on a new and more powerful dimension. Even as the African American literary and cultural conception of the antebellum South obviously runs sharply contrary to the prevailing privileged white narrative, the swamp itself carries profoundly different significance for groups not included in the idealized Southern society. While the swamp represents to the dominant white Southern imagination a place of mysterious menace, it is also a haven for escaped slaves, who, as narratives such as *The Confessions of Nat Turner* (1831) and abolitionist novels such as Harriet Beecher Stowe's *Dred: A Tale of the Great Dismal Swamp* (1856) tell us, could disappear into the swamp with a level of effectiveness that far exceeded any physical distance they may have traveled. As Cowan points out in "The Slave in the Swamp: Affects of Uncultivated Regions on Plantation Life," "[T]he swamp was a place where enslaved Africans could seize the opportunity afforded them by the environment to survive and strike back against the institution of slavery. The region certainly could fill them with dread as it would have the planters, yet the spark it must have caused in the imagination would not be one of romantic self-reflection but of possibilities" (204). Thus, the swamp, though still mysterious and fearsome, also becomes a sort of home for the disenfranchised—and, as such, a harbor for the "germs" that threatened to infect the purity of Southern plantation civilization.

Harriet Jacobs's *Incidents in the Life of a Slave Girl* (1861), one of the most noted and powerful first-person articulations of slave life, provides a powerful image of the ambivalent significations of the swamp for the escaped slave. During an escape attempt, slaves hide Jacobs in the aptly named "Snaky Swamp," where they know no white men will look for her. Jacobs's experience is a virtual catalogue of swamp terrors, though it is largely free of the superstitious and metaphorical evils that characterized not only white swamp mythologies but also African American ghost stories.[1] Jacobs' horrors are more potent for their practicality. Her initial fears are based in personal experience: "My fear of snakes had been increased by the venomous bite I had received, and I dreaded to enter this hiding-place. But I was in no position to choose, and I gratefully accepted the best that my poor, persecuted friends could do for me" (113). A literal nest of serpents, then, becomes preferable to recapture for Jacobs.

Once in the swamp, Jacobs experiences a nightmarish barrage of its terrors: she is devoured by mosquitoes, surrounded by snakes, which she and her companions are "continually obliged to thrash . . . with sticks to keep them from crawling over us," and eventually stricken by fever, which she attributes to the swamp environment. Jacobs endures the worst the swamp has to offer but still chooses its dubious shelter over return to captivity: "even those large, venomous snakes were less dreadful to my imagination than the white men in that community called civilized" (113). Accounts like Jacobs's delineate the beginnings of a troubled link between menacing swamps and African

American freedom; a link which will be explored in myriad ways, with varying rhetorical intent, over the next century.

While the shelter that Jacobs finds in Snaky Swamp is dubious at best, the
swamps' role in harboring escaped slaves notably influenced popular swamp
representations. Novels, newspaper stories, and magazine accounts reinforced
the idea of the menacing swamp dweller, generally figured as an elementally
powerful, quasi-wild escaped slave: a vision that resonated to some with ideals
of the Noble Savage, to others (typically Southerners) with images of unchecked
savagery and danger. The image of the Maroon, or long-escaped slave fiercely
removed from civilization, took a strong hold on the Southern and national
psyche—as Kirby points out: "By the end of the antebellum era . . . swamp
maroons were legendary in the United States" (168). Porte-Crayon presented
one of the most famous and resounding representations of the archetypal
Maroon in his portrait of the escaped slave Osman in his piece entitled
"The Dismal Swamp," which appeared in *Harper's New Monthly Magazine*
in 1856. In it he describes an encounter with a vigorous middle-aged black
man, "gigantic," with "purely African features . . . cast in a mould betoken-
ing, in the highest degree, strength and energy," bearing an expression "of
mingled fear and ferocity, and every movement [betraying] a life of habitual
caution and watchfulness" (452–53). It is not clear whether Porte-Crayon's
description and accompanying illustration are based in fact, but his vivid and
rhetorically inflected description indicates the imaginative hold that the
Maroon image had on the white imagination: the Maroon, with his power,
ferocity, and stylized elemental "Africanness," became both Southern bogey-
man and abolitionist icon.

In his famous 1856 study *A Journey in the Seaboard Slave States*, a collection
of pieces written for the *New York Daily Times* between 1853 and 1854,
Frederick Law Olmsted remarks, in slightly less sensational but more com-
pellingly factual fashion, on the phenomenon of the swamp-dwelling escaped
slave: "The Dismal Swamps are noted places of refuge for runaway
negroes. . . . Children were born, bred, lived, and died here. Joseph Church
[a slave hired out for swamp labor who accompanied Olmsted for a time]
told me he had seen skeletons, and had helped to bury bodies recently dead.
There were people in the swamps still, he thought, that were the children of
runaways, and who had been runaways themselves all their lives. What a life
it must be; born outlaws; educated self-stealers; trained from infancy to be
constantly in dread of the approach of a white man as a thing more fearful

than wild-cats or serpents, or even starvation" (1: 177). Joseph Church's descriptions underscore the threatening nature of the escaped slaves to the ideal of controlled social relations, pointing out that "some on 'em would rather be shot than took, sir" and attesting to physical markers of their difference from more domesticated slaves:

> *Joseph said that it was easy for the drivers to tell a fugitive from a regularly employed slave in the swamps.*
> *"How do they know them?"*
> *"Oh, dey looks strange."*
> *"How do you mean?"*
> *"Skeared like, you know, sir, and kind o' strange, cause dey hasn't much to eat, and ain't decent [not decently clothed] like we is" (1: 179; bracketed passage original).*

Whether vigorous or half-starved, the swamp Maroons create an impression of uncontrollable savagery lurking just beyond the bounds of carefully cultivated civilization, physically marked as categorically distinct from the docile slave. Olmsted remarks on the topic of slave uprisings that rebellions are almost always betrayed by domestic servants (1: 20): in this respect, the Maroon represents the furthest remove of the enslaved African American from domesticity and control, the polar opposite of the "loyal" turncoat domestic.

Olmsted also recounts a conversation with an unnamed Virginia gentleman who describes a more common but less permanent form of escape afforded by the swamp to slaves hired out by their masters: "But a more serious loss frequently arises, when the slave, thinking he is worked too hard, or being angered by punishment or unkind treatment, 'getting the sulks,' takes to 'the swamp,' and comes back when he has a mind to. Often this will not be till the year is up for which he is engaged, when he will return to his owner, who, glad to find his property safe, and that he has not died in the swamp, or gone to Canada, forgets to punish him, and immediately sends him for a year to a new master" (1: 112–13). Thus, the swamps provided slaves with both temporary and permanent refuge and often disrupted the commercial relations that defined the slave as exchangeable commodity.

Aside from the specter of the escaped slave, swamp dwellers of various kinds emerge repeatedly as ideological and practical threats. One of the most threatening aspects of the swamp, paradoxically, is its very bounty—the effortless "living off the land" that enchanted William Bartram as he observed the habits of swamp-dwelling Native Americans and that disgusted Byrd as he observed the same "savages" and derided the leisurely white "lubbers" for their lack of industry. Olmsted recounts a conversation with Mr. R., a plantation owner and his host during his visit to South Louisiana, that brings home the ideological as well as the practical consequences of the swamp-borne leisure enjoyed by a nearby group of Acadians: "Mr. R. described them as lazy vagabonds, doing but little work, and spending much time in shooting, fishing, and play. . . . Why did he so dislike to have these poor people living near him? Because, he said, they demoralized his negroes. The slaves seeing them living in apparent comfort, without much property and without steady labor, could not help thinking that it was not necessary for men to work so hard as they themselves were obliged to; that if they were free they would not need to work" (2: 332–33). Thus, the temptation of the swamp's natural bounty represented a genuine problem for the slaveholder at the swamp's border, and not merely an affront to an intangible cultural work ethic. Kirby describes the swamp's significance for those who, while not enslaved, were excluded from the master narrative of Southern civilization and society: "This same wetland environment rendered free humans freer to resist both bourgeois society and the agronomic reformers. . . . In and near the Great Dismal, especially, woods-burning and hog-running country folk might live their 'careless' lives . . . and still raise cash at will, on the periphery of the world's market order" (161). By its very fecundity, the swamp threatened the crucial order of the plantation system, sowing discontent among the enslaved through the example of those who lived outside the system they were compelled to perpetuate with their labor and providing limited prosperity to those excluded by the Southern order.

Compounding the menace of the swamp is the fact that it seems only navigable by those that society rejects. Again and again in antebellum Southern literature, the figure of the swamp guide emerges as a misshapen, typically either black or criminal-class white man who is either grotesquely comical or who exudes palpable menace. The cavalier figures, otherwise masters of nature, are obliged to turn over their fates to these unwanted ones who alone can navigate the otherworldly swamps (an exception to this rule appears in the work of William Gilmore Simms, whose own unique engagement with the swamp and its relationship to Southern identity I will examine shortly). To enter the swamp, for the gentleman, is to surrender the control that is, ideally, his greatest and foremost attribute to one of those unfortunate creatures whom his system has forced into mastering this undesirable domain. The swamp becomes a persistent reminder of the limits of civilization's conquest of nature and of the divine right of social class.

The swamp can be seen as the essence of nature, as distinct from and unassimilable into the literary and cultural construct of Southern civilization. It, like the animal self always battled and denied by the cavalier, was in many ways the essence of the Southern problem: it had no place in the myth of self-creation that constituted the ideal South, and yet it remained utterly inalienable from the South itself and therefore ingrained into Southern identity from the very beginning. The remainder of this chapter examines how key antebellum writers and thinkers dealt with the swamp as trope, symbol, signifier, and problem and how, even in the most archetypal Cavalier or plantation romances of William Gilmore Simms and John Pendleton Kennedy, the swamp consistently reemerges as an insurmountable problem.

One writer, well outside the tradition of antebellum myth making, rendered a vision of the swamps—and of Southern society—that ran directly counter to the Cavalier constructions that characterized most Southern literature of the era. In *Odd Leaves from the Life of a Louisiana Swamp Doctor* (1850), Henry Clay Lewis, a Louisiana humorist, creates an image of the swamp and the society around it that not only satirizes the conventions of polite Southern society but also gives a sense of the genuine horrors that the swamps held for those who attempted to navigate them. In the tradition of Southwest humor, Lewis skewers hypocrisy from the very beginning of his work. His collection of stories opens with a brief excursus entitled "The City Physician vs. The Swamp Doctor," in which he consciously distances himself from gentlemanly pretense: "The city physician must be of polished manners and courtly language: the swamp doctor finds the only use he has for bows, is to escape some impending one that threatens him with Absalomic fate; the only necessity for courtly expression, to induce some bellicose 'squatter' to pay his bill in something besides hot curses and cold lead" (22).

Even as Lewis's narrator, Madison Tensas, does away with gentlemanly pretense on his own behalf, he criticizes it roundly in others—the humor in many of his stories comes in part from "unmasking" the "planters" around him. He describes the area where he practices in much the same way that Cash would critique Southern society almost a century later: "The country adjacent to the village where I was studying, is, on two sides, swamp of the vilest, muddiest nature imaginable, with occasional tracts of fine land, generally situated on some bayou or lake; frequently an 'island' of tillable land will be found rising out of the muddy swamp, accessible to footmen or horse only, when the river is within its banks . . . and, wherever existing, generally occupied by a small *planter*. Every farmer in the South is a planter, from the 'thousand baler' to the rough, unshaved, unkempt squatter, who raises just sufficient corn and cotton to furnish a cloak for stealing the year's supply" (Lewis 87).

Lewis's tales present a vision of the rural South that contradicts Cavalier mythology at virtually every turn. His doctor's first call in the swamp is to an older lady whose real problem is that she has run out of whiskey and is going through delirium tremens—his dilemma becomes how to treat her without admitting the nature of her ailment to her or her cohort of ladies. In "A Man of Aristocratic Diseases," he presents us with Major Subsequent, a man who "[finds] his chief glory in the possession of loathsome and incurable afflictions" (157) and who takes pride in the fact that, while his family is riddled with various diseases, "not one of them had ever had a plebeian or unfashionable disease" (159): "The blood of his family was so pure, that only aristocratic diseases could make any morbific impression on their susceptible systems. . . . Every twinge of the gout was a thrill of exquisite pleasure, for only high living and pure blood could have the gout. His eldest son had the King's Evil—the King's Evil, mind you! Major Subsequent was one of those that believed that kings existed in a perpetual atmosphere of delight, and that consequently the King's Evil was only a play-synonyme for the king's pleasure" (160). Lewis unsparingly attacks not only the pretense that accompanies Major Subsequent's questionable claims to royal lineage but the very conception of "pure blood" itself: if pure blood carries with it a host of gruesome disorders, then how pure, finally, can it be? Given the various racial mythologies of pure Anglo-Saxon ancestry purveyed by Southerners in the decades before the Civil War as claims to regional superiority, Lewis's parody of gentlemanly pretense carries genuine subversive power.[2]

Lewis's swamps are vehicles not only for social satire but for terror as well. In "A Struggle for Life," Lewis provides a particularly vivid scene of the swamp guide's potential for horrific violence, and the danger inherent in surrendering one's control to such a being, as the African dwarf who has guided him through the rapidly flooding swamp turns on him. Notice the complete inversion of the traditional power relationship playing out in a matter of moments:

> *Breaking off a cane, I told him that if he spoke to me in that manner again I would give him a severe flogging.*

. . . 'I will kill you,' he again screamed, his fangs clashing and the foam flying from his mouth, his long arms extended as if to clutch me and the fingers quivering nervously.

I took a hasty glance of my condition. I was lost in the midst of the swamp, an unknown watery expanse surrounding me, remote from any possible assistance. The swamps were rapidly filling with water, and if we did not get out tomorrow or the next day we would in all probability be starved or drowned. The Negro was my only dependence to pilot me to the settlements . . . but oh! Awful were my thoughts at dying in such a way— suffocated by a hellish Negro in the midst of the noisome swamp, my flesh to be devoured by the carrion Crow, my bones to whiten. (198–200).

In *Odd Leaves from the Life of a Louisiana Swamp Doctor*, Lewis undercuts many of the underpinnings of the Cavalier myth when it is transposed into the wild, vile, and muddy swamps that provide the setting for his grotesqueries. Here, the masks of honor are poorly maintained, becoming ludicrous claims to aristocracy; further, the swamps themselves are not places to be dominated by crusading cavaliers, but places where the social order loses its power and the lowest of creatures determine the fates of their masters. Significantly, the gentlemanly response to such writings appears to be disdainful silence: Simms, perhaps the foremost spokesman for the mythic South of his era, said in a review of Lewis's work that it was "one of a class to which we do not seriously incline. . . . [T]he less we say the better."

Whatever their menace or mystery, the Southern swamps were clearly men's domain. The discourse of domestic writing, the dominant mode for the Southern antebellum woman writer, largely and rather categorically ignored the swamp. Reasons for this general omission may lie in the very nature of the Southern ideal of womanhood, described vividly by Ann Goodwyn Jones in her 1981 study of Southern women writers, *Tomorrow is Another Day*. Jones points out that, while Southern womanhood shared with ideals of British Victorian and American womanhood the idea that women should be "sexually pure, pious, deferent to external authority, and content with their place in the home," the ideal Southern lady is fundamentally different in that she "is at the core of a region's self-definition; the identity of the South is contingent in part upon the persistence of its tradition of the lady" (4). Jones puts the same essential idea more bluntly in stating that "in general, historians agree that the function of Southern womanhood has been to justify the perpetuation of the hegemony of the male sex, the upper and middle classes, and the white race" (10). It is clear, then, that the swamp in its various significations runs directly counter to ideals of Southern femininity—the very centrality of these ideals to the project of Southern cultural self-creation explains the distance of the idealized feminine from swamp discourse. Further reason for the general distance between white Southern womanhood and the swamp is the necessity of shelter to the fragile feminine ideal. As Jones puts it, "[S]he embodies virtue, but her goodness depends directly on innocence—in fact, on ignorance of evil. She is chaste because she has never been tempted" (9). Thus, distance from such a threatening and morally inflected region as the swamp was not only a matter of categorical separation of the ideological elements of a created civilization from the untamable wilds but of preserving the very vulnerable essence of Southern womanly virtue.

David Miller offers a reading of the swamp in Lydia Sigourney's short story "The Patriarch" (1848) that defines the role of the swamp in much sentimental and domestic fiction: "The obvious allusion is to the Israelites in the wilderness. The encircling swamp is in one sense a relic of the adversity suffered by those who aspired to the righteous life. The colony occupies a circle of purity; it is a refuge from the ambiguity (both moral and physical) of the swamp" (79). The swamp represents the profoundly antidomestic, for reasons the foregoing discussion makes clear; therefore, domestic fiction deals with it primarily as a boundary. It is the province of the cavalier to explore this no-man's- (or woman's-) land: as a genre, the domestic novel had little room to investigate the swamp's secrets.

The most extensive treatment of the Southern swamp as metaphorical and physical entity by an antebellum woman writer comes in what is generally considered to be a lesser novel by a non-Southerner: *Dred*, by Harriet Beecher Stowe. Stowe, who never actually saw the swamps she describes, relies on cliché and convention to invest them with a stridently moralistic symbolic valence: "The wild, dreary belt of a swamp-land which girds in those states scathed by the fires of despotism is an apt emblem, in its rampant and we might say delirious exuberance of vegetation, of that darkly struggling, wildly vegetating swamp of human souls, cut off, like it, from the usages and improvements of cultivated life" (274). The religious overtones of Stowe's statement resonate throughout the novel. Dred, the escaped slave turned swamp-dwelling prophet, becomes a strange version of Milton's Satan as Stowe undermines the Christian underpinnings of slave society: better to reign in his swampy hell than to serve in their unjust "heaven." Dred describes his own condition in opposition to Southern psuedo-Christianity quite dramatically: "I have been a wild man—every man's hand against me—a companion of the dragons and owls, this many a year. . . . I have found the alligators and snakes better neighbors than Christians. They let those alone that let them alone; but Christians will hunt for the precious life" (359).

Stowe's implicit ideal of order, cultivation, and control in *Dred* bears closer investigation in order to situate the swamp's conventional status in the context of the domestic and to explicate the swamp's general lack of investigation by women writers who generally endorsed the Southern system. Stowe situates her societal ideals squarely in the person of Clayton, the devoted reformer who wins the heart of her short-lived heroine, Nina. Clayton's plantation is an ideal of order (391–92), and he devotes himself to "cultivating" slaves. He comments on the negative aspects he perceives in slave behavior: "[W]e are not to judge of it by the rules of cultivated society. In well-trained minds every faculty keeps its due boundaries; but, in this kind of wild-forest growth, mirthfulness will some-times outgrow reverence, just as the yellow jessamine will completely smother a tree" (367). Clayton's philosophies regarding an end to slave society lie in edu-cating and cultivating the slaves, who, while they will never overcome their nat-ural inferiority, can be trained to live in civilized society: as Clayton puts it, "There is no use in trying to turn negroes into Anglo-Saxons, any more than making a grape-vine into a pear tree. I train the grape-vine" (420).

Nina's dreams of a laborless, pastoral, ordered idyll, where there is "no labor, and no trouble, and no dirt, and no care" (409), reflect a naive version of Stowe's implicit ideal. The swamp, as a literal region of unchecked growth and as symbolic correlative to the untrained savagery of neglected, uncultivated slaves, is something to be eliminated through a process of ordering, education, and cultivation. Nina's comments about Tiff, an old slave who earnestly wants to see his children converted to Christianity, sum up her perspective on the tragedy of the transplanted and untutored slave: "Tiff seems to me just like those mistletoes that we see on trees in the swamps. He don't seem to have any root of his own; he seems to grow out of something else" (367). A large part of the evil of the slave system, then, lies in the slaves' lack of rootedness, of proper cultivation and tending. The solution, for Stowe, seems to rest in the placement of proper pruners in Simpson's Garden of the Chattel.

Another work by a woman author of the period, though written by an out-sider, gives at least indirect insight into how Southern women of the upper class may have experienced the swamps—as well as a clear indication of how quickly the swamps could be rhetorically transformed from exotic, fairy-tale settings to mirrors of cultural degradation. Frances Kemble's *Journal of a Residence on a Georgia Plantation*, though not truly representative of a Southern lady's perspective because of both the origins and sympathies of its author, nevertheless proves instructive both as an outsider's account of plantation culture and as a practical depiction of how upper-class Southern ladies dealt with the swamps in everyday life—something that lay outside Stowe's experience until after the Civil War. Kemble was an English actress who entered into the Georgia planter aristocracy by marrying George Butler, a rice planter on the Altamaha river. Kemble's account is travel literature, an account of the scenery, customs, and practices of a place by an outsider—and, as Nelson points out, "Fanny is clearly an outsider—she was never again allowed back onto the Georgia plantations after her visit" (xxv). Kemble was strongly opposed to slavery, and her narrative openly and powerfully critiques the society she observes; further, her critiques are not limited to moral outrage but bespeak a pervasive cultural snobbery: at one point, she refers to the plantation and its environs as "this *ultima thule* of all civilization" (80). At the same time, her position as a privileged participant in that culture gives her a unique perspective among travel writers of her time. The length of Kemble's residence, and her halting but substantial acculturation into the day to day role of a privileged planter's wife, distinguish her account from those of contemporaries who made briefer and more superficial visits. Her account becomes, in ethnographic terms, the work of a participant-observer and as such provides a number of intriguing insights into the relationship of the swamp to the aristocratic Southern woman.

On her initial approach to the settlement that contains Butler's plantation, Kemble's reaction to the swamps seems typical of outside accounts, emphasizing their forbidding, negative aspects: "[I] pursued my way along a narrow dike— the river on the one hand, and, on the other, a slimy, poisonous-looking swamp, all rattling with sedges of enormous height, in which one might lose one's way as effectually as in a forest of oaks" (18). As she settles in to plantation life, the swamps emerge to her as virtual barriers, limiting her walks around the grounds: "My walks are rather circumscribed. . . . On all sides lie either the marshy rice-fields, the brimming river, or the swampy patches of as yet unreclaimed forest, where the hugh [*sic*] cypress-trees and exquisite ever-green undergrowth spring up from a stagnant sweltering pool, that effectually forbids the foot of the explorer" (19).

While Kemble feels effectively excluded from the swamps that surround her new plantation home, she also perceives in them a kind of alien, otherworldly beauty, particularly striking in its uniqueness to the South: "[The Magnolia Grandiflora] grows to the size of a forest tree in these swamps. . . . Under all these the spiked palmetto forms an impenetrable covert, and from glittering graceful branch to branch hand garlands of evergreen creepers. . . . I . . . look round on this strange scene . . . and feel very much like one in another planet from your-self" (20). Kemble views the swamps from their edges, looking down upon them from dikes that serve as bulwarks separating the plantation world from the wilds beyond. To her, the swamps become impenetrable and fascinating; they are poisonous and threatening, but idyllic, wild, and otherworldly. Her fascination, clearly, is born from a sense of exoticism, which she admits evokes an amused curiosity among her neighbors, and sets her apart from the native Southern lady of her era. She makes an effort to bring some of the swamp's exotic beauty to the plantation, going to areas she calls "swamp reserves," tamer, partially cleared, and more easily accessible parts of the swamp, and returning various bushes and trees to plant on the premises. When she does so, her workers disparage her choices for their commonness, "for, though the tree is beautiful, it is also common, and with them, as with wiser folk, 'tis 'nothing pleases but rare accidents' " (69). The swamp's beauty depends, Kemble acknowledges, upon its exoticism; what strikes the outsider as beautiful is commonplace to the native.

Perhaps the most telling single episode regarding the relationship between Southern female gentry and the swamp comes as Kemble rides out to survey the property in hopes of finding an apt spot for a garden. Coming up on a seemingly impassable swamp, she begins to turn back. At this point, a slave woman calls to her: " 'You hab slave enough, nigger enough, let 'em come, let 'em fetch planks, and make de bridge; what you say dey must do—send, missus, send, missis!' It seemed to me, from the lady's imperative tone on my behalf, that if she had been in my place, she would presently have had a corduroy road through the swamp of prostrate 'niggers,' as she called her family in Ham, and have ridden over the sand dry-hoofed" (255). This offer, which Kemble rejects, is intriguing in its insistence—to the woman who calls out, it seems only natural that the slaves should be called upon to build the lady a path through the swamp, laying down planks, or, as Kemble imagines it, their own bodies for her horse to pass over unmolested. The practical problems of the swamp should not be a concern for a lady to deal with—she has slaves enough; let them bear the hardship, as she passes over the obstacle literally on their backs.

Kemble, instead, seeks another way around but, unfortunately, "finds swamp the second, and out of this having been helped by a grinning, facetious personage, most appropriately named Pun, I returned home in a dudgeon in spite of what dear Miss M– calls the 'moral suitability' of finding a foul bog at the end of every charming wood path or forest ride in this region" (255).

While Kemble's experiences give a possible indication of the practical day-to-day relationship between the swamp and the Southern lady, her more rhetorically and politically charged moments transform the swamps entirely. The "moral suitability" allusion here proves characteristic of her attitudes toward Southern society, and the intersections between her impressions of the swamps and her depictions of Southern culture provide some of the most interesting moments in her work. Kemble's social commentary, in contrast to her aesthetic appreciation of the swamps' exotic beauty, follows the abolitionist trend of using the swamps as apt metaphors for a civilization in moral and cultural decay. She makes this moral link clearest as she calls the South "a scene of material beauty and moral degradation, where the beauty itself is of an appropriate character to the human existence it surrounds: above all, loveliness, brightness, and fragrance; but below! It gives one a sort of melusina feeling of horror—all swamp and poisonous stagnation, which the heat will presently make alive with poisonous reptiles" (187). She recounts an instance in which a slave, Louisa, tells of running away into the swamps to escape the taskmaster's lash; incredulous, Kemble asks whether she was afraid of the "dreadful rattlesnakes" that infested them. " 'O, missis,' " the girl replies, " 'me no tink of dem; me forget all 'bout dem for the fretting' " (175). Here, as in Stowe and Jacobs, the snake-ridden swamps emerge as preferable to the everyday horrors of slavery. The fragrant beauty she observes from her vantage point on the protective dikes fades, as well, as she discusses the swamps in the context of slave labor conditions: though rice cultivation is a purportedly unhealthy process, she says, "it seems to me that even the process of soaking the rice can hardly create a more dangerous miasma than the poor creatures must inhale who live in the midst of these sweltering swamps, half sea, half river slime" (187–88).

The swamps' charms end, for Kemble, with their connection—whether actual or metaphorical—to Southern culture. She goes on a lengthy tirade against the squalid white settlers who live on others' land in the pine barrens and swamps: "These wretched creatures will not, for they are whites (and labor belongs to blacks and slaves alone here), labor for their own subsistence. They are hardly protected from the weather by the rude shelters they frame for themselves in the midst of these dreary woods. Their food is chiefly supplied by shooting the wild-fowl and venison, and stealing from the cultivated patches of the plantations nearest at hand. Their clothes hang about them in filthy tatters, and the combined squalor and fierceness of their appearance is really frightful" (76). Kemble does not dwell on the poor swampers out of sheer disgust at their poverty; she goes on to claim that "this population is the direct growth of slavery" (76). However aesthetically bewitching the swamps may be, when called to the aid of social critique they assume all the classic negative tropes: they are hellish shelters for runaway slaves; places of poisonous, malarial sickness; and havens for the lazy, impoverished dregs of Southern civilization.

Kemble's true target in her negative depiction of the swamps is always the culture that surrounds them. This fact becomes clearest as she expresses what seems to be a nascent ecologist's perspective on the clearance of the swamps along the road: "They have almost stripped the trees and thickets along the swamp road since I first came here. I wonder what it is for; not fuel surely, nor to make grass-land of, or otherwise cultivate the swamp. I do deplore these pitiless clearings; and as to this once pretty road, it looks 'forlorn,' as a worthy Pennsylvania farmer's wife once said to me of a pretty hill-side from which her husband had ruthlessly felled a beautiful growth of trees" (262). At times, for Kemble, the swamps embody and mirror the wickedness of the local culture; at others—when the swamps fall victim to that very culture—they become helpless, lamented victims of its "pitiless" advance.

By the end of her stay, Kemble has clearly compartmentalized her appreciation and pity in favor of making full rhetorical use of the swamps. A letter to the editor of the London *Times*, written after her return to England, makes pointed use of the swamp landscape to depict the Southern people. They are "a nation, for as such they should be spoken of, of men whose organization and temperament is that of the Southern European; living under the influence of a climate at once enervating and exciting; scattered over trackless wildernesses of arid sand and pestilential swamp; intrenched within their own boundaries; surrounded by creatures absolutely subject to their despotic will; delivered over by hard necessity to the lowest excitements of drinking, gambling, and debauchery for sole recreation; independent of all opinion; ignorant of all progress; isolated from all society—it is impossible to conceive a more savage existence within the pale of any modern civilization" (302). Kemble's writings depict a swamp that is by turns exotic and enticing, pestilential and blighted. Her participant-observer status as a "temporary" Southern lady gives us glimpses of how the swamps may have appeared to those whose gender and class typically kept them from exploring them, or from thinking of them as anything but impenetrable barriers. Her outsider status, however, gives rise to the contradictory tropes that emerge in her work: the swamp as a place of otherworldly beauty, and the swamp as metaphor for moral decadence.

Stowe, in dealing with the swamp in a semidomestic, heavily conventionalized manner as an unambiguous metaphor for the evils of Southern society, and Kemble, in portraying the swamps as unsurpassable obstacles best used as metaphorical ammunition for attacks on the South, may suggest why antebellum writings by Southern women largely neglected the swamp as anything but a boundary. While Stowe's novel and Kemble's polemics warn that the swamp's evils already pervade and permeate Southern culture, that culture's staunchest adherents—those most devoted to defending the apex of Southern civilization, the hallowed female, domestic space—properly relegated the untamed wilderness to a position that was, by definition, beyond the margins of the world they described. If the swamp embodied the perceived sins and ills of their civilization, they would ignore it as they ignored those ills.

It has become a truism that the female domestic finds its opposite number in the masculine drive to explore, to conquer, and to subjugate. However simplistic such a formulation may seem, it is undeniably true that the writings of Southern males, both fictional and otherwise, describe a much more direct confrontation with the swamp on its own terms than do those of Southern women. It is through tracing the writings of those who, as the dominant gender and class, were the most self-conscious inventors and definers of Southern identity that the vexed relationship of the swamp to that identity becomes clearest.

Most Southern scholars date the inception of the Cavalier myth, a cultural myth that served as the underpinnings for Old South culture as we now know it, in the early 1830s. As we have seen, that myth was as pivotal in defining Southern identity in relation to the swamp as it was in so many other aspects of Southern life. However, a few very meaningful and influential early encounters with the Southern swamp have proven resonant in establishing the relationship between Southern Man and Southern Swamp that would persist into the twentieth century. Before the Cavalier myth that came to govern much of Southern self-conception came into its own in the early 1830s, mercantile, scientific, and poetic engagements with the Southern swamps would cast the die for future understandings of Southern selfhood.

As romantically lauded or superstitiously demonized as the swamp would come to be in the South, the earliest notable colonial excursions into it were utilitarian. In fact, New World swamp discourses from the very earliest English settlements were actively sanitized by the trading companies who sought to profit from New World development, leading to an early war of words in representing the American swamps. As Stephen Adams describes in his 2001 book *The Best and Worst Country in the World: Perspectives on the Early Virginia Landscape*, a propaganda war characterized early English representations of Virginia: "Alongside the upbeat, propagandistic view of Virginia as Eden, Promised Land, gold mine, commodity warehouse, pastoral paradise, there emerges from the surviving texts another, opposite view of Virginia. This pictures the land as a hellhole where people die quickly and miserably and in breathtaking numbers—Virginia as a death trap and slaughterhouse" (156). The Virginia Company of London made concerted efforts to minimize these reports, censoring and suppressing them and "[distracting] attention from Virginia itself by focusing on the veracity, morals, and intentions of those who reported trouble in the land" (158). In the course of this war of representation, we see a nascent sense of defensive regional identity emerging: "Francis Wyatt (1624) identifies other slanderers of Virginia [than those who actually settled there]: 'Some disparage the Plantation in generall, who are fomented perhaps by those, who desire to raise the Northern Colony by the disgrace of ours.' Damn Yankees were suspected of hostility toward Virginia from the very beginning" (115, 158).

Health problems in Jamestown were an undeniable reality, and the swamps, contaminated by human factors, played a definite role in the pestilence, as Adams explains: "[T]he island itself was a marshy lowland, over one-half swamp. . . . The settlers, prevented by Indian attacks from getting their water elsewhere, contracted from their contaminated water the diseases that took such a heavy toll those first years, especially dysentery, salt poisoning, and typhoid fever" (165). The swamps became a central locus for debates over the healthiness of the New World. Contemporary representations of the health problems emergent in the Virginia colony followed strategies that the South would later adopt in ideological defense of its own culture. William Strachey tried to put the swamps in perspective as an unwholesome part of a much larger and more varied area: "[N]o more let us lay scandal, and imputation upon the Country of Virginia, because the little Quarter wherein we are set downe (unadvisedly so chosed) appears to be unwholesome, and subject to many ill ayres, which accompany the like marish places" (qtd. in Adams 166).

Strachey further places a kind of self-serving spin on the causes of "swamp-borne" diseases by placing the blame on the "idleness and mismanagement of the colonists themselves" (Adams 166)—a charge clearly motivated by marketing and propaganda concerns but closer to accurate than the tradition that would emerge of blaming the swamps themselves for naturally emanating unhealthy air. Early colonial representations of the swamp were primarily motivated by practicality, and even by the time of Byrd, the potent mythologies that would surround the swamps were secondary to practical concerns.

Both Byrd's attempts to demarcate between North Carolina and Virginia and the Great Dismal Swamp Company's efforts to drain and farm the swampland share the basic assumption that the swamp was an obstacle that could and would be overcome by the efforts of gentlemen (more directly, of course, of those working for them) in an effort to create an ordered "landscape of the mind" in the service of either King and country or of monetary gain. Byrd, despite the sexual frankness of his diaries and his theoretical opposition to the institution of slavery, was in many ways an early prototype of the ideal chivalric Southern gentleman. A brief examination of his early life reveals how appropriate his adoption as that prototype truly is: Byrd's self-creation was as self-consciously literary and as driven by inflexible codes as that of the Cavalier South itself. Although Byrd's self-fashioning long predates the construction of the Cavalier myth, the defensiveness of his posture as a cultured gentleman in a savage land, and his self-professed desire to bring the wilderness under civilized control, make him a microcosmic template for the eventual project of antebellum Southern identity and account for his influence over such later Southern spokesmen as Edmund Ruffin and Simms.

At the age of seven, Byrd was sent to England by his father, an ambitious middle-class Virginian, to receive the kind of schooling befitting a proper English gentleman. In part, Byrd's father made the decision in response to Bacon's Rebellion in 1681—an event perceived by many in both England and the colonies as a rising of the "rabble" that cast doubt on Virginia's fitness as a place to breed gentlemen. Kenneth Lockridge, in *The Diary, and Life, of William Byrd II of Virginia, 1674–1744*, explains the rationale for Byrd's uprooting: "If, in rowdy and rebellious Virginia, the potentially gentle family his father was creating was to acquire the polish and influence which would enable it to consolidate its gains—the polish to impress the turbulent populace, the influence to obtain from the crown positions of profit and power— . . . then William Byrd II must be sent to his mother's Cavalier family and to their school. Measuring up to this goal became young William's way of explaining to himself the hurt of a rejection, his exile, which was no less profound for being somewhat in keeping with the mores of gentle Englishmen then and now. . . . To 'improve,' as his father put it, meant first of all to be what Felsted school was intended to create, a gentleman" (21). Presented poetically, as Lockridge presents it, Byrd's early life seems almost Faulknerian: the young Southerner, exiled from his birthplace and family, strove to meet his father's expectations but had no real idea how to do so. He would only see his father twice more in his life, though some accounts report that late in life he disinterred his father's corpse to seek advice in its "wasted countenance" (Lockridge 12). In the absence of any clear male role model, Byrd set about the vague task of "improving himself" by turning to books: "[B]ooks were all he brought with him out of his school years, books and the personality they helped him shape" (20). Byrd turned to works like Sir Thomas Elyot's *The Boke Named the Governour* and Richard Brathwaite's *The English Gentleman*, whose doctrines in many ways extol the virtues that would eventually be associated with the Southern Cavalier: "Both Brathwaite and Elyot recommended above all else moderation, temperance, and self-control. For both, the great enemy is passion. They prescribe examples of how all passions may be controlled" (Lockridge 24). From these works, the solitary Byrd constructed a self as close as he could attain to what he perceived as the cryptic object of his "improvement."

On his return to Virginia, Byrd followed his literary idea of gentlemanly behavior ever more closely: "The shock of Virginia seems to have turned a stiff view of the gentleman's role into an unvarying daily routine which had compulsively to be reviewed in secrecy" (50). Lockridge portrays Byrd as a man whose private self becomes subsumed in his obsessive attempts to embody the ideal of the proper English gentleman. In discussing Byrd's diary, written in a shorthand code, Lockridge observes: "Byrd's very behavior was encoded. . . . Plainly, what the diary describes are the expected behaviors of an eighteenth-century gentleman repeated and obsessively reviewed" (6). An often quoted passage in his diaries reveals his morning regimen: "I rose at 4 o'clock this morning and read a chapter in Hebrew and 400 verses in Homer's *Odyssey*" (qtd. in Lockridge 6), a self-conscious devotion to classical education that will mark the archetypal Southern gentleman at least until the era of Jason Compson. Key to Byrd at all times were equanimity and composure—the maintenance of his "good humour," as he puts it, which amounts to subduing passion. In many ways, Byrd seems to have almost thoroughly written himself into being: as Lockridge suggests, "The behavioral routine and the emotional restraint are so deeply engrained that they raise the possibility that beneath the codes there *was* nothing to hide. William Byrd was his secrecy, his routine, his restraint" (8). Through obsessive adherence to codes, constant self-review, and a stringent and inflexible response to a constant creeping uncertainty that he was indeed a gentleman, Byrd became a breathing embodiment of his codes— a self-made, meticulously maintained gentleman of a kind that resonates strongly with future Southern archetypes.

Not surprisingly, in his writings other than the coded journal, Byrd comes across as acutely conscious of his own gentility. *A History of the Dividing Line* depicts Byrd as the chivalric knight, trusted with a crucial task and willing to carry it out regardless of the risk. His literary persona "was a gentleman who was representative of a class of men which alone could direct the running of coherent lines through an incoherent wilderness. . . . The line this leader ran was, ultimately, a social line. On one side was a social order, emanating in its essence from men like himself. On the other, was the social chaos of lubberland" (141). Byrd emphasizes the swamp's mystery, remarking that even those who lived at the swamp's edges could tell him nothing of what lay within: "It is hardly credible how little the bordering inhabitants were acquainted with this mighty swamp, notwithstanding they had lived their whole lives within smell of it. . . . In short, we saw plainly that there was no intelligence of this *terra incognita* to be got, but from our own experience" (53). Byrd reinforces his image as knight-errant, if somewhat self-parodically, in describing the locals' reactions to his group: "They looked upon us as a troop of knights-errant who were running this great risk of our lives, as they imagined, for the public weal; and some of the gravest of them questioned whether we were not all criminals, condemned to this dirty work for offenses against the state" (45). This brief passage from his *History* introduces three themes that will recur in Southern understandings of the swamp: first, that the swamp is a place of death; second, that it is the domain of self-sacrificing knightly heroes; and finally, that it is the rightful abode of society's dregs—a place of condemnation for criminals against the state.

Byrd's conscious self-creation in his diaries makes his accounts of swamp cultures particularly intriguing from an ethnographic standpoint. In recent years, anthropologist James Clifford, at the forefront of a broad trend, has pointed out the instability of the distinction between literary and ethnographic representation. As he points out in *Writing Culture*, no written representation of a culture can be strictly mimetic: ethnography, as a product of writing, "is always caught up in the invention, not the representation, of cultures. . . . Literary processes—metaphor, figuration, narrative—affect the ways cultural phenomena are registered, from the first jotted 'observations,' to the completed book, to the ways these configurations 'make sense' in determined acts of reading" (2–4). Clifford underscores the crucial power dynamics underlying the ethnographic process: "Ethnographic work has indeed been enmeshed in a world of enduring and changing power inequalities, and it continues to be implicated. It enacts power relations" (9). Richard Fox agrees, stating in *Recapturing Anthropology: Working in the Present* (1991) that "writing ethnography is always . . . an assertion of power, a claim to 'authority' that, when successful, becomes an 'authorization.' . . . [A]n ethnographic text, most of us would agree, works to construct the very society and culture under study" (6). Further, Clifford's 1988 work *The Predicament of Culture* examines the tendency toward appropriation, distortion, and intellectual imperialism that often, consciously or not, distorts the ethnographer's work. For Clifford, ethnography tends to cast cultures into ideological molds: ethnographers reflect more of themselves and their own cultures in their representations than the cultures they purport to depict. Ethnography, then, tells us as much about the surveyor as the surveyed: as Clifford claims, ethnography often "[throws one] back on a relentless self-ethnography—not autobiography but an act of writing [one's] existence in a present of memories, dreams, politics, daily life" (14). Byrd's representations of swamp cultures reinforce his autobiographical aims—he defines himself in terms of the Other, even as he blazes the line of civilization through the swamp wilderness.

From the beginning, Byrd is unequivocal about the foulness of the swamp that he must navigate, making repeated comments that the swamp is a more appropriate domain for vermin and amphibians than for men. Most intriguing, though, are those moments when the understandable frustration of one sent to perform an onerous task in inhospitable surroundings takes on a moral, and even religious, dimension—particularly because, in each case, Byrd's condemnation of the swamp or of its people is tinged with some acknowledgment of the swamp's sinister beauty or of the temptations of its wild bounty. Beginning what will prove a long tradition, he derides the "lubbers"—his term for people on the edges of the swamp—for their laziness, which he sees as rising directly from the generous natural yield of the swamp he seeks to tame: "[D]rones . . . are but too common, alas, in that part of the world. Though, in truth, the distemper of laziness seizes the men oftener much than the women. These last spin, weave, and knit, all with their own hands, while their husbands, depending on the bounty of the climate, are slothful in everything but the getting of children, and in that only instance make themselves useful members of an infant colony" (59). Thus, Byrd, in a mood either proleptically Victorian or belatedly Puritan, perceives the lassitude of the locals as moral failing and blames that flaw on the region's very fecundity. Further, he blames the men in particular for failing to be industrious, for falling short of the drive to produce that will characterize the Cavalier gentleman. Byrd is even more vividly judgmental of a landowner who has built his plantation on the very edge of the swamp to exploit its bounty: "This, I own, is some convenience for his purse, for which his whole family pay dear in their persons, for they are devoured by mosquitoes all the summer, and have agues every spring and fall, which corrupt all the juices of their bodies, give them a cadaverous complexion, and besides a lazy, creeping habit, which they are never rid of" (65). The swamp breeds both physical sickness and moral decay; Byrd links both to the effort to profit from the swamp's natural bounty. Byrd blasts the frontier "lubber" society along the swamp's borders, claiming that "[s]urely there is no place in the world where the inhabitants live with less labor than in North Carolina" and that the men's lack of industry makes them "just like the lazy Indians" (185). We see here an early instance of the persistent idea—recounted by Olmsted in his conversation with the Louisiana planter—that swamp-dwelling peoples outside the white Anglo-Saxon mainstream present dangerous examples to those who, though less "noble" than the Southern gentleman, are nevertheless part of the dominant system. To Byrd's classically trained mind, the swamp becomes a menacing nymph, whose gifts always come with a moral and physical price. The fact that the swamplands provide ample bounty without agricultural effort emerges as a threat to the soul—indeed, the swamp becomes paradoxically deleterious both in its enabling of, and resistance to, various forms of agriculture.

Also compelling are the moments when a paranoid religious mysticism colors Byrd's fascination with, and revulsion toward, the swamp: "Doubtless, the eternal shade that broods over this mighty bog, and hinders the sunbeams from blessing the ground, makes it an uncomfortable habitation for anything that has life. . . . It had one beauty, however, that delighted the eye, though at the expense of all the other senses: the moisture of the soil preserves a continual verdure, and makes every plant an evergreen, but at the same time the foul damps ascend without ceasing, corrupt the air, and render it unfit for respiration. Not even a turkey buzzard will venture to fly over it, no more than the Italian vultures will over the filthy lake Avernus, or the birds in the Holy Land, over the salt sea, where Sodom and Gomorrah formerly stood" (62). This tendency to imbue the swamp with religious significance would hardly be limited to Byrd—generations of writers, from Bartram to Stowe to Sidney Lanier, would treat the swamp as a primordial place vested with daunting spiritual significance, and it became a commonplace to refer to the alligator, the most notorious of swamp fauna, as "leviathan." There is, however, a palpable air of self-dramatization in Byrd's writing, justifying his status as a gentleman crusader that was threatened by his dwelling in the New World. The more horrible, both physically and spiritually, this terra incognita becomes, the more admirable is Byrd's errand into the wilderness, and the more implicitly distant he becomes from the sallow-faced drones who live slothfully off the swamp's poisoned bounty. Though Byrd composed his *History of the Dividing Line* with no real intent that it ever be published, for one whose personal diary so painstakingly records his efforts to sustain his status as gentleman, even private reaffirmations seem significant. The swamp is unsuitable for human life, to Byrd, but most especially for the more refined sensibilities of the Englishman—he claims at one point that in the Great Dismal Swamp "the soil was so full of water, and the air so full of damps, that nothing but a Dutchman could live in them" (103).

Byrd's perception of the swamp's dangers was not entirely the product of philosophical predisposition. Malaria had been not only a vague superstition but a real threat linked with the swamp for centuries. Contemporary science bore out the indeterminate variety of physical, mental, and moral illnesses that Byrd feared emanated from the swamp, and would until Alphonse Laveran's 1880 discovery of the actual cause of malaria, the parasite *plasmodium* (Poser and Bruyn 20). Before that time, malaria described any illness thought to result from the swamp's "bad air" (*mal'aria*), or miasma, the etymological root of malaria. As Charles Poser and George W. Bruyn point out in *An Illustrated History of Malaria*, "During most of the 19th century, malaria was not used as the name of a disease; it referred to a noxious material, presumably gaseous, which emanated from swamps or from rotted vegetation or decaying animal carcasses" (22). Byrd, classical scholar that he was, was no doubt familiar with the quasi-mystical, inchoate menace whose association with the swamp's "exhalations" dates back to the ancient Greeks. Upon completing his task, Byrd is as pleasantly surprised that none of his company was taken ill as he is that the job proved a relatively quick one.

Byrd's studiously refined sensibilities are perhaps most evident as he describes the Indians who dwell in the swamps, whose cruelty vies with their lack of gentlemanly honor for Byrd's disapproval: "And (what shows the baseness of the Indian temper in perfection) they can never fail to treat those with greatest inhumanity that have distinguished themselves most by their bravery; and, if he be a war captain, they do him the honor to roast him alive, and distribute a collop to all that had a share in stealing the victory" (157). It would be banal to attribute Byrd's revulsion at witnessing acts like these to mere cultural chauvinism, and to his credit he follows his indictments with a note that even the mighty Achilles and Alexander the Great were cruel to their enemies in battle. Nevertheless, Byrd's writings show a clear conception of the swamp-dwelling Native Americans, whose individual tribes he only occasionally makes clear, as purely savage, distilling swamp-born lassitude and moral lack. He notes that the Indians have no sabbath and explains that "[i]ndeed these idle people have very little occasion for a sabbath to refresh themselves after hard labor, because very few of them ever labor at all. Like the wild Irish, they would rather want than work, and are all men of pleasure, to whom every day is a day of rest" (194). Byrd's values emerge in sharp relief here: torture and cannibalism, he may excuse with a classical comparison; sloth garners pure disapproval and a comparison to the Irish.

As a kind of archetypal Southern gentleman, whose works were widely read after their publication in 1841, Byrd undoubtedly influenced the perceptions of the Southern lettered class. He underscores or inaugurates the ideas that swamp dwellers are not only physically but morally imperiled; he feeds the idea that the swamp is not only dangerous but profoundly unholy, its apparent gifts like a serpent's apple to the farmer better served by diligent toil. Alongside his warnings and deprecations, Byrd continuously asserts the supremacy of the Southern gentleman—himself—over the various swamp subalterns, underscoring the gentleman's ability to triumph over and to reform both human and geographic recalcitrance. As Lockridge puts it, Byrd's story of taming the swamp is also "the epic of William Byrd's natural mastery of those around him on their great journey" (132). Ultimately, despite the success of his mission and the continued health of his men, Byrd's judgment on the swamp is unequivocal: "The exhalations that continually rise from this vast body of mire and nastiness infect the air for many miles round, and render it very unwholesome for the bordering inhabitants. It makes them liable to agues, pleurisies, and many other distempers, that kill abundance of people, and make the rest look no better than ghosts. It would require a great sum of money to drain it, but the public treasure could not be better bestowed, than to preserve the lives of his majesty's liege people, and at the same time render so great a tract of swamp very profitable" (74). Byrd's plans here express the second of Douglas's cultural means of dealing with troubling ambiguities: the effort to master or destroy them physically. This trend dominates early notable Southern encounters with the swamp, and Byrd, as we shall see, influenced many subsequent approaches. Perhaps most importantly, Byrd clearly defines the gentleman's role as tamer of the swamp, the one who ventures in and demarcates and the one who, ultimately, should see to the draining of this unhealthy and unhallowed morass, for public good and personal profit.

The distinct Southernness of Byrd's encounter with the swamp and the influence of his experience come into sharper focus alongside the work of another early swamp explorer with a decidedly different agenda: the Philadelphia-born naturalist William Bartram. Venturing into the wetlands of Florida, Georgia, and the Carolinas in 1791, Bartram had few of the practical concerns that weighed on Byrd and his society—he was a naturalist, not a planter, and instead of Byrd's proto-Victorian disapproval of the lassitude of swamp dwellers and the savagery of its native Indians, he brought distinctly romantic sensibilities to his study of the swamplands.

In many ways, Bartram represents the polar opposite of Byrd's self-conscious Southern gentleman. Bartram was a Quaker, a member of a religious group famously antagonistic to the Southern slave society. In *Poquosin*, Kirby explains the affinity of Quakers, who rejected slavery and rigid class distinctions, for the Southern swamp: "That Quakerism flourished not on the upper Elizabeth but at the foot of the cross, in the remote swamps, may be more than coincidence. . . . Here was a countercultural place, where people removed themselves from disagreeable institutions economic and social and where enslavement was visible but relatively unimportant" (11). Though he nominally belonged to the Philadelphia Quaker "elite," Bartram's indifference to social standing and prestige sets him markedly apart from Byrd. Although Bartram was elected in 1768 to a prestigious group that would merge with the American Philosophical Society, whose members included such luminaries as Ben Franklin, he never attended a meeting. Also, Bartram concerns himself comparatively little with slavery in his writings and indeed provides little historical or cultural context for his writings at all (his *Travels* does not even mention the Revolutionary War, though the majority of it was written between 1773 and 1778). Bartram's account is almost thoroughly removed from culture and history, while Byrd's fairly creaks beneath the weight of cultural expectation.

Bartram's work had a profound impact upon its publication in London in 1792. While reviewers, particularly in America, typically tempered their praise with mild criticism of Bartram's uncritical ebullience about nature and "indulgence" toward the natives, these were exactly the characteristics of his writing that appealed to the Romantics he influenced most: as Francis Harper points out, his descriptions of the swamp and of the swamp's denizens influenced Coleridge, Wordsworth, Shelley, and Southey, among others, as well as American romantics such as Emerson and Thoreau (xxvii). Bartram's *Travels* intriguingly combines scrupulous detail and scientific empiricism with romantic wonder and awe. Early in his work, Bartram reveals his fundamental philosophy of human nature—upon meeting a gentle Indian in the swamp, Bartram asks, "[C]an it be denied, but that the moral principal, which directs the savages to virtuous and praiseworthy actions, is natural or innate?" (15–16). The contrast with the soon-to-develop Victorian idea that natural impulses were inherently savage and evil is immediately clear: for Bartram, outsider and naturalist, nature needs no taming. Bartram waxes poetic about the natural virtues of the Cherokee: "O Divine simplicity and truth, friendship without fallacy or guile, hospitality disinterested, native, undefiled, unmodified by artificial refinements" (222). The impact of Bartram's presentation of what would become the "noble savage" in the Romantic imagination underscores his opposition to Byrd's goals in literature and in life: while Byrd strove to carry out the paternal imperative to prove that the civilized gentleman could and did inhabit the Southern "wilds," Bartram's visions of the native restored an image of an aboriginal New World that ran distinctly counter to the Southern gentlemanly drive to legitimize his civilization in the eyes of a judgmental and metropolitan Britain. If Byrd's *History* can be characterized as the epic of a gentleman imposing order and mastery on the people and landscape around him through sheer force of personality, Bartram's *Travels*, in presenting a world largely untouched by European culture or the vicissitudes of history, seems to erase any trace of that civilizing power.

Bartram's sharpest direct contrast with Byrd comes as he describes the Seminoles who live off the swamp without agricultural labor. While Byrd condemns those who live without industry, Bartram exalts the situation in ironically classical tones: "How happily situated is this retired spot of earth! What an elisium it is . . . where the wandering Siminole, the naked red warrior, roams at large. . . . Here he reclines, and reposes under the odoriferous shades of zantholixon, his verdant couch guarded by the deity; Liberty, and the muses, inspiring him with wisdom and valour, whilst the balmy zephyrs fan him to sleep" (69). The swamp provides secure repose and inexhaustible sustenance, "such a plenty and variety of supplies for the nourishment of varieties of animals . . . that no part of the globe so abounds with wild game or creatures fit for the food of man" (134). Bartram's Indian is no torturing cannibal, but noble savage; his swamp is not a polluting temptress, but a bountiful Eden. In many ways, Bartram can be considered a proleptic multiculturalist, even planning in his representations to stave off the unjust judgments that his European readers were likely to pass on the Native Americans he described. Gregory Waselkov and Kathryn Braund state that Bartram "unquestionably endeavored in his writings to present Native Americans in a way that his readers would find appealing and morally correct, especially in regard to practices that white society found reprehensible. In his mind, a society should be judged, at least initially, by its own standards" (17). Adopted now as a kind of progressive hero by a school of approving academics, Bartram seems, in his very "primitivism," to have been a harbinger for the contemporary left: aside from his nascent multiculturalism, he was, according to Harper, "simply two or three generations ahead of his time in his appreciation of nature" (xxvi).

Essentially, Bartram exalts the very elements that the Cavalier mentality sought to master and control. Further, Bartram at times directly inverts the typically Southern idea that swamp peoples and cultures can pollute mainstream Southern culture through their moral lassitude and slothful examples. At some points, Bartram denies the generally accepted necessity of religious conversion and cultural instruction for the Muscogulges, or Creek and Seminole Indians: "If we consider them with respect to their private character or in a moral view, they must, I think, claim our approbation, if we divest ourselves of prejudice and think freely. As moral men they certainly stand in no need of European civilization" (310). In another passage, Bartram goes a step further, displaying a rare degree of consideration for the Native Americans' perspective on socialization into European mores: "In the consideration of this important subject it will be necessary to enquire, whether they were inclined to adopt the European modes of civil society? Whether such a reformation could be obtained, without using coercive or violent means? And lastly, whether such a revolution would be productive of real benefit to them?" (xxxiii). Not only does Bartram question what Byrd and his ilk took to be self-evident—that dominion and conversion of the swamps and the swamp peoples were not only desirable but a kind of divine destiny—he ultimately suggests that white culture, not the culture of the swamp-dwelling Indians, is the true polluter. He points out that the Creek Indians' vigorous hunting "is indeed carried to an unreasonable and perhaps criminal excess, since the white people have dazzled their senses with foreign superfluities" (214). From Bartram's perspective, white civilization despoiled the natural ideal, positioning him at the opposite ideological pole from the standard-bearers of Southern culture.

Bartram's account of the swamps is not all starry-eyed paean to natural beauty. He has moments of genuine fear at being in the swamps alone, surrounded by marshes that "seemed to have no bounds," and confesses at one point that "constant watching at night against the attacks of alligators, stinging of mosquitoes and sultry heats of the day; together, with the fatigues of working my bark, had almost deprived me of every desire but that of ending my troubles as speedy as possible" (86). He also reports that some of the Indians he meets with have had to move their town because of the unhealthy rot and exhalations of the swamp (123). At one point, seeming to echo Byrd, Bartram describes an awful ulcerating disease among cattle who live off the rich water-grass of the swamp as "a sacrifice to intemperance and luxury" (132). The swamp's menaces, though, are always secondary to its gifts for Bartram. His accounts contain just hint enough of the terrors of the swamp, and of its traditional association with death, to maintain the tension necessary for the true pastoral. In one key passage about a feast in the swamps, the landscape's inherent duality comes through most clearly. He and his companions are "in the midst of plenty and variety, at any time within our reach, and to be obtained with little or no trouble or fatigue on our part," but he remains conscious of "the vultures and ravens, crouched on the crooked limbs of the lofty pines, at a little distance from us, sharpening their beaks, in low debate, waiting to regale themselves on the offals, after our departure from camp" (114). Bartram's swamp, though it maintains an air of sublime mystery and awesome fear, is ultimately a cornucopia. For those who are attuned to it, and who know how to live in it and avoid its dangers, it is Elysium. Bartram's perspective, influential as it was both overseas in Britain and in the United States, stands as virtually antithetical to the practical, proto-Victorian mindset that characterized the plantation South even before the turn of the nineteenth century.

For the final touchstone pre-Cavalier encounter with the Southern swamp, we turn to the efforts of perhaps the foremost gentleman in early American history—George Washington, cofounder of the Great Dismal Swamp Company. Perhaps the most famous mercantile endeavor in the early history of the Southern swamp, the Great Dismal Swamp Company officially announced itself in 1763. It was a consortium of distinguished gentlemen whose goal was essentially to follow through on Byrd's prescription for the swamplands—to drain them and farm them for the common good and, of course, for what they hoped and fervently, illogically, and eventually mulishly believed would be rich profits.

Washington's perspective on the land itself diverged markedly from conventional wisdom. In *The Fabulous History of the Dismal Swamp Company* (1999), Charles Royster, with a hint of foreshadowing futility, recounts Washington's earliest encounters with the swampland: "Most soil along the road into North Carolina was sandy and poor. Yet Washington was sure that within the swamp all was black and fertile. . . . Though local people thought it 'a low sunken Morass, not fit for any of the purposes of Agriculture,' Washington felt certain that it was 'excessive Rich'" (82). The swamp's gifts, to Washington and the Company, were not to be given at the swamp's discretion to the slothful, disease-ridden, and morally questionable parasitic edge dweller, as they were in Byrd's journals. They were to be systematically and industriously taken, while the swamp itself was leveled, drained, and plowed into a proper and profitable garden. The perspectives, opinions, and even claims of those more familiar with the territory mattered little to the politically potent gentlemen of the company, who acted with equally powerful and only problematically distinguishable moral, political, and commercial mandates. Royster reveals the blurring of the lines between Byrd's (and the Great Dismal Swamp Company's) two chief goals in draining the swamp, the "public good" and profit. In 1764, the House of Burgesses and Council approved a Company-proposed law giving them the right to dig canals in the swamp and stating that "[t]he company must submit to arbitration to determine compensation due to any property-holder claiming to have suffered loss. But property-holders could not sue the company because, the law read, rendering the swamp fit for cultivation 'will be attended with public utility'" (89). From its outset, then, the Great Dismal Swamp Company's history underscores the encoded caste system underlying antebellum Southern social and political dynamics. Although historical record, the journals of Byrd, and the law itself acknowledge that a certain (comparatively low) class of landowner might have a vested interest in the swamp, the acts of the gentlemen, of the cultivators and tamers of wildness, truly represented the public good.

For over forty years, the Company sent its inexhaustible army of slave laborers to toil in the swamps. This group of laborers, however, was not so fortunate as Byrd's seemingly blessed company, who emerged from the swamp's pestilential heart relatively unscathed. As Royster recounts, the efforts of the Great Dismal Swamp Company took a brutal toll on its laborers: "Suffering, disease, and deaths among slaves working on the Jericho Canal appeared in stories told by people in Nansemond County for generations—stories of 'chain-gangs of slaves': 'They say the poor creatures died here in heaps from swamp fever. But that didn't make any difference to their owners. They was made to dig right into the heart of the swamp to get at the juniper trees' " (422). And still, the goal of draining the swamp to create farmland eluded the Company, whose only real profits came from the shingles made from the inexhaustible trees that their laborers felled.

At the same time, echoing the ambivalent signification of the swamp for the slave that Cowan describes, the swamp labor that white men shunned led those slaves who escaped the swamp's plagues to a strange liberty. As long as the workers were productive, the whites allowed them leisure time: "If they produced their shingles in five days, they took two days for themselves outside the swamp. Some weeks they took three. Their owners and other whites in and near Suffolk complained that the shingle-getters had 'too much leisure time,' which they spent 'improperly' " (419–20). While it would be absurd to compare the experience of these laborers with true freedom, in one sense the swamp here does afford privileges to the oppressed who work within it. The vexed complaints of their owners, largely powerless to do anything about the leisure that sparks their disapproval, underscore the real, if limited, role of the swamp in undermining Southern power relations—the physical disorder of the swamp transfers into the societal disorder created by efforts to tame it. Kirby describes the situation as indicative of "[a] paradox of slavery and swamps. The latter were refuges to renegades and revolutionaries near and far. But to those regularly engaged in industrial labor inside the swamps, the environment (and the relatively high value of all labor) guaranteed a life close enough to freedom to discourage renegadeism" (168). Kirby provides an intriguing portrait of the hired slave shingle-getter's unique situation: "They were both property, productive and valuable, laboring in an environment conducive not only to limits but also to privileges and immunities seldom seen on upland plantations. They were, as Olmsted said so well, quasi-free, which is certainly better than unfree" (168). Olmsted adds another peculiar element to the shingle-getter's relationship to the swamp: "They almost invariably have excellent health. . . . [T]hey all consider the water of 'The Dismals' to have a medicinal virtue, and quite probably it is a mild tonic" (1: 173). Though the sheer numbers of slaves who succumbed to swamp-related illnesses casts doubt, to say the least, on the efficacy of the waters as tonic; the slaves' belief that it worked as such further underscores the swamp's imaginative signification for the enslaved African-American as profoundly different from that of his master: for the white Southerner, the swamp was a place of pestilence and an obstacle to cultural progress; for the hired shingle-getter, it was a place of at least limited self-determination and a source of health.

For all the eminence of its founders, the purported high-mindedness of their ideals, and the awful toll taken on the enslaved laborers carrying out its efforts, the Great Dismal Swamp Company never managed to conquer the swamp. In 1804, several years before the company finally dissolved, their decision to sell all their slaves "ended all vestiges of the original scheme devised by the elder William Byrd. . . . The partners at last admitted that for years they had not envisioned a self-supporting, growing population of company slaves who would turn the Dismal Swamp into farmland to make shareholders rich" (Royster 420). Ironically, the wealth that the company did generate was essentially that same bounty that Byrd so decried in his judgments of the morally degenerate swamp profiteers: "[T]heir true source of profit had always stood fully grown in the swamp" (420). Finally abandoning their initial goal of draining the swamp for the public good, the company survived by harvesting naturally occurring swamp riches. In its era, long before humankind would pose a genuine threat through deforestation, the history of the Great Dismal Swamp Company can best be understood as a kind of stalemate with the swamp, which remained, as it was in Byrd's time, both a source of wealth and an untamable obstacle.

Nevertheless, the Company's efforts, and their brutal legacy of disease and death among the workers, would leave some mark on the swamp, if only on its imaginative significance to later generations. In closing his account of the death toll among slaves working for the Company, Royster includes an anecdote: "Early in the 20th Century, the tourist entering the Dismal Swamp by the Jericho Canal asked her guide, a young white Virginian, why a swamp so filled with color, sunshine, and bird calls was named 'dismal.' 'There's more to it than shows just at first, ma'am,' he answered. 'There are more sad stories about this swamp than all the sunshine can make bright'" (422). This legacy stands in sharp contrast to Washington's better-known gesture of freeing his slaves in his will, countering that symbolic gesture with the very real toll of his ill-fated endeavor. In the context of the Southern imaginary construction of the swamp as dark nemesis of the plantation ideal, this legacy represents the swamp's greatest victory over the Great Dismal Swamp Company on the ideological, if not commercial, level: all their efforts to domesticate the swamp only reaffirmed and underscored its forbidding menace.

The ultimate image of the swamp that emerges from these three early encounters underscores Schama's statement that landscape is essentially an imaginative creation. Depending on the values a culture imports, the swamp's character changes drastically. As Bartram's work and, ironically, the history of the Great Dismal Swamp Company attest, the swamp can be a cornucopia if left on what we might simplistically call its own terms. The effort to transform its natural state into the pastoral garden, however, transforms the swamp into a deadly and intractable foe. Approached with a romantic sense of nature as inherently benevolent, the swamp becomes a shady paradise. With the onset of the Victorian drive to subdue the natural, particularly in the South, where, as Singal tells us, Victorian ideals were typically distilled into simplest terms, the swamp would remain as Byrd designated it—a moral and commercial enemy.

As the Civil War approached and the South found itself compelled to articulate and defend its cultural values more energetically, the swamp's status in relation to Southern identity became more problematic and, consequently, more intriguing. Union rhetoric increasingly followed the trend we have observed in Stowe's *Dred*, generalizing the conventionally negative characteristics of the swamp into statements about Southern moral character. Miller cites Daniel Webster's use of swamp imagery to characterize secession: "[B]ut secession and disunion are a region of gloom, and morass and swamp; no cheerful breezes fan it, no spirit health visits it; it is all malaria. It is all fever and ague. Nothing beautiful or useful grows in it; the traveler through it breathes miasma, and treads among all things unwholesome and loathesome" (qtd. in Miller 10). Webster's description of a nation marred by disunity would not seem out of place among Byrd's descriptions of the Virginia and Carolina swamps; intriguingly, though, Southern rhetoric often adopted terminology that spoke directly to the idea of the Union's metaphorically putting Byrd's ideas of drainage and cultivation into process. Robert Toombs, for example, in a speech delivered on November 13, 1860, calls the treasury "a perpetual fertilizing stream to them and their industry, and a suction-pump to drain away our substance and parch up our lands" (Commager 38). Henry Benning also employs images of forced desiccation and drainage in his November 19, 1860, speech, in which he describes various expenditures forced on the South by the North as "drains" and claims that "we may now form some estimate of what the South would gain by the separation from the North for [by] the mere act of separation all these drains would stop running, and the golden waters be retained within her own borders" (Commager 142). Thus, even in a culture characterized by an obsessive drive to order, a need to master the savage and promote the civilized, the idea of being cultivated by an outside, exploitive entity became anathema. While the Southerner might seek to drain his own lands, he would not stand to have them drained by anyone else.

Edmund Ruffin and William Gilmore Simms represent transitional figures in defining the evolving literary and cultural relationship of the swamp to Southern identity for different reasons. Although their careers and viewpoints were markedly different, each bridges a kind of gap in Southern understandings of the swamp in terms of identity. Moreover, each man's writings can be considered representative of an opposing pole in perceptions of the Southern swamp: Ruffin, the man of science, entered the swamp with an attitude of scientific and agricultural empiricism, which remained largely uninflected by his passionate proslavery and pro-Southern views as they emerged in the 1850s, while Simms, though less politically passionate about the Southern system for which he had been elected de facto literary spokesperson, created a romantic vision of a swamp divorced from reality, a swamp that, for all its terrors, showed a peculiar obedience when confronted by the archetypal Cavalier's force of character. Considered together, Ruffin and Simms represent a transitional point as Southern approaches to the swamp's anomalous ambiguity evolved from physical to linguistic strategies.

Ruffin's earliest encounters with the Carolina swamplands predated his true obsession with protecting Southern identity and culture: they were primarily commercial. Ruffin only later realized what was ultimately at stake in preserving and improving Southern agriculture by drawing marl from the swamps. Simms, on the other hand, provides a peculiarly retrospective view of the swamp's role in the formation of Southern identity. In works such as *The Partisan* and his *Biography of Francis Marion*, Simms explores the seemingly paradoxical connection between the Southern gentlemen whom he credits with founding American (and, more importantly, Southern) culture and the wild swamps which nurtured their cause—ultimately, in creating a continuity between the Southern revolutionary war hero and the Cavalier-era Southern gentleman, he is forced to create a strange discontinuity between the swamps that served as the war heroes' fortresses and those generally agreed upon to be a thorn in the side of contemporary Southern prosperity. Ruffin dealt with real swamps, eventually in the interest of a very real quest to maintain the South he so loved and so passionately defended, while Simms created romanticized netherworlds whose passing he could, in true Southern literary style, passively and wistfully lament.

Ruffin, prior to adopting his political role as Fire-Eater and defender of slavery and Southern culture, was primarily a geological and agricultural surveyor. His personal attitudes were far removed from the all-consuming class consciousness that Byrd manifested and that Cash lampoons as Southern pretense. As Kirby points out, Ruffin preferred to call himself a "farmer" than a planter: "The plainness of the words convey [sic] his disdain for conspicuous consumption and preoccupation with display of his wealthier neighbors and the parvenus of the cotton and sugar belts to the south" (Poquosin 61). His chief cause was marling and soil reform, the process of harvesting rich, fecund soils to rejuvenate "dead" farmlands. The swamps contained great reserves of this marl, and Ruffin's strategies ranged, over the course of his career, from harvesting marl from the swamps to draining and cultivating the swamps themselves. The ideological underpinnings of Ruffin's devotion to agricultural reform are crucial to understanding the significance of his swamp encounters to the larger question of Southern identity. Unless we consider them, Ruffin's typically unemotional, almost purely scientific accounts of the swamps he surveyed seem to carry little rhetorical weight until late in his career. Key to understanding Ruffin, for my purposes, is the link that developed in his imagination between draining and cultivating the swamps, maintaining slavery, and saving Southern culture. Ruffin was hardly alone in emphasizing agriculture as key to the South's cultural survival. As William Mathew points out in *Edmund Ruffin and the Crisis of Slavery in the Old South* (1988), "A good many people sensed that perhaps the only way to save slavery within the union lay through the fundamental, local processes of farm reform. . . . Agricultural improvements presented a difficult means of rescue, but as Southern slavery was essentially a plantation institution, the productive power of the land was utterly vital" (23). Ruffin's eminently practical approach to the swamps exemplifies this attitude. A reluctant and ineffective speaker until late in life, Ruffin devoted himself to saving the abstract and ideal through the tangible and real.

At the root of all his writings is Ruffin's abiding belief that in one crucial sense the future of agriculture depended directly upon the very earth in the swamp. His swamp explorations were devoted to discovering and mining calcareous marl, a substance in rich supply in swampy soils that Ruffin believed could literally rejuvenate infertile soil. Ruffin saw in swamp soil the hope for Southern agriculture: he repeatedly attributes the success of the rice plantations he surveys to the "close proximity of the marl to the surface of the swamps" (*Agricultural, Geological, and Descriptive Sketches* 163) and believed that if that essential element of swamp soil could be harvested and introduced into poor or fallow fields Southern agriculture would be invigorated and rejuvenated. In his book *Ruffin: Family and Reform in the Old South*, David Allmendinger explains that Ruffin "assumed quite consciously that without rejuvenation, Virginia, Maryland, North Carolina, and South Carolina would soon confront a Malthusian crisis, with a growing slave population consuming a declining supply of food, leading in turn to an exodus by whites and the end of slavery" (114). By 1850, Ruffin's agricultural agenda had merged consciously and completely with a very clear idea of the future of Southern society; to his understanding, political, racial, and cultural order were inseparable from the health of the land.

Ruffin's emphasis on social order through development of the land shows Byrd's influence. Indeed, as Kirby points out, "Byrd—the quintessentially cosmopolitan Anglo-Virginian gentleman—was often on Ruffin's mind. . . . He was (to someone unable to read the encoded 'Secret Diary') altogether an inspiration for Ruffin's century" (79–80). Nevertheless, Ruffin's earlier writings remain as free of Byrd's all-consuming, literarily inflected prejudices as did his self-presentation. Ruffin's empirical early work shows no consistent pattern in his thinking about the swamp—he neither demonizes it nor romanticizes it with any consistency, though he does both at various times. His 1843 diary, reissued and retitled *Agriculture, Geology, and Society in Antebellum South Carolina* in 1992, shows a degree of scientific detachment only occasionally colored by the author's aesthetic or cultural predispositions. This work, composed early enough that it is largely uninflected by the secessionist passions that would eventually consume Ruffin, is a fairly straightforward scientific account, largely untouched by the kind of personal asides and familial digressions that characterize Ruffin's later and more famous diaries. Ruffin admires the rice plantations that can thrive in an only partially drained and cultivated swamp: "There can scarcely any where be found more elaborate & perfect culture, & more exercise of skill, intelligence & industry, than in the rice culture of this region. . . . And the immense value of this culture, & the quantity of rich tide swamp land devoted to it may be inferred, from the fact of the great quantity of rice exported from lower S.C. notwithstanding the general barrenness & waste condition of most of the other land, & the bad cultivation & poor products of that which is not waste & useless" (*Agriculture, Geology, and Society* 63). Further, Ruffin expresses a kind of romantic admiration for the swamp's history as he reflects upon the part of the Santee swamp that served as Francis Marion's chief fortress: "Here, he was safe from the pursuit of the enemy, no matter how much superior their force; & ready to sally forth & fall upon them whenever there was an opportunity to strike with effect" (*Agriculture, Geology, and Society* 162).

Although Ruffin acknowledges the dangers of malaria and repeatedly laments the perils of improper drainage, he never indulges in the kind of dramatic rhetoric that characterizes either Byrd's demonizations or Bartram's romanticizations of the swamp. Even as he describes an episode when his carriage sank into the swamp, Ruffin maintains an air of humor seemingly untouched by popular rhetoric of the swamp's foulness: "If my wagon body did not keep water *out*, it kept it in admirably" (*Agriculture, Geology, and Society* 147). Ruffin's early approach to the swamp is simple: its inherent goodness or evil is not an issue, and his appreciation for it remains directly proportionate to its productivity. In fact, an 1837 piece for the *Farmer's Register*, in a rare moment of subjective indulgence, expresses a profoundly evenhanded aesthetic approach to nature and civilization: "It seems unfortunate, that the first approach to the swamp, of almost every person hereafter, will be the rapidly moving railway train. The savage gloom of the face of nature is altogether unsuited to the highly artificial facilities by means of which the traveller is flying past—and the discordance serves to lessen the high gratification which either the conveyance or the scene alone would cause, when new to the observer" ("Observations" 516). Intriguingly, Ruffin's sensibilities are not offended by one extreme or the other but by an inappropriate blurring of nature and civilization. This response is particularly anomalous in one who saw harvesting wilderness areas as key to the advancement and perpetuation of civilization itself. Still, Ruffin's response reflects a balanced appreciation of the virtues of both elements in his tableau. Only later, as abolitionist rhetoric and the threat of secession have made him more acutely aware of how genuinely threatened the Southern system actually was, did emotion begin to inflect Ruffin's treatment of the swamp.

Even very late in his career, audience and genre considerations kept Ruffin's vigorous politics from influencing much of his strictly scientific work. His

1861 book *Agricultural, Geological, and Descriptive Sketches of Lower North Carolina and the Similar Adjacent Lands* studiously avoids lapses into rhetoric; while his focus has clearly changed from harvesting marl to wholesale draining and conversion of swampland into farmland, Ruffin remains empirical in his approach, save for the occasional expression of aesthetic appreciation for the beauty of both wild and drained swamps and for his references to any hindrance to productive cultivation as an "evil." When Ruffin addresses a crowd, though, the changes in his emphasis and his concept of his plans' significance become apparent. In his 1853 piece entitled "Southern Agricultural Exhaustion and its Remedy," Ruffin gives perhaps the clearest indication of his concept of the swamps' relationship to Southern identity, allowing emotion and judgment free reign in a manner sharply divergent from his scientific prose. This article, originally presented as an address in Charleston, South Carolina, before its publication in *DeBow's Review*, clearly expresses the larger significance that Ruffin perceived in his agricultural endeavors. Agriculture, for Ruffin, is central to culture itself: "The destructive operations of the exhausting cultivator have a most important influence far beyond his own lands and his own personal interests. He reduces the wealth and population of his country and the world, and obstructs the progress and benefits of education, the social virtues, and even moral and religious culture. For, upon the productions of the earth depend, more or less, the measure to be obtained, by the people of any county, of these and all other blessings which a community can enjoy" (37). Having established agricultural prosperity's centrality to civilization's health and quality, Ruffin claims that "[a] great resource . . . is presented in your great inland swamps, now only wide-spread seed-beds of disease, pestilence, and death; and which, by drainage, with certainty and great profit, might be converted to dry fields of exuberant fertility" (41) and asserts that, with the passage of legislation facilitating drainage, "improvements might be permitted and invited which would render these now worthless and pestilential swamps as fruitful as the celebrated borders of the Po" (41). To Ruffin, the swamps' "evil" persists only in a lack of cultivation. Because the swamps have not been conquered, acculturated, and assimilated into the agrarian system, they remain a pestilential evil; simple (conceptually if not practically) drainage and cultivation could, in his view, transform the unknown, the anticivilized, into the hope for civilization's salvation. The swamps, for Ruffin, hold the key to maintaining agriculture in the face of exhaustion and entropy; agriculture holds the key to maintaining Southern civilization. For the eminently practical man of science, the swamps not only had to be included in the Southern agricultural system but were essential to its survival.

It is important to note that Ruffin's venom in discussing the pestilential swamps had been influenced, by 1852, by the loss of two infants to malaria. Eliminating mill ponds, which were essentially stagnating collections of swamp water, became one of his foremost crusades. According to Kirby, for Ruffin, "elimination of 'marsh miasma' was an urgent requisite for a civilized South Atlantic" (137). Thus, appropriately, Ruffin's transition from unemotional empiricist to condemnatory rhetorician in describing the swamp has its roots in an ideological fervor based on objective, if tragic, personal experience.

Ruffin's agricultural ideas were never broadly implemented, and he gained considerably more notoriety as a defender of slavery and advocate of secession—although his agricultural ideas were inextricably linked to his stance on these issues, history has generally managed to prise the two apart, understandably devoting more attention to Ruffin's more explicitly political work. The crucial point here, though, is the fact that to him the two were essentially inseparable: as the land goes, as the swamp goes, so goes the essence of Southern identity. Ruffin's eventual suicide in 1865, a response to his beloved South's subjugation by the Yankees he came to despise, indicates a further, more intensely personal dimension of the continuum: as the South died, so died Edmund Ruffin.

Ruffin's views of the swamp represent one dimension of its relationship to Southern identity: the realm of the commodifiable and practical. If the South was defined by Cavalier myth, it was at least as much defined by the agricultural and slave systems that enabled that myth's promulgation. Ruffin chose to ignore the idea that the swamp's wildness was somehow outside the realm of Southern civilization and evaluated it by a standard that fused moral and commercial criteria so that the two became indistinguishable. Ruffin believed the swamps' riches could be had easily enough—all that was needed to ensure the South's agricultural and cultural survival was concerted drainage and cultivation. Ruffin's beliefs that the South could be reinvigorated through concrete, quantifiable actions and that the swamp could be demystified and subjected to agriculture compounded his horror and despair at the slaveholding South's undeniable end.

Simms, the erstwhile bard of the antebellum South, stands in sharp contrast to Ruffin, defining a profoundly different view of the swamp's relationship to Southern identity. Ruffin's swamp was scientific fact; Simms's was romantic fiction, literally shaped by force of dominant personalities into a palpable embodiment of the pathetic fallacy.

Simms's sensibilities differed profoundly from Ruffin's. Author of works that he insisted be recognized as romances, Simms fleshed out in literature the archetypal Cavalier ideal. The cavalier, as Singal has pointed out, was a fundamentally antibourgeois creation, a defender of the values generally associated with English country gentry. In devoting many of his novels to creating such a mythic hero, Simms clearly did not concern himself with the South as a commercial entity. If Ruffin staked the survival of the South on agricultural and commercial prosperity, Simms articulated, in the romantically decadent style that has become a hallmark of Southern literature, the fading, glorious ideals of days gone by, the romantic, impractical hyperreality of Cavalier Southern archetype.

Although Simms is the apocryphally designated inventor and promulgator of true Southern literature, his devotion to the South seems more problematic than Ruffin's fiery, uncomplicated zeal. Simms disdained the anti-intellectual and antiliterary trends he perceived in the South, complaining repeatedly in his correspondence that the South has no moral bedrock and that Southerners "want fixed principles and leading and high purposes" (qtd. in Miller 85). As Miller points out, "Simms related this weakness to the low regard for literary pursuits held by most Southerners" (84). Simms describes the literary as connected to what he calls "The Ideal," which is "a correlative against the dangers of the *REAL*" (qtd. in Miller 84). What troubled Simms, then, was the distance between the real bourgeois, anti-intellectual South and the romantic Cavalier South in the legends he in large part helped to create.

Miller's *Dark Eden* offers a compelling analysis of the swamp in Simms's work, claiming that the swamp's moral ambiguity troubled Simms, as it was irreconcilable with the sharp moral distinction in his mind between Cavalier and Yankee, and that he ultimately repudiated the swamp as amoral (85–88). Miller may well be correct, but there is another dimension to Simms's literary relationship with the swamp that sheds a clearer light on its relationship to his perception of Southern identity—a question that lies largely outside Miller's concerns, but which is clearly central to my own. For Simms, the swamp does indeed change, as Miller suggests; however, there is a consistency to its nature that clarifies Miller's assertion that "the moral status of the swamp in Simms' romances . . . changed in accordance with the author's predominant rhetorical concern" (88). The significant change, for Simms, occurs not so much in the nature of the swamp itself but in the character of the men who seek to command it. Simms's concern with the essence of the Southern gentleman, with the power and prevalence of the Cavalier hero, with the ability of this archetype to shape nature itself in a manner that echoes Byrd's self-representation in his *History of the Dividing Line*, stands as the preeminent driving force in his fiction. The ambiguity that came to trouble Simms inheres not in the swamp itself but in the changes he perceived in Southern manhood. Simms responded to these changes with what has become a familiar reaction—through nostalgic evocations of a past greatness, of an idyllic, pastoral cultural order that has always already begun to fade.

The archetypal cavalier's moral transcendence lies in his ability not only to resist nature but to subjugate it to his will. Simms's tales of cavaliers, notably *The Partisan* and *Life of Francis Marion*, transplant this intellectual and moral ideal to the physical realm of an oddly unreal swamp. A passage from *The Partisan* works to situate Simms's swamp in relation to his much derided "real": "The gloomy painter would have done much with the scene before us. The wild and mystic imagination would have made it one of supernatural terrors; and fancy, fond of the melancholy twilight, would have endowed the dim shadows, lurking like so many specters between the bald cypresses, with a ghostly character, and most unhallowed purpose" (72).

Simms' invocation of a painter is interesting here, especially in light of Poe's apt criticism of *The Partisan*: "[S]ome passages of swamp imagery are exquisite. Mr. Simms has evidently the eye of a painter. . . . Perhaps, in sober truth, he would succeed better in sketching a landscape than he has done in writing a novel" (897). Even in historical fiction, Simms evokes images of the unearthly and the unreal. Further, this swamp is no natural shelter, as Miller would characterize its role in Simms's early romances. It will become a shelter but only through the intervention of the Cavalier hero.

Simms provides another image, shortly after the one quoted above, that clarifies his idea of the swamp's role in defining the character of the revolutionary heroes who become his prototypical cavaliers: "Here, the rank matter of the swamp, its slime and rubbish, resolving themselves by a natural but rapid decomposition into one mass, yield the thick luxuriance of soil from which springs up the overgrown tree, which throws out a thousand branches, and seems to have existed as many years—in whose bulk we behold an emblem of majesty, and, in whose term of life, standing in utter defiance of the sweeping hurricane, we have an image of strength which compels our admiration, and sometimes the more elevated acknowledgement of our awe" (72). In the context of Simms's archetype-driven heroic hagiography, the symbolism here is hardly subtle. In the image of the oak, majestic, defiant, growing strong and regal both because and in spite of the swamp that nourishes its roots and overgrows its branches, he justifies the gentleman hero's thriving in the same wretched surroundings.

Significantly, rather than relying on the swamp's natural benevolence, Simms's Cavalier hero masters and transcends an environment that Simms designates in no uncertain terms as foul. Its shelter must be won through toil, self-mastery, and the triumph of civilization over nature. Simms aptly characterizes the meeting of civilization and swamp in his biography of Francis Marion, the historical model for the swamp-sheltered patriots in his fiction: "To subdue the forest, of itself, to European hands, implied labors not unlike those of Hercules. But the refugees, though a gentle race, were men of soul and strength, capable of great sacrifices, and protracted self-denial . . . the toil of felling trees . . . the constant danger from noxious reptiles and beasts of prey . . . and, most insidious and fatal enemy of all, the malaria of the swamp, of the rank and affluent soil, for the first time laid open to the sun; these are all only the ordinary evils which encountered in America, at the very threshold, the advances of European civilization" (16). The evil swamp becomes a home and a haven only because these determined men of "gentle race" have forced it to be so. It certainly has no beneficial moral or spiritual effects on those Simms calls "the half-human possessors of the same regions, the savages" (23), whose unpredictable attacks help to train the stalwart Europeans for war.

Simms's biography of Marion repeatedly underscores the idea that the swamp is wickedness brought to heel and shaped by force of character. Perhaps in response to European perceptions of America as a land of savages, Simms takes great pains to liken Marion to a European lord, and his swamp den to a castle—as he claims, "in this snug and impenetrable fortress, he reminds us very much of the ancient feudal baron of France and Germany, who, perched on castled eminence . . . marked all below him for his own" (166). Simms's swamp, duly subjugated to the gentleman warrior's will, becomes a fortress with the same artistic features that mark European civilization's most elaborate creations: "the massive pine, the gigantic Cypress, and the stately and Evergreen laurel, streaming with moss, and linking their opposite arms, inflexibly locked in the embrace of centuries, group together, with elaborate limbs and leaves, the chief and most graceful features of Gothic architecture" (177). For the heroic cavalier, Marion, nature itself takes on the dimensions and aesthetic appeal of a grand fortress.

For all Simms's attempts to romanticize Marion's swamp, he must eventually recognize its realities. The swamp that these men have tamed and transformed into their personal stronghold no longer exists, Simms suggests: "Such a place of encampment, at such a season, would hardly commend itself now to the citizen of Carolina. The modes and objects of Culture, and probably the climate, have undergone a change. The time was autumn, the most sickly period of our year; and, to sleep in such a region now, even for a single night, would be considered certain death to the white man" (278). Simms presents a landscape that he admits no longer exists, bent to the will of heroic archetypes who he, with his insistence that his works be read as romances rather than as novels, must admit bear little relation to the real. His Cavalier heroes elevate the swamp from dire and pestilential reality into the realm of the ideal.

Simms's treatment of the swamp in his 1854 novel *Woodcraft* is less evidence of his changing perspective on the swamp's moral status than part of his overall commentary on the changing nature of Southern character and culture. *Woodcraft* does not feature Simms's usual irreproachable, stalwart heroes but instead focuses on the Falstaffian Porgy, a character who is, for all his broad bluster, more recognizably human than Simms's usual icons. As John Caldwell Guilds describes him in *Simms: A Literary Life* (1992), Porgy is "a blustery, comic, lovable figure of a man who lends credibility and humanity to the Southern aristocratic tradition as does no other character in our literature. Compared to Lieutenant Porgy, philosophical but laughing and relaxed leader of guerillas, the other gentlemen characters seem wooden indeed—Major Singleton, the dauntless hero . . . not excluded" (68). In a novel that takes place in the aftermath of a myth-making war, Simms backs away from his chivalric icons in favor of a gentlemanly, yet comically flawed protagonist. The air of nostalgia for a better, more noble society that permeates all of Simms's novels here becomes part of the novel's present: as Porgy laments, "The curse of my generation was that our fathers lived too well, were too rapidly prosperous, and though they did not neglect the exercise of a proper industry in themselves, they either did not know how to teach it to their children, or presumed on the absence of any necessity that they should learn" (206). Porgy, the Southern gentleman of the post-revolutionary era, finds his values challenged by the forces that many of Simms's era saw threatening the South as a whole, as Millhouse, the money-grubbing pragmatist who gauges the value of any endeavor solely by its potential profitability, becomes an antagonist to Porgy's wistful but impractical aesthetic sensibility. The specter of practicality, a vulgar manifestation of the real, haunts Simms's largely comic novel.

Because the villainous squatter Bostwick finds some shelter in the swampy quagmire that surrounds him, Miller reads an implicit repudiation of the swamp into Simms's novel. I contend that the swamp, as such, does not truly change; the fault lies with Bostwick, who, with his repulsive bourgeois concerns and his very status as squatter, the antithesis of the gentleman landowner, cannot hope to dominate the amoral wilderness in the same way that Simms's cavalier heroes do. Bostwick, from his first mention in the novel, comes across as a betrayer of the proper social order—the parasite who shows no appreciation for the fruits of Mrs. Eveleigh's *noblesse oblige*: "The ungrateful wretch; and I have fed his family for years; his wife and child—when they were sick and starving. Oh! What a frightful, fiendish thing is poverty, when it is linked with ingratitude" (12). The swamp, for Simms, has always been fundamentally amoral— the difference, the degradation, lies entirely in the devolution he perceives in Southern character and in the great gulf between the Cavalier ideal and a profoundly unromantic reality. Bostwick does find nominal shelter in the swamp, but his flight into the wilderness takes its toll: by the time he emerges, Simms says that "in truth, his appearance was that of a diseased and almost deranged man. His face burned with fever, his eyes were bloodshot and prominent, almost seeming to start from his head; his mouth lay open, and he panted with the least exertion" (474). In an era that no longer lends itself to the archetypal heroes that people his earlier works, the swamp, too, loses its mythic status. No longer a gothic fortress, arranging itself castlelike around its masters, Bostwick's swamp is merely a hole that insures solitude for his dissolution. Simms's swamp becomes a mirror unto human nature, shaping itself to the will of those worthy to command it and mirroring the degradation of those who are not. It is not the reality of the swamp that intrudes on Simms's romanticism, rendering his symbol inoperative; it is the reality of what he perceives as a declining Southern people, bereft of the literary sensibility crucial to a romantic understanding of the world. As the latter phenomenon occurs more frequently in his later and less romantic fiction, it only clarifies the bard of the Confederacy's growing pessimism about a society that had become, to him, all too "real."

Southern literary scholarship generally situates John Pendleton Kennedy and Edgar Allan Poe as opposites, almost bookends, in the antebellum Southern literary universe. Kennedy emerges as the quintessential spokesman for the Southern gentry—his *Swallow Barn* the most eloquent tribute to the fiction of the plantation South as pastoral idyll—writing his world in the dilettante-like style that its code demanded of a gentleman scholar. Appropriately enough, Kennedy's work resembles that of Meriwether, the genial lord of the manor who presides over Swallow Barn: "He rambled with wonderful assiduity through a wilderness of romances, poems, and dissertations, which are now collected in his library." His introduction sums up his approach—his work is a play of images, "presenting as I make bold to say, a faithful picture of the people, the modes of life, and the scenery of a region full of attraction, and exhibiting the lights and shades of its society with the truthfulness of a painter who has studied his subject on the spot" (10). Kennedy's description of his own project in the context of a comparison with Poe cannot help but bring to mind Poe's evaluation of Simms's *Partisan*, that perhaps Mr. Kennedy, too, "would succeed better in sketching a landscape than he has done in writing a novel" in Poe's stylistically obsessed estimation (897). While critics continue to argue about how much structure actually underlies Kennedy's self-described perfunctory skim over his society's surface, his philosophy of composition remains clearly at odds with Poe's. Further, while Kennedy is a self-appointed spokesman for, and documentarian of, mainstream (that is to say, dominant and privileged) Southern society, Poe rather notoriously seems to ignore the society of his birth in his writings, except in veiled metaphor or indirect suggestion.

However pronounced their differences in literary style, approach, and philosophy, Poe and Kennedy display a certain similarity in their treatment of the swamp and its relationship to Southern identity. Although their overarching implications remain profoundly different, each presents the swamp in his work as a signifier of chaos, an element beyond control of both the mind of the individual and the mind of the South. Predictably enough, though, Poe's vision of the swamp goes beneath the surface that Kennedy skims: the swamp becomes not an unknown quantity behind a carefully guarded boundary but a physical exemplar of a more pervasive chaos infecting the very heart of Southern society.

Throughout most of Kennedy's *Swallow Barn*, the swamp remains a felt presence at the edge of the idyll, a mildly unpleasant but picturesque element of plantation life that can be accommodated with a minimum of effort. We discover, for example, that it is Meriwether's custom "to journey over the mountain to the Springs, which he is obliged to do to avoid the unhealthy season in the Tidewater region" (34). The swamp at the edge of Swallow Barn's land is part of a kind of continuum, a natural arrangement that, in its gentle opposition to agrarian prosperity, provides the formal tension needed to establish Kennedy's work as a true pastoral, by the definition Frank Kermode and others have articulated. For the most part, Kennedy's visions of natural order and chaos are as mild as in his description of the vines that overgrow part of the plantation: "[A]round this window grows a profusion of creeping vine which is trained with architectural precision along the wall to the roof. . . . Here and there, however, an intruding Rose has stolen a nest among its plexures, and looks pleasantly forth from this sober tapestry" (46–47). Kennedy gives us an exceedingly mild version of the conflict between order and chaos in nature: echoing Simms, he gives us vines that grow with "architectural precision," and the only hint of the chaotic comes with the welcome intrusion of the impudent rose. Throughout most of the novel, Swallow Barn is a world of trained vines and impudent roses—of peaceful coexistence with a capricious, not chaotic, nature.

The episode in the aptly named Goblin Swamp, however, changes the tenor of Kennedy's work considerably. As the aristocratic protagonists venture into the swamp, they experience the swamp as a place of genuine fear despite their initial bluster: "Here and there a lordly Cypress occurred to view, springing forth from the stagnant pool, and reposing in lurid shade. Half sunk in ooze, rotted the bole and bough of fallen trees, coated with pendent slime. . . . This dreary region was neither silent nor inanimate; but its inhabitants corresponded to the genius of the place. . . . The foxfire,—as the country people call it,—glowed hideously from the cold and matted bosom of the marsh; and, far from us, in the depths of darkness, the screech-owl sat upon his perch, brooding over the slimy pool, and whooping out a dismal curfew, that fell upon the air like the cries of a tortured ghost" (261). Kennedy echoes Byrd's assessment of the swamp as a place marked not only by disease and physical danger but by supernatural moral evil. The appearance of Hafen, the poor man for whom the swamp holds no terrors, echoes two other aspects of traditional swamp representations: first, that the swamp is home to the dispossessed, and ironically masterable only by those excluded from the master class, and second, that the swamp is a place of evil that somehow cannot affect a virtuous man. As Hafen claims, "The swamp is a very good mother to me, although I am a simple body and can pick up a penny where rich folks would never think of looking for it. . . . I never saw anything in these hobgoblins to make an honest man afraid. All you have to do is to say your prayers, and that will put any dev-ilish thing out of heart" (257–59). Hafen becomes a crucial guide for Ned and Mark, who would otherwise be lost within the swamp. Ned blusters, as he loses his way in the seemingly shifting swamp, that diabolical forces are at work: " 'What ho, good Mr. Belzebub!' He cried out jocularly, 'have you no mercy on two foolish travelers?' " (252). Soon enough, his bluster fades into a more serious apprehension at the swamp's potential for danger. Even with Hafen to lead the way, the two aristocrats eventually succumb to their trepida-tion, and find themselves reduced to silence: "We trudged briskly upon our way, but almost without exchanging words; for the assemblage of striking objects in the scene had lulled us into silence. I do not wonder that a solitary traveler should grow superstitious, amid such incentives to his imagination" (261). Significantly, the company waits until they have returned safely to Swallow Barn to speak of the swamp and its legends. Ned and Mark, members of the plantation aristocracy that was essentially, as so many have argued, a lit-erary and therefore linguistic creation, find themselves unable to speak in the thick of the swamp. Language breaks down, and thus, implicitly, the very sub-structure of the highly literary Southern Cavalier aristocracy breaks down, when one strays beyond the plantation boundaries into the swamp.

The tale of Mike Brown and the devil with which Hafen entertains Ned and Mark in the comfort and safety of the plantation veranda further establishes the swamp's subversive potential to Southern society. The story is essentially a humorous bit of folklore about Mike Brown, a blacksmith, who meets the devil in the swamp. In one sense, the telling of the tale represents a reclamation of swamp terrors by language: filtered through the traditional structure of the deal-with-the-devil tale at some physical remove, the swamp's dangers can be converted into language and therefore controlled. On the other hand, though, Hafen's tale illustrates both the swamp's connection to earthly and unearthly evil and the futility of civilized convention and chivalric tradition in the face of the swamp. The devil first tempts and humiliates Mike by convincing him, after a night of drinking, that the bottom of a pond is covered in gold. Mike, taking the moon's fragmented reflection in the water for the glitter of riches, goes through a series of ignominious attempts to rake the gold pieces out of the pond before the episode rather predictably culminates with his falling in and realizing he has been had. Meeting the devil in the swamp a second time, Mike challenges him to a duel to avenge his humiliation. The devil, however, chooses the ground on which they fight: his own land in the heart of the swamp.

Here, Mike finds himself defeated, and the honorable conventions of the duel literally undermined, by the ground itself, as he sinks into the muck until he cannot move. The devil and the swamp have gotten the better of him twice, and he becomes the stuff of humorous cautionary tales.

However comical the story of Mike and the devil becomes, at the heart of it are two key points: the swamp thwarts Mike in both commercial endeavors (one wonders how amused the founders of the Great Dismal Swamp Company would be by the accounts of Mike's failed attempts to draw gold from the swamp bottom) and in his efforts to uphold chivalric tradition through the convention of the duel. The diabolical swamp subverts both efforts to amass material wealth and attempts to defend and uphold personal honor endorsed by a carefully created and defensively maintained system of public honor; thus Kennedy, for all his seeming insouciance, establishes the swamp as anathema to both the mercantile and the poetic aspects of the created Southern self.

Poe also presents the swamp as a subversive influence on Southern society; however, his swamp is more an emblem than a physical presence, and the works of his that comment most significantly on the Southern system meta-phorically engage the issues that Kennedy presents as artistically rendered but largely mimetic images. In his 1997 book *Pastoral and Politics in the Old South*, John Grammer casts light on Poe's unusual status among Southern authors in describing his modernity: "Only a handful of Southern writers—Edgar Allan Poe is the chief example—really regarded themselves as artists in quite the modern sense, the sense Charles Baudelaire had in mind when he declared that 'the man of letters is the world's enemy.' For the South preserved, longer than other sections of the country, the antique idea of the man of letters as public man, with public responsibilities" (3–4). Because of his disdain for this idea, Poe alienated many more ideologically driven Southerners. Ruffin claims in a diary entry dated September 7, 1857, that "[w]hatever of genius, or other talent, his strange writings may exhibit, they are as monstrous & abominable as his morals, & as absurd as his course of life" (*Agriculture, Geology, and Society* 102). Ruffin's combination of his criticism of Poe the author and Poe the man under-scores the lack of separation between writer and work that Grammer charac-terizes as peculiarly Southern. As Poe lies profoundly outside the mold of Southern writer as public figure, much of his best work exemplifies an internal paradox that makes his writing more meaningfully antithetical to Kennedy's than any comparison of real or perceived "Southernness" might. Where Kennedy presents his observations in a good-natured ramble, Poe dedicates himself to singleness of purpose and to tightly and deliberately organized action, as his "Philosophy of Composition" makes famously clear. The central and often recognized irony of Poe's style, though, comes in his application of rigorously controlled expressive techniques to explicate the impossibility of controlling or even understanding various natural and supernatural phenomena. Louis Rubin has remarked on the inconsistency of Poe's authorial philosophy and his own life in *The Edge of the Swamp* (1989): "Little knowledge of psychology is needed to grasp the obvious fact that fixation upon authorial control, upon the necessity for employing calculation rather than emotion when composing a poem or story, the constant insistence that the writer must be absolute master of his material and shape everything in the work toward a predetermined end, are the expression of a dire personal need on his own part, and represent his effort to enforce such discipline upon his own very intense emotional life" (129).

The horror at the heart of Poe's most famous stories comes from contemplating madness, the ultimate loss of the personal control so central to the Cavalier ideal. In many notable cases—"The Tell-Tale Heart" and "The Black Cat," among others—the loss of control plays out on the most intimate and internal level as we witness firsthand accounts of disintegrating sanity and self-destruction. At times, though, Poe demonstrates the breakdown of men's (the gendered term here is not an oversight, as most of Poe's women are either dead, dying, or returning from the dead, and therefore agents of little other than ghostly revenge) attempts to control elements outside themselves. Although few of Poe's stories have an explicitly Southern setting, his ideas must bear significance in the context of a society so profoundly and explicitly constructed around ideals of mental, moral, and environmental control.

In most of Poe's work, the swamp only emerges in hints and brief, indirect images. As Rubin has pointed out, Poe rarely devotes time to natural description; in fact, in Poe's works, "[t]he natural world is not so much recreated as bizarrely imagined" (*Edge of the Swamp* 137). Poe, like Simms, creates his own nature in accordance with his own aesthetic—one which proves strikingly different from Simms's. "The Facts in the Case of M. Valdemar," a story in which the narrator, a mesmerist, attempts to prolong the life of his dying friend through a process of mental control, hints at Poe's understanding of nature's controllability. The story recounts the mesmerist's efforts, which preserve Valdemar in a kind of "undeath" for a time, and the action culminates with the attempt to awaken Valdemar's unnaturally preserved corpse. At the last, Valdemar protests that "*I am dead!*" (57) and the indomitable natural forces of entropy intrude hideously: "[H]is whole frame at once—within the space of a single minute, or even less, shrunk—crumbled—absolutely *rotted* away beneath my hands. Upon the bed, before that whole company, there lay a nearly liquid mass of loathsome—of detestable putridity" (57).

While this passage is obviously interesting for the swamplike resonance of Poe's description of Valdemar's dissolution, the tale's real significance to my argument lies in its assertion that man's efforts to halt the natural processes of entropy and decay are doomed to failure—a poignant and pointed fear in the minds of Southerners beginning to dread the possible destruction of their society.

Rubin's convincing reading of Poe's story "The System of Dr. Tarr and Professor Fether" as an allegory for a Southern slave rebellion in *The Edge of the Swamp* supports the idea that Poe may have layered coded critiques of the Southern system in his works. The surface horror of the narrator's discovery that lunatics are not only running the asylum but are indistinguishable from the putative authorities meant to control them can only be compounded in the mind of a Southerner reading the story with its coded slave context in mind. Like many of Poe's stories, "The System of Dr. Tarr and Professor Fether" deals with the troubling breakdown of boundaries; if those boundaries can be read not only as institutional but as racial, as the seeming authorities become indistinguishable and inseparable from those they had once contained, Poe's story takes on a new and much more disturbing dimension to the order-obsessed Victorian Southern mind. Rubin's reading of "The System of Dr. Tarr and Professor Fether" establishes Poe's penchant for veiled critique of the Southern system; one that sheds additional light on his most explicitly Southern and most explicitly swamp-related story, "The Fall of the House of Usher."

Before entering into a specific discussion of "The Fall of the House of Usher," it is important to understanding both the contrast between Kennedy and Poe and the role that the swamp plays in Poe's story that we understand more fully the Southern philosophy that Poe so powerfully assails. In *Pastoral and Politics in the Old South*, Grammer describes what he calls the closest thing to a collective Southern myth of identity: an ideology he calls "pastoral republicanism." Grammer describes the antebellum Southern mind as one that links personality to property, endorses and believes in the pleasures of rural settlement, and strongly leans toward a theory of entropy—the idea that a perfect agrarian society will always tend toward decay and thus time and history are its enemies. Both *Swallow Barn* and "Usher" acknowledge entropy and present the Southern system as doomed, but Kennedy attributes its demise to the inevitability of out-side encroachment on an insular system—to a kind of outside "infection"—while Poe suggests that the infection is bred by the system's very insularity. *Swallow Barn*, with its numerous wistful statements that the perfect way of life it describes must fade, reflects a nostalgic form of pastoral republicanism. "Usher" provides a considerably darker commentary on the philosophy. In form and content, these texts can be regarded as antitheses: one, a love letter to a gracefully dying tradition; the other, a chilling account of a tradition's cataclysm.

Underscoring Wyatt-Brown's statements about the predominance of familial purity and the sacredness of the Southern bloodline, the residents of Swallow Barn are all related in some manner to its owner. The plantation embodies the insular, pastoral republican ideal of Southern society and will only end as a result of history's inevitable entropic progress. Poe's tale systematically under-cuts the philosophy suggested in *Swallow Barn*. In "Usher," Poe criticizes the underside of the very aspects of Southern life that Kennedy, and the South as a whole, seem to elevate. In so doing, he sets his tale in the midst of a dark "tarn," a setting in which nature itself seems diseased and poisonous. While a tarn is not technically a swamp, but a small mountain lake, the images of pestilential vapors and miasma enact the kind of transposition that Rubin observes in "The System of Dr. Tarr and Professor Fether"—such language could not fail to evoke a sense of the Southern swamps that had become so laden with rhetori-cal significance. While Kennedy's work, with its suggested sense of eventual decay, roughly fits Leo Marx's formulation of the "machine in the garden," or the destruction of pastoral innocence by the encroachment of technological progress, Poe's story undercuts the pastoral by implying that the seeds of destruction lie within nature itself and that the attempt to protect a system's insularity is itself a form of personal and cultural suicide.

Arthur Hobson Quinn rightly claims that the essence of "Usher's" horror lies in contemplating a loss of identity: "The loss of spiritual identity is natu-rally the final human danger, and Roderick lives in its shadow" (285). Poe's narrative strategy deconstructs the meticulously created Southern identity in microcosm: in setting the stage for his tale, Poe first makes a point of stripping away the layers of imagination and romance that typically obfuscate portraits of the South. Poe's distaste for Simms's work, outside the area of description, indicates his lack of patience for that style of presentation, and as his narrator first approaches Usher's decaying mansion, he repeatedly indicates that he is seeing through to the truth at its heart. On the narrator's first approach to the house, he describes a "sense of insufferable gloom" that overcomes him, made insufferable because "the feeling was unrelieved by any of that half-pleasurable, because poetic, sentiment, with which the mind usually receives even the sternest natural images of the desolate or terrible" (216). He likens the sight before him to waking from an opium dream, "the hideous dropping off of the veil" (216). Thus, Poe establishes from the beginning that his tale will be unvarnished by the trappings of poetry and will be utterly and unpleasantly real. This is a South unmediated by literary interposition—Usher's situation is a horrific waking from a collective dream.

As in Kennedy's work, the narrator encounters a house populated by a closed familial system, enacting the purity of familial line hinted at in the more heterogeneous but still explicitly pure-blooded community of Swallow Barn. Here, though, the isolation, the unvarying line of Usher inheritance, has been carried to a hideous extreme. The Usher family embodies the ideals of Southern civilization—artistic and intellectual accomplishment, generosity and magnanimity, and, most importantly, purity. As Poe's narrator points out, "the stem of the Usher race, all time-honored as it was, had put forth, at no period, any enduring branch" (218). The Usher family represents a genteel, tradition-rich, and ultimately closed system. Shortly after revealing this detail, Poe, with his exacting eye for compositional detail, reinforces the negative sense of stagnation with an image of miasma outside: "[A]bout the whole mansion and domain there hung an atmosphere peculiar to themselves and their immediate vicinity—an atmosphere which had no affinity with the air of heaven, but which had reeked up from the decayed trees, and the gray wall, and the silent tarn—a pestilent and mystic vapor, dull, sluggish, faintly discernible, and leaden-hued" (219). The fanatical purity of the Southern system, reproduced in microcosm in the House of Usher, breeds its own pestilence, its own stagnation and decay, transforming the very foundations of idealized Southern culture into their own disease-breeding swamp.

Poe's description of the Usher family's inbreeding evokes images of stagnant water; as he states that "the stem of the Usher race, all time-honored as it was, had put forth, at no period, any enduring branch," he brings to mind not only the traditional image of the family tree but also, particularly in light of its juxtaposition with the image of the silent tarn, the image of a body of water with no outlet. While many critics have characterized the wasting diseases that afflict many of Poe's characters as consumption, Usher's physical condition, in fact, mimics the symptoms of malaria, as Poe transfers the natural malady to the realm of supernatural punishment. "Malaria weakened and dispirited, imposing limits on human effort and expectation," Kirby relates; Usher's condition, marked by "a cadaverousness of complexion . . . a finely moulded chin, speaking, in its want of prominence, of a want of moral energy . . . [and] the now ghostly pallor of his skin" (221), coupled with his swampy domicile, strongly suggest malaria. Malaria, of course, is particularly apropos in Poe's scheme of imbuing the natural with supernatural significance: what better to afflict the last of a dying, stagnant line than a disease thought to be caused by respiration of decaying matter? The pursuit of purity again breeds it own corruption, mirroring the very pestilence against which Ruffin so wholeheartedly campaigned.

In setting his tale by a tarn whose very air seems to breathe corruption, Poe collapses the distinction between prosperous, ostensibly "pure" agrarian Southern society and the foul, unconquerable wildness of the swamp. Intriguingly, Poe's swamp is not itself the source of infection but its symbolic emblem. A system so devoted to maintaining pure blood breeds its own plague. It is then significant that, for all the story's "swamp" imagery, Poe locates it not in a physical swamp but by a mountain tarn: the foul exhalations that surround this house come not from nature, but from a corrupted culture. Thus, the true "swamp," in the trope-laden sense of the site of disease and death, is inextricable from the Southern way of life itself. The final, personal destruction that Usher's suggested incest brings upon himself and his sister is not a blow against a natural, pastoral system but a last desperate defense against an unnatural self-perpetuation. Thus, Poe critiques the pastoral republican resistance to outside adulteration by showing a perverse insularity as the ultimate destroyer of the literal and figurative House of Usher.[3]

In this sense, Poe's commentary on the system idealized in Kennedy's novel contributes to a general understanding of the swamp as paradoxically alien and antagonistic to, yet inseparable from, Southern culture—the same paradox that we encounter again and again in antebellum Southern literature. Never quite assimilable into mainstream narrative or endeavor, whether literary or commercial, the swamp, like an element in the collective Southern psyche imperfectly repressed, remains a mercurial but undeniable element in defining a culture to which, in both practical and literary dimensions, it was both progenitor and antagonist.

Poe's and Kennedy's works, taken side by side as a kind of culmination of antebellum swamp representation, indicate a final stage in the prewar South's attempts to reconcile the swamp's ambiguity. After abandoning efforts to drain the swamps—the effort to master and destroy them physically, according to

Douglas's paradigm—the struggle to reconcile the swamp with the rigid, slow-evolving creation of Southern identity moved from the physical realm to the realm of language and ideology. Ruffin, after a lifetime of earnest efforts to use the swamplands as a means of perpetuating the Southern agrarian way of life, at last came to embrace a demonizing rhetorical perspective in response to personal and impending cultural tragedy. Simms created a fantasy world in which the swamp proved malleable before the iron will of the Cavalier archetype, but his romances were always consigned to a distant and better past. Acknowledging the swamp's essential indomitability, Kennedy adopts a strategy of exile: he depicts the swamp as emphatically beyond the ruling class's physical and linguistic control, a space that reduces them to silence and must be rendered and characterized through the folktales of the ungentlemanly Hafen Block. Utterly beyond the gentleman's experience, the swamp can comfortably remain a place of mystery so long as its removal from the plantation life can be underscored and its "evils" defused through comic storytelling. And yet, as Poe's chilling tale underscores, this ideological exile remained artificial and imperfect. The swamp, in all its significations, remained—not only at the edges of Southern civilization but beneath its very foundations, threatening to subvert the structures of a tenuous ideological creation and ultimately to bring the entire mythopoetic house down.

NOTES

1. Post–Civil War interviews with former slaves reveal a host of swamp-oriented ghost stories and superstitions. Camilla Jackson, an eighty-year-old former slave interviewed by the Federal Writers' Project in 1938, gives a characteristic one: "During slavery and since that time, if you should go out doors on a drizzling night for any thing, before you could get back Jack O'lantern would grab you and carry you to the swamps. If you hollowed and some one bring a torch to the door the Jack O' lantern would turn you aloose."

2. Ritchie Watson provides an excellent overview of the various pseudoscientific claims of pure Anglo-Saxon and/or Gallic descent in the South.

3. While the issue of incest in this story remains a subject of critical debate, and the story offers no concrete evidence of physical incest between Usher and his sister, Gerald Garmon presents a compelling argument for the incest—and Roderick's inability to perpetuate it with his sister, as a result of the very heightening of sensation that incest breeds in its offspring—as the ultimate cause of the House's downfall.

Chapter Two

THE SOUTHERN SWAMP IN THE CIVIL WAR, RECONSTRUCTION, AND BEYOND

For the antebellum South, the swamp began as a region of both danger and great promise—the inspiration for ambitious plans and ultimately a source of frustration for such luminaries as William Byrd II and George Washington. As it proved ever more stubbornly intractable to practical efforts to reap its riches and even, in its breeding of disease and sheltering of runaway slaves, became a kind of loosely personified antithesis of the civilized South, the swamp emerged in literature as a supernatural nemesis to genteel Southern society. Whether it was an entity to be overcome by heroic will, as in Simms's revolutionary romances, a subversive zone of chaos and devilry, as in Kennedy's *Swallow Barn*, or, most troublingly, a symbolic embodiment of a self-destructive element within the social order itself, as in Poe's "The Fall of the House of Usher," the swamp always manifested opposition to Southern civilization.

This chapter considers a variety of shifts in swamp representation as the South itself transformed radically with the coming of the Civil War, Reconstruction, and the halting emergence of the "New South" at the end of the nineteenth century. The writings considered here fall into three basic categories: those that concern themselves with the present (Civil War era memoirs that show radical reconceptions of the swamp landscape and its role in Southern culture), the past (the tradition of plantation novels and nostalgic evocations of a glorified, lost South), and the future (the works of social reformers, such as George Washington Cable, who make rhetorical use of swamp imagery to promote social change, and those of Sidney Lanier, who takes a step toward divorcing the swamps from the cultural baggage that has come to accompany them). As the South undergoes the most dramatic changes in its history, the swamp adapts in various discourses to fit practical and rhetorical needs: it becomes, by turns, a tool of war, a boyhood Eden, an exiled space, a signifier of social decay, and an erstwhile escape from the tropes of civilization, depending on the perspective of its chronicler. The late nineteenth century saw a series of radical revisionings of the swamp landscape, which accompanied radical revisionings of Southern culture itself.

With the coming of the Civil War, the practical exigencies of swamp navigation and combat in some ways shifted popular perceptions of the Southern swamp, stripping away the aura of superstition that had come to characterize it for North and South alike. As soldiers were compelled to regard the swamps as necessary elements in battle strategy, and as definite obstacles to be overcome, the swamps' aura of demonic menace gave way, for both North and South, to more empirically justifiable demonizations.

At the same time, the fading, sinister tropes gave way in the memoirs and journals of many Southern noncombatants to revised, often more accepting visions of the swamps, again driven by emerging practical exigencies. Writings of the time reveal an increased sense of aesthetic appreciation and cultural ownership of these formerly derided spaces. While the old tropes persist in intriguingly modified ways, the swamps enjoyed a period of new acceptance among both Northerners and Southerners during and after the war.

For soldiers on both sides, though, the swamps were, first and foremost, obstacles. The popular Northern and abolitionist derogation of the South as a swamp in its entirety seemed to gain practical support as Union troops found their horses, wagons, and even themselves mired in ill-kept roads deluged with heavy rains. The most spectacular failure to result from this phenomenon is General Ambrose Burnside's infamous "mud march" in January of 1863, when mules, artillery, and soldiers, attempting to outmaneuver Lee's army and take Richmond, sank into the hopeless morass that has since been dubbed "Burnside's Quagmire" as heavy rains soaked the soil outside Fredericksburg.

Within the figurative swamp of the South, literal swamps posed problems of their own. Ulysses S. Grant, always an archetypal pragmatic realist, renders his army's struggles with the swamp terrain among the bayous outside Vicksburg in a way that, despite its lack of emotion or inflection, conveys the Union's general frustration on encountering the very intractability that had long vexed the Southern planter: "Bayou Baxter . . . disappears entirely in a cypress swamp before it reaches the Macon. . . . To get through it, even with vessels of the lightest draft, it was necessary to clear off a belt of heavy timber wide enough to make a passable way. As the trees would have to be cut close to the bottom—under water—it was an undertaking of great magnitude" (299). Testaments from soldiers in the field are less detached and reveal the swamp's dangers from a personal as well as strategic standpoint. Union soldier Thomas Mann's memoirs report the health problems that the Chickahominy Swamp in Virginia caused northern troops unaccustomed to the climate: "The Chickahominy Swamp was not conducive to good health, and northern men were commencing their first summers' experience in the South under these adverse malarial surroundings. . . . Of the 600 out of every 1000 who did take some part in the prolonged struggle, many were weakened by the hydra-headed forms that the Chickahominy malaria took so as to incapacitate in degrees varying from slight indisposition to an almost helpless state" (68). The shift from a superstitious and rhetorical Northern understanding of the swamp to a more practical and fact-based assessment did not necessarily redeem the swamp's image and reputation. To Mann, the actual devastating effects of malaria (still believed to be caused by breathing swamp air) were sufficiently horrific to draw monstrous comparison. As hundreds died from malaria and hundreds more were consigned to inhuman prison camps based in or near swamps—most notoriously Andersonville—practical horrors blended with and underscored the formerly abstract derogations of superstition.

One of the most detailed, dramatic, and painful accounts of imprisonment at Andersonville comes from the memoirs of Charles F. Hopkins, most recently printed in a piece entitled "Hell and the Survivor" in *American Heritage* magazine. Hopkins describes Andersonville as encompassing part of the swamp on whose borders the camp was constructed: a full third of the camp consisted of porous, undrained, swampy ground. Added to this was human waste, left to fester in the swampy ground, creating an incubator for various diseases, debilitating and often killing the inmates: "Death at the hand of the guards . . . was merciful beside the systematic, studied, absolute murder inside, by slow death, inch by inch. . . . [O]ne-third of the original enclosure was swampy—a mud of liquid filth" (83). The horrific swamp emerges again in Hopkins's account as he and some companions manage to tunnel out of the camp into the surrounding swamps, leading to perhaps the most shocking moment in Hopkins's tale: "The crawl was a horror—through the mud and filth . . . and lastly into the water, covered with frog spawn, bri-ars, and rushes—simply a nasty, shallow mudhole backed by a swamp reek-ing with the seepings through dead vegetation of generations. . . . We reached a strip of swamp and entered but a short distance when the weak comrade sank helplessly down and died, while we waited, hoping to be missed by the hounds" (89–90). Hopkins's nonfiction account is, at times, as lurid and frightening as anything from Poe's *oeuvre*. For the Union soldier in the Southern swamp, even as the real and empirical swamp replaced the abstract and rhetorical one, the intrinsic horror of the swamp remained undimin-ished—indeed, it was, in most cases, intensified.

In at least one account, we even see an African American Southerner using his knowledge of the swamps to help the Southern cause. In *Fagots from the Campfire*, his 1881 memoir of his experiences as a Confederate scout during the war, journalist-turned-soldier Louis Dupré recounts a tale told by a Lieutenant Hughes, a captured Union officer, of "a negro's treason to the Union":

Of course the black rascal was my guide to the guerilla Clark's hiding place. My force was compelled to follow a narrow path across the swamp. Any deviation from the track, only wide enough for one horseman, was almost certain death. Quagmires were bottomless. . . . It occurred to me that we had traveled ten or fifteen, when the negro had said we need only go eight miles. . . . Within twenty minutes I heard the report of a pistol, and riding rapidly forward I encountered a corporal, who said that the negro had taken advantage of his perfect knowledge of the paths through the swamp, and of the different appearances of miry and of hard ground, and had sep-arated himself and the sergeant from the main body of my command, and that the "black rascal had shot the sergeant dead and disappeared." (177)

While we can only speculate as to the motivations of Hughes's nameless "negro," this anecdote, in its vivid and dire characterization of the swamp's menace, as well as its evocation of the man's "perfect knowledge" of the swamp paths, provides a telling testament to the subversive power of the swamp in the face of both Southern aristocrat and Northern invader.

For all the toll the swamp took on Union forces, it was generally no friend to the Southern cause, either. In his *Reminiscences of the Civil War* (1904), Confederate soldier John Brown Gordon provides a vivid account of his time stationed on the banks of the Chickahominy. Standing guard in the "dreary darkness and sickening dampness of its miasmatic swamps, hurrying to the front through the slush and bogs that bordered it, fighting hip-deep in its turbid waters," Gordon describes the swamp as pure misery lightened only by the grim humor of one private's cartoons of "this or that comrade with a frog-like face and the body and legs of a frog, standing in deep water, with knapsack high up on his back, his gun in one hand and a 'johnny-cake' in the other—the title below it being Bill or Bob or Jake 'on picket in the Chickahominy'" (54–55). Familiarity, it seems, was not sufficient to render the swamps comforting fortresses, in the manner of Simms's depictions of Marion's domain, to the Confederate troops.

The story of Acadian involvement in the Confederate army underscores the distance between swamps and swamp cultures and the rigid model of Southern identity dictated by antebellum social codes. In his 1992 book *Acadian to Cajun: Transformation of a People, 1803–1877*, Carl Brasseaux recounts that the Acadians were generally divided into two geographically and culturally divided groups. River Acadians were typically large planters who modeled their lives on the plantation system: "Automatically elevated in social status through the acquisition of their human chattel, these Acadian slaveholders soon aspired to the rarefied social position of Creole planters, which necessitated their adoption of the materialistic values and life-styles of their slaveholding neighbors" (6). This lifestyle, understandably, excluded the undeveloped swamps: despite the wealth to be had from exploiting the swamps' considerable bounty, few of the Acadians included in the official census lived off the swamps or identified themselves with them: "In 1860, only two Acadians east of the Atchafalaya were designated as 'hunter-fowlers,' and only one, an Iberville Parish resident, was listed as a 'swamper.' This swamper, however, owned $10,000 in real estate and $1,000 in personal property" (14). The planter Acadians, understandably, supported and felt part of the Confederate cause.

Swamp-dwelling Acadians, however, were considerably less inclined to involve themselves in the world beyond their self-sustaining communities. Vaughn Baker describes the insularity of many swamp-dwelling antebellum Cajuns in his article "In and Out of the Mainstream: The Acadians in Antebellum Louisiana" (1983). As he explains, many Acadians were separated from the rest of America by "the almost impenetrable barrier of the Atchafalaya Swamp" and "had little part in the emerging cultural pattern loosely termed 'American.' . . . Since their lives were essentially unmarred by the broader social or economic patterns and processes, they developed no higher loyalty than to their own community and in many cases the ultimate loyalty remained to the family" (103). The poorer prairie and swamp Acadians, often excluded from the official census, felt equally excluded from the cause of the Confederacy: "[W]ishing only to be left alone, the insular, poor, nonslaveholding . . . Acadians viewed the war as an elitist cause" (Brasseaux 62). While the river planters enlisted as officers, their poorer cousins shunned the war effort. With the passage of the Conscription Act of 1862, the Acadians outside planter society adopted an attitude of "open hostility" and regarded forced recruitment as "an intolerable intrusion into their peaceful lives" (63). Those forced into service consistently mutinied, even collectively throwing down their guns and running at the Battle of L'Abadieville (64). Deserters, and others reluctant to be impressed into military service, used the swamps in the same way that slaves did, fleeing into the vast Atchafalaya basin where even efforts to "[hunt] them down with dogs, like slaves" proved generally fruitless. By 1865, "desertions became so numerous that for the first time conscription parties were dispatched into the Atchafalaya swamp" (74), with limited results. In Louisiana, then, the swamps persisted in undermining the Southern cause throughout the Civil War.

In other Southern accounts, however—particularly those of non-combatants—the role of the swamp undergoes an intriguing change during the Civil War. Memoirs surviving from the Reconstruction and post-Reconstruction eras reveal an evolving conception of the swamps informed both by practical necessity and even a sense of ownership of lands that had so long been spurned. Some of this change can be attributed to the fact that these writers were not, generally, as driven to idealize their land as Southern fiction writers were, and some, no doubt, to the undeniable reality of the circumstances the writers faced. A few notable accounts by both male and female authors reveal a more complex vision of the swamps than we have seen in most Southern writing to this point—a mix of the old fears and demonizations with a kind of reclamation and even, in the notable case of Eliza Andrews, a drive to protect these formerly menacing spaces.

One of the more intriguing accounts is *The Autobiography of Joseph LeConte*, published posthumously in 1903. LeConte, a Georgia native who studied medicine, zoology, and geology, runs the gamut in representing the swamps as he knew them both in his youth and as an adult during the Civil War. He begins by crediting the proximity of his youthful home to Bulltown Swamp with his early academic learnings: "The situation was not healthy for whites. . . . [T]he children all suffered more or less from malarial fevers, which were sometimes hard to break. Ill health in my case led to contemplative, reflective, introspective habits. From this cause or from natural tendency, I early became interested in philosophical subjects" (15–16). LeConte's linking of an unhealthy swamp atmosphere with a heightened intellectual life might have proven an ingenious argument against earlier Northern propaganda linking swamp air to physical, mental, and moral lassitude; in this context, though, it becomes only one of several visions he provides of the swamp in everyday Southern life.

LeConte's swamps are not all miasma and pestilence. In fact, he recalls a childhood fascination with exploring the swamps near his home: "[W]hole days were spent in the exploration of the great swamp on which the plantation was situated. I am sure we felt, on a small scale, all the joy and pride of discoverers of unknown lands" (27–28). Freed from the constraints of literary propagandizing, accounts like LeConte's begin to reveal a much more congenial relationship between even plantation gentry and the swamps than we have yet seen. The swamps were dangerous, yes, but for boys, they represented fertile hunting grounds, mysteries to be explored, and even places to be appreciated for their beauty. Robert Q. Mallard recounts similar sentiments in his 1892 memoir *Plantation Life before Emancipation*: "As we grow older, our sisters and our boys begin to separate in our pursuits. . . . Now comes the savage age, the period of traps and bows and arrows. . . . Well do I remember the day when two fortunate successive shots brought me nine fat ducks, five of which I shouldered. . . . I felt proud as Julius Cæsar decreed by the Roman Senate a triumph, and coming home from the war of Gaul or of Britain" (23–24). Mallard's characterization of the period in his youth as the "savage age," and his clear distancing of his and his brothers' pursuits from those of his sisters, gives a logical explanation for the aristocratic Southern boy's appreciation for the much-derided and menacing swamps: they are wild spaces to be explored and conquered, if only on a small and personal scale. While LeConte, with his philosophical bent and stereotypically un-Southern interest in scientific matters, may have fancied himself a "discoverer," Mallard becomes a conquering Caesar. While the grand conquests envisioned by Byrd and Ruffin had been thwarted, postwar memoirs reveal that the swamps still tempted Southern boys to exploration and conquest.

A later episode in LeConte's memoirs heralds a more significant revisioning of the swamps in the face of wartime exigency. LeConte, in hiding from

Northern troops, learns from "three of the negroes" that the Yankees are on his trail. Faced with discovery and capture, LeConte trusts his fate to the "faithful and affectionate" slaves, who hide him in the swamp so effectively that he is able to forget his situation: "Soon the Yankees were swarming in the fields on both sides of me, popping at everything they could see; but I became so absorbed in one of James's novels . . . that I entirely forgot their presence" (192). Here, motivated by the dangers of war, the Southern aristocratic man of letters takes to the very swamps that sheltered escaped slaves as refuge from the Union soldiers. Far from representing the swamp hideout as menacing or malarial, Le Conte, ironic humor notwithstanding, presents an eminently civilized scene, as he peruses amid whizzing bullets a novel given to him by a friend named James.

This newfound sense of the swamp as protection—rarely before seen outside Simms's romances—resonates in many Civil War memoirs. Significantly, the idea is not limited to writings by Southern men, whose boyish adventures, we might expect, would make them more receptive to such ideas. Southern women's memoirs reveal perhaps the most dramatic reconceptions of the swamps brought about by the Civil War. Mary Boykin Chesnut, in her *Diary from Dixie* (1905), alternates between immediate, personal dread of riding through "swamps of pitchy darkness" with "the coachman as our sole protector" (221) and a broader strategic conception that elevates the swamps to logistical assets and even to benevolent expressions of nature's goodwill. For her, the swamps become a rallying point for the Southern cause: "To my small wits, whenever people were persistent, united, and rose in their might, no general, however great, succeeded in subjugating them. Have we not swamps, forests, rivers, mountains, every natural barrier" (147–48). Later in her diary, she reinforces the idea of the swamps as natural blessings: "It rains a flood, freshet after freshet. The forces of nature are befriending us, for our enemies have to make their way through swamps" (341). Inspired by a greater cause, Southern women began to move beyond their preconceptions about the blighted swamps—if only to regard their terrors as obstacles to invading forces rather than to Southern agriculture.

A more thorough reconception of the swamps comes in Eliza Frances Andrews's *War-Time Journal of a Georgia Girl, 1864–1865* (1908). Andrews was born in Washington, Georgia, which, as Jean Berlin tells us, was "an area favored by lowcountry dwellers for retreat from the miasma of the coastal areas in the summer" (vi). Andrews was, in many ways, profoundly atypical among Southern women of her era. She was fascinated by science and botany and was awarded membership in the International Academy of Science (Berlin vii). This fact alone makes her an atypical Southerner: as Kenneth Greenberg points out, "the lack of interest in . . . secrets of nature was characteristic of the antebellum South" (7), a fact that set Southern culture apart from much of the nineteenth century Western world. In other respects, Andrews is something of a contradiction. Her diary reflects a peculiar mixture of conservative reaction and progressiveness: though she was a suffragette and publicly proclaimed socialist, she used Marxism as a defense of slavery, explaining that in the South the transition from chattel slavery to wage slavery had not yet occurred (vii).

Andrews's odd Marxism is further complicated by the fact that she was a proud aristocrat. She praised the planter class effusively, seeing virtue in its rarefied status and quasi-familial bonding in its exclusivity: "To use a modern phrase, we were intensely 'class-conscious,' and this brought about a solidarity of feeling and sentiment almost comparable to that created by family ties. Narrow and provincial we may have been, in some respects, but take it all in all, it is doubtful whether the world has ever produced a state of society more rich in all the resources for a thoroughly wholesome, happy, and joyous life than existed among the privileged '4,000' under the peculiar civilization of the Old South" (2–3). Confident in the "solidarity of feeling" that united the Southern aristocracy, Andrews proclaims herself exemplar of its sentiments, claiming in her journal that "the experiences recounted are such as might have come at that time, to any woman of good family and social position; the feelings, beliefs, and prejudices expressed reflect the general sentiment of the Southern people of that generation" (4). While the limitations inherent in her self-definition as a "woman of good family and social position" belies her claim's implicit universality, Andrews's conception of her experiences and reactions as typical—and her willingness to speak for her people—make the swamp representations in her diary compelling for those examining the collective myth of the unified Southern mind.

Like many Civil War memoirs by women, Andrews's diary is largely a chronicle of the burdens and abasements endured by high-born women due to the hardships of war. Andrews laments the collapse of class divisions and social rituals: "these are unceremonious times, when social distinctions are forgotten and the raggedest rebel that tramps the road in his country's service is entitled to more honor than a king" (120). While Andrews willingly sacrifices social distinction and ceremony among her fellow Southerners, she shows a decidedly different reaction to the Union's destruction of racial and spatial divisions. She complains, once the Union has established a commanding presence in her town, that freed blacks overrun the streets, celebrating their liberty in what had been the favored spots among the aristocratic whites. Her entry for the Fourth of July, 1865, acutely displays her feelings: "They had a nigger barbecue out at our old picnic ground. . . . They have strung up one of their flags across the sidewalk, where we have to pass on our way to the bank, so I shall be forced to walk all around the square, in future, to keep from going under it" (329–30). Andrews's outrage becomes all the more acute when occupying Union forces, both white and black, seek to invert the traditional relationship between Southern gentleman protector, imperiled Southern lady, and marauding Northern invaders: "They say that they come for peace, to protect us from our own lawless cavalry—to *protect* us, indeed! With their negro troops, runaways from our own plantations! I would rather be skinned and eaten by wild beasts than beholden to *them* for such protection" (213). Andrews adopts the classic rhetoric of savage and civilized, casting her erstwhile protectors as worse than wild beasts, in resistance to the new social order forced upon her. Moreover, she expresses resistance in the only way available to her—a willingness to sacrifice herself in the interest of her cherished social ideals.

This sense of self-sacrifice pervades Andrews's account, though she generally avoids the hand-wringing martyrdom of many contemporary pieces. In service and deference to the common cause, Andrews repeatedly sets aside aristocratic pride—sometimes by choice but more often by necessity. As she eats a meal in hiding from the Yankees, she recalls searching her plate "for a clean spot on which to deposit my share, and, finding none, dabbed it down at random, and went for it, dirt and all, for I was desperately hungry" (163). The diary is full of such small humiliations, which Andrews recounts with candor. Andrews carries a zealot's appreciation of antebellum aristocratic ideals into an era in which, as she recognizes, they cannot be maintained. Throughout her diary, she embraces her abasement as a personal sacrifice in the service of an intangible and increasingly lost cause.

Alongside her stoic acceptance is a clear aesthetic appreciation of the Southern swamps. While any direct causal relationship between the two is clearly tenuous, a number of practical, situational factors combine to make such a shift in the perspective of a self-proclaimed exemplar of Southern female gentility understandable and significant: the erosion of social categories; the new wartime necessity of practical experience in the swamps; Andrews's intellectual interest in botany, itself a sign of progressive times; and a nascent sense of the swamps as fragile, Southern-identified spaces made newly valuable by their vulnerability to outside invasion.

Often, in Andrews's diary, the swamps are practical obstacles: her carriages slosh through them; her party gets lost in them as they flee the Yankees; they flood and block her way. Her descriptions, however, retain a balanced quality that generally avoids clichéd condemnations. Even as she describes a particularly difficult swamp crossing, during which "we came near upsetting twice, and the water was so deep in places that we had to stand on top of the trunks to keep our feet dry" (47), she appreciates the beauty around her: "Every few hundred yards we crossed beautiful, clear streams with luxuriant swamps along their borders, gay with shining evergreens and bright winter berries" (47). When Andrews does indulge a bit of poetic license in describing the swamps, any implicit judgment of them depends entirely on situational exigency. At one point, she echoes Chesnut in appreciating them as natural barriers: "We are safe from [the Yankees] for the present, at any rate, I hope; the swamps of the Altamaha are so flooded that it would take an army of Tritons to get over them now" (66). A bit later in the work, as Mr. Warren, her company's African American guide, becomes lost in a storm, the swamps understandably become somewhat more menacing: "At last he confessed that he had lost his way. . . . As there was nothing else to do, we concluded to follow the blind path we were in, hoping it would lead somewhere. It did lead us with a vengeance, through ponds and bogs and dismal swamps where the frogs filled our ears with unearthly noises" (113).

When Andrews can appreciate the swamps at leisure, though, she regards them with aesthetic appreciation and a botanist's fascination. She describes the environs of Coney Lake as "a beautiful place. Great avenues of Cypress extend into the shallow waters near the shore, where we could float about in shady canals and gather the curious wild plants that grow there" (106). These accounts express none of the fear stereotypically attached to swamp encounters: in fact, the excursion during which she and her escort are "followed by an alligator" is the trip that she "[enjoys] . . . more than any" (107). Andrews, her representativeness perhaps marred by a characteristically un-Southern interest in the scientific, regards the swamps for the most part with pleasure and fascination; no devils or leviathans surface to remind her that Southern women should fear them.

Perhaps the most significant moment in Andrews's account comes as she rides the railroad between Smithville and Cuthbert and perceives the early encroachment of New South development on the pristine natural world of the Old. Looking out on the surrounding swamps, she observes, "My taste may be very perverted, but to my mind there is no natural scenery in the world so beautiful as a big Southern swamp in springtime. It has its beauty in winter, too. . . . The railroad from Smithville to Cuthbert is lined on both sides with saw mills, getting out lumber for the government, and they are destroying the beauty of the country" (132). Andrews, in this brief moment, articulates an early sense of nascent Southern ecological consciousness. The swamp here emerges not as a practical obstacle or as a terra incognita to be explored but as a place of beauty, made more precious by its increasing vulnerability to the timber industry and, tellingly, to the government. A kind of solidarity with the native swamps emerges here—a sense that they, like the culture she so loves, are doomed by the encroachment of industrial Northern society. While Andrews acknowledges the entrenched negative swamp stereotypes by admitting that her taste "may be very perverted," she shows a willingness here to admit the swamps, which she personifies in terms ("somber," "stately") that evoke aristocratic virtues, into the fading collective myth of the victimized South.

Civil War era memoirs mark a significant, if halting, evolution in the ways that Southerners viewed the long-demonized swamps. In most, rhetoric fades in deference to practicality; they become defensive and strategic assets and natural rather than supernatural problems. While the swamps remained understandably nightmarish to those, both Union and Confederate, who fought among them, a gradual sense of appreciation and cultural ownership emerges in the writings of noncombatants—particularly those of women, the ordained keepers of Southern culture.

By the end of her account, Andrews embraces her newfound poverty with a kind of wistful pride: "It is more graceful and more sensible to accept poverty as it comes than to try to hide it under a flimsy covering of false appearances. . . . For my part, I am prouder of my poverty than I ever was of my former prosperity, when I remember in what a noble cause all was lost . . . I thank Heaven that I was born a Southerner,—that I belong to the noblest race on earth—for this is a heritage that nothing can ever take from me" (380). Andrews's quotation here signifies a key moment in the evolution of Southern mythology. While scores of critics, ranging from H. L. Mencken and Cash to more contemporary scholars such as Singal, Edward Ayers, and Steven Stowe might characterize the entire cultural creation of the Southern aristocracy as "a flimsy covering of false appearances"—though, clearly, with differing perspectives on its nature and significance—Andrews makes a transition here that encapsulates exactly the shift that had to happen to maintain and invigorate the myth of the Cavalier South. As Southerners were relieved of the necessity of demonstrating the validity of their current culture in the manner of George Fitzhugh's "Cannibals, All!" they were able to accomplish through retrospective deification and fictitious embellishment what was always an imperfectly realized task in the present: essentially, writing the South as it should be. Contemporary humility about the state of a fallen Southern gentility only elevated the prelapsarian South further, and the absence of pressing military or secessionist threat made the mythic, picturesque vision available to North and South alike.

No longer faced with the rhetorical need to demonize a defeated South via morally loaded descriptions of its landscape, freed of scientific misinformation that connected swamps to pestilence, and distanced from wartime swamp miseries, Northern writers became fascinated with the swamp as a place of beauty and even recreation. Even the real dangers represented by the swamp's creatures became vastly downplayed from their early leviathan-like characterizations. A typical period guidebook presents the danger of alligator encounters on a trip to Florida in terms more evocative of Southwest humor than of biblical significance: "You had better not take a dog, unless you dislike him and want to lose him: he will feed the first alligator you meet in fording a stream" (qtd. in Rinehart 27).

Key to the swamp's appeal for Northern writers, painters, and journalists was its very removal from the Southern society they so deplored. As Ann Vileisis explains, the previously maligned swamps were untouched by the ravages of war: "By the time that Grant and Lee met at Appomattox, towns and plantations had been destroyed, but most of the enormous cypress forests of the Southern river swamps stood intact" (117). Unencumbered by the need to employ swamp imagery in the service of abolitionist rhetoric, Northerners visiting the South saw in the swamps an area virtually untouched by what they perceived as a morally bankrupt civilization and thus a space that could be regarded and presented positively without stigma. Even Stowe, who had in many ways been foremost in demonizing the Southern swamp, calling it "an apt emblem . . . of that darkly struggling, wildly vegetating swamp of human souls, cut off, like it, from the usages and improvements of cultivated life" (*Dred* 274), made a home in Florida after the war and delighted in the surrounding swamps, as she recounts in her 1877 book *Palmetto Leaves*.

David Miller describes a veritable "swamp vogue" that arose shortly after the Civil War, fed primarily by Northern writers' representations and artists' swamp portraits for a curious Northern public fascinated by an element of Southern exoticism independent of civilization. St. Louis artist Joseph Rusling Meeker, who had served in the Union navy, made a career of exploring and painting the swamps along the Mississippi, emphasizing their mysterious mists and mosses. William Cullen Bryant edited a multivolume collection of art, *Picturesque America* (1872), which included a number of romanticized representations of Florida swamp landscapes. A. R. Waud, whose regular articles about the conditions Northern troops faced in Louisiana for *Harper's Weekly* during the war had initially demonized the swamp in conventional fashion, dwelling on the "alligators and rattlesnakes abound[ing] in the bayous and in the swamps, and all manner of unpleasant creeping, flying, and walking creatures swarm[ing] under the luxuriant tropical vegetation" (302), altered his representation of the swamps considerably after the war. His postwar articles about the Louisiana landscape in fact represent "an effort . . . to recreate the delicate impressions conveyed by a world very much alive, sacred, and self-absorbed" (Miller 59). The swamp, no longer a mire charged with all the corruption of Southern social sin, began to appeal to cultivated sensibilities. As a result, as Miller tells us, Northern tourists—even, remarkably, "a host of consumptive invalids seeking a healthy climate"—flocked to Florida after the war's end (60).

Accompanying this swamp vogue was, inevitably, a focus on a class of Southerners largely ignored in the plantation fiction and Confederate hagiographies dominating immediate postbellum Southern literature. Though both genres found broad markets in a North more forgiving of the Old South than accepting of the New, much of the most noteworthy writing about the present-day South by Northern journalists and other writers focused on the yeoman farmer, poor relation of the plantation aristocracy. Aristocrats had generally shunned swamps, so writers treating the swamps tended to focus on poorer rural Southerners, either praising the yeoman farmer or caricaturing "crackers." Again, this shift in literary emphasis from wistful plantation romance indicates the South was losing control over the literary and linguistic creation of its culture—an element of that culture arguably as constitutive as the economic system that was the most conspicuous, but not the sole, casualty of war.

Perhaps the most encyclopedic and best-regarded of the spate of Southern travel guides produced in the decades following the Civil War is Edward King's

Great South. initially published as a series of articles in *Scribners* in 1873 and 1874 and released in book form in 1875. Born in Massachusetts, King was a profound Unionist, strongly devoted to the reconciliation of North and South. Generally, his assessments of Southerners, both white and black, depend on their prospects for quick and thorough assimilation into the new nation. He enthusiastically proclaims, for example, that the "citizens of Alabama, as a mass, are as loyal to the idea of the Union to-day as are the citizens of New York" (340–41) and looks with particular approval upon the few "large manufacturing towns" he encounters as "evidences of thrift, industry, and investment" (694). Deeply critical of the cotton economy and the plantation system, King shifts the heart of Southern culture from the plantation aristocracy—the class that had the most invested in the old Southern system and thus the strongest investment in Southern separatism—and emphatically places the yeoman farmer at the center of Southern culture, invoking a tropic connection of the Southerner and the land that would become an enduring way of understanding Southern culture. Additionally, he expresses much concern about the status of freed slaves in the South and praises the instances that he observes of blacks advancing through improved education and political involvement, even as he disparages those who remained uneducated and, to his eyes, morally degenerate. Education, industrialized agriculture in place of immoral slavery, and general "northernization" are key to King's ideal Southern future.

In light of these ideas, King's depictions of the Southern swamps contextualize the aesthetic value postwar Northerners perceived in them. King's brief but compelling swamp descriptions indicate the attraction the mysterious landscapes offered Northern visitors and, more importantly, delineate the profoundly un-Southern terms of that attraction. King paints an ambivalent but picturesque portrait of one Louisiana swamp. He begins by calling it a "tract of hopelessly irreclaimable, grotesque water wilderness, where abound all kinds of noisome reptiles, birds and insects," but then exhorts that

> [o]ne should see such a swamp in October, when the Indian summer haze floats and shimmers lazily above the brownish-gray of the water; when a delicious magic in the atmosphere transforms the masses of trees and the tangled vines and creepers into semblances of ruined walls and tapestries. . . . As far as the eye can reach you will see hundreds of ruined trees, great stretches of water, forbidding avenues which seem to lead to the bottomless pit, vistas as endless as hasheesh visions; and the cries of strange

birds, and the bellowings of the alligator, will be the only sounds from life. You will be glad to steal back into the pure sunlight and the open lowland, to the river and the odors of many flowers—to the ripple of the sad-colored current, and the cheery songs of the boatmen. (70–71)

King curiously combines Byrd's disdain for the swamp's irreclaimability, Bartram's extolling of the swamp's mysterious beauty, and Poe's supernatural *frissons d'horreur*. These mingled responses reflect King's distinct subject position as a Northern Unionist encountering a landscape that is, to him, thoroughly alien. His initial disdain for an expanse that cannot be domesticated can be read as stemming from his fervent wish that the South be brought into line, economically and socially, with the rest of the nation: a seemingly endless and hopeless swamp represents a lost space in that regard. The blend of horror and fascination that follows can be classified as a kind of Northern aesthetic of ruin that developed after the Civil War regarding the defeated South. The decay and ruination he perceives—simultaneously "forbidding" and "delicious"—would appeal only to the victor surveying a defeated land; not to an explanter living in what in many ways was a "ruined" life in a "ruined" South. King's aesthetic responses to the swamp run counter to the Old South ideology of order and strict classification that rendered the swamp such a literal and figurative problem. The distinction becomes more pronounced as King surveys the swamps on the banks of Florida's St. John's River: "It is not grandeur which one finds on the banks of the great stream, it is nature run riot. The very irregularity is delightful, the decay is charming, the solitude is picturesque" (384). King's initial swamp description presents the postwar decadence of the swamps that Simms's Cavaliers ordered into "walls and tapestries," now doomed to ruin by the fall of the system he championed. King's second description finds beauty in a tableau explicitly untouched by any sense of grandeur, instead manifesting the ultimate fear of the Cavalier— "nature run riot."

Tellingly, King's perception of beauty in ruins extends to his encounters with the least regenerate Southern cities. As he describes his approach to St. Augustine, he revels in its decay: "The vegetation takes on a ghostly aspect; the black swamp canal over which the vehicle passes sends up a fetid odor of decay. . . . Ah! Here is a half-ruined cottage built of coquina, with a splendid palmetto overshadowing its remains, and some vines which I cannot identify in the darkness, creeping about the decaying windows!" (388). This aesthetic of chaos underscores that the swamp's appeal was categorically different from that of the popular plantation fiction that found a broad Northern audience during and shortly after Reconstruction.

Now perforce a part of a national progressive narrative rather than a regional pastoral, the South began to resemble in the eyes of the progressively minded North its own swamp—an intractable element in the advancement of a great nation, a necrotic space resisting cultivation and meaningful inclusion. King's qualified optimism aside, Northern observers generally viewed the defeated South as a wasteland. Some regarded it as irredeemably degraded, morally degenerate, and unfit for assimilation into a progressive nation: as one unnamed editorialist for the *New York Tribune* said in 1879, "Wherever slavery existed, there the moral sense was so blunted and benumbed that the white people as a whole is to this day incapable of that sense of honor which prevails elsewhere" (qtd. in Ladd 30). In the face of such criticisms, a body of literature emerged in defense of Southern culture, glorifying Old South society and meeting with considerable success in regenerating its image in the national imagination. In contrast to most Northern representations, these texts painted the South as a unique and noble culture, tragically lost forever. And yet, even in these wildly popular works, the swamps remained a potentially subversive force, threatening the pastoral visions that rehabilitated the image of a defeated South.

Of the vocal and influential group of Southern writers who took on the task of writing *for* the South—either rehabilitating its image, deploring its adulteration, or dwelling wistfully on idealized bygone days—Thomas Nelson Page stands preeminent. He crafted stories that appealed both to Southern nostalgia and to Northern curiosity about a faded, mythologized culture. For the most part, Page's picturesque and nostalgic representations steer clear of the swamps that historically challenged such a view of the South. However, when the swamp does emerge in his stories, it becomes both vehicle and repository for all the troublesome ambiguities that complicate his idealizing vision.

Page was, as Clyde Wilson attests, "the most popular and representative Southern writer of his time and one of the few Southern writers of any time to achieve the fullest measure of recognition and worldly success in his own lifetime" (xi). While Thomas Dixon, Page's contemporary, focused his fiery novels on political problems and racist paranoia, Page was a diplomat, appealing both to North and South: "For Northerners Page provided reassurance that sectional conflict was not intransigent, that the South had accepted restoration of the Union in good faith. For Southerners, he satisfied the desire to establish that they had not been dishonorable in their motives and conduct in the war and that the South had not really been the domain of diabolism of lurid abolitionist and Black Republican propaganda" (Wilson xiv). For the most part, Page's 1887 short story collection *In Ole Virginia, or "Marse Chan" and Other Stories* bears out Wilson's claim. Page's work is exceedingly genial, providing visions of the Old South that combine wistful idealization with placating perspective. In "Marse Chan," the most famous of the stories, Page muses on the old Southern aristocracy: "Their once splendid mansions, now fast falling to decay, appeared to view from time to time, set back far from the road, in proud seclusion. . . . [T]ime was of no consequence to them. They desired but a level path in life, and that they had, though the way was longer, and the outer world strode by them as they dreamed" (1). This is a fading South of lost dreams, a prelapsarian space where, as Matthew Martin observes in his 1998 article "The Two-Faced New South: The Plantation Tales of Thomas Nelson Page and Charles W. Chesnutt," the sins of slavery are generally effaced: "Like the Biblical Eden, the pre-war South here exists in another time, in a kind of world that has since been fundamentally altered. Like Eden it is a world of perfect order, in which both sin and labor are nonexistent" (22).

One story in Page's collection, though, stands out sharply from the others. "No Haid Pawn," the fifth story, immediately stands apart stylistically: it is the first that de-emphasizes the black dialect pervading the others and reassuring readers about the peaceful coexistence of races in the plantation South. In his article "The Other Side of Slavery: Thomas Nelson Page's 'No Haid Pawn,'" Louis Rubin has remarked at the story's radical departure from the others in Page's collection, pointing out that in the midst of Page's "tribute to the golden days before the Fall" there lurks, "seemingly unrelated to the life described in all the other stories[,] . . . this terrible tale of horror, guilt, fear, and depravity" (99). Significantly, it is also the only story to mention the swamps that surround the plantation Eden.

Other Southern writing of Page's generation goes out of its way to ignore or deny the swamps: Dixon, for example, virtually erases the swamps in his work, despite their Carolina settings. Now that web technology has made such things practicable, a search of his two most noted novels, *The Leopard's Spots* and *The Clansman*, reveals that neither volume contains a single instance of the word "swamp"; it seems as if Dixon, so focused on the polluting legacy of the Union interlopers, excises the rhetorically loaded landscape features entirely from his vision of the South.

However he may quarantine it in a single, uncharacteristic story, Page treats the swamp directly in "No Haid Pawn." In so doing, he creates the most complex and potentially troubling story in his collection. The tale is, on the surface, a traditional ghost story, dealing with a haunted manor house deep in a virtually impenetrable swamp, and a young Southern gentleman compelled to spend a night there. Encoded in this classic formula, though, is a subtle and complex acknowledgment of the less picturesque elements of the antebellum South: violence, racial tensions, the brutality of slavery, and the looming fear of insurrection. The story revives old, negative, swamp-centered tropes about Southern culture even as it distances them from mainstream Southern culture. As in Kennedy's Goblin Swamp episode in *Swallow Barn*, Page cloaks his brief critique of the South's underside in layers of removal from the Virginia society he idealizes; however, as in Poe's "Usher," he sews a troubling undercurrent of social critique into his tale of terror.

"No Haid Pawn" refers to an abandoned, dilapidated plantation house built in the heart of a particularly vile swamp. Page makes a point early on of distancing the place from mainstream 1850s Southern culture: not only is it "as much cut off from the rest of the country as if a sea had divided it" (163), but its owners were strangers to the area, and "no ties either of blood or of friendship were formed with their neighbors, who were certainly open-hearted and open-doored enough to overcome anything but the most persistent unneighborliness" (166). In fact, as we discover, the place has never had a local owner: its most notorious owner was a West Indian, and its current owners, "if there were any[,] . . . were aliens" (163). Page carefully distances the terrors he will discuss from the idyllic, pastoral society of his other stories.

Page also consciously distances the haunted swamp from the other, more picturesque swamps on his narrator's property: "I knew every foot of ground, wet and dry, within five miles of my father's house, except this plantation, for I had hunted by day and night every field, forest, and marsh within that radius; but the swamp and 'ma'shes' that surrounded this place I had never invaded" (162). The swamps around No Haid Pawn, in contrast to the rest of the plantation, are heavily exoticized: as the narrator traverses them, he uses "jungle" and "swamp" interchangeably, underscoring the racial overtones that become so important to understanding the tale: "Old logs thrown across the miry canals gave me an uncomfortable feeling as I reflected on what feet had last crossed on them. On both sides of this trail the marsh was either an impenetrable jungle or a mire apparently bottomless" (176). While Page shows a hint of the post–Civil War tendency to rehabilitate the images of some swamps as hunting grounds for the gentry, he quarantines this spot, loading a single swamp beyond his protagonist's purview with all the traditional demonic swamp tropes. In "No Haid Pawn," Page creates a kind of überswamp, one whose fears outstrip the horrors of slavery for the local slaves: "Even the runaway slaves who occasionally left their homes and took to the swamps and woods, impelled by the cruelty of their overseers, or by a desire for a vain counterfeit of freedom, never tried this swamp, but preferred to be caught and returned home to invading its awful shades" (164).

Page invests this swamp with supernatural terror—the slaves tell us that "hit's de evil-speritest place in dis wull" (162)—but, significantly, its terrors come less from the landscape than from the decayed reminders of its prior master: "[T]he place, by reason of the filling up of ditches and the sinking of dikes, had become again simple swamp and jungle, or, to use the local expression, 'had turned to ma'sh,' and the name applied to the whole plantation" (165–66). This swamp houses a man-made evil, and Page's descriptions collapse the distinction between the house and the swamp that surrounds it.

The house's history is singularly hideous, marked by a series of disasters in its construction that cost the lives of many slave laborers: one is crushed beneath the cornerstone; a scaffold collapses and kills several more. Disturbing the ground itself breeds pestilence: disturbing and reclaiming the land "proved unhealthy beyond all experience, and the negroes employed in the work of diking and reclaiming the great swamp had sickened and died by the dozens. The extension of this dangerous fever to the adjoining plantations had left a reputation for typhus malaria from which the whole section suffered for a time" (168). Even as the sickness bred by No Haid Pawn spreads throughout the entire surrounding area, the slaves attest to its uniqueness: its ubiquity "did not prevent the colored population from recounting year after year the horrors of the pestilence of No Haid Pawn as a peculiar visitation, nor from relating with bloodcurdling details the burial by scores, in a thicket just beside the pond, of the stricken 'befo' dey *daid*, honey, befo' dey *daid!*'" (168).

The property's terrible beginnings are compounded by the arrival of a new owner, "more gloomy, more strange, and more sinister than any who had gone before him" (168). Again, as he does with the property itself, Page takes pains to assert the fundamental alienness of this creature: he is "a man whose personal characteristics and habits were unique in that country. He was of gigantic stature and superhuman strength, and possessed appetites and vices in proportion to his size" (168–69). The villain in this legend of a fallen plantation is, fittingly, a kind of anti-Cavalier, possessed of great force but no character or control. He is uncultured and uneducated, speaking "only a *patois* not unlike the Creole French of the Louisiana parishes" (169), and is brought down by "a brutal temper, inflamed by unbridled passions," which lead him to "an act whose fiendishness surpassed belief" (169), for which he is ultimately hanged. The role of intemperance in his crime is even more emphasized as his slaves lament his death, claiming that "he was a good master when he was not drunk" (170). Thus does Page set the scene for his tale of horror: a site marked by the cruel deaths of mistreated slaves—but under the ownership and direction of people alien to the region; and a brutal, murdering plantation owner—but a foreigner, and the antithesis of the Cavalier upon whom the system that Page idealizes was built.

After this set-up, the events of the tale are fairly simply retold. A young man on his father's plantation, frustrated with a series of poor hunts, decides to venture into the forbidden swamps around No Haid Pawn to improve his luck. After a difficult journey through the dark and dangerous swamp, he arrives at the house itself. A brutal storm breaks out, forcing him to seek shelter in the house for the night. After nervously settling in for sleep, he is awakened by a "very peculiar sound . . . like a distant call or halloo" (183). Looking out the window, he sees a shadowy boat with "a man in it, standing upright, and something lying in a lump or mass at the bow" (184). He waits in terror as he hears someone enter the house and hears "a string of fierce oaths, part English and part Creole French" (185), which he naturally takes to be a sign that "the murderer of No Haid Pawn [has] left his grave, and that his ghost [is] coming up that stair" (185). At last, with a thunderclap and flash of lightning, the creature is revealed: "Directly in front of me, clutching in his upraised hand a long, keen, glittering knife, on whose blade a ball of fire seemed to play, stood a gigantic figure in the very flame of the lightning, and stretched at his feet lay, ghastly and bloody, a black and headless trunk" (186). The details of his escape are left ambiguous, and the house is blasted by lightning and sinks into the swamp: ultimately, in an echo of "Usher," "No Haid Pawn had reclaimed its own, and the spot with all its secrets lay buried under its dark waters" (186).

On this level, the tale seems a simple ghost story, but, as Rubin and others have pointed out, the true tale lies beneath the supernatural histrionics. Furthermore, however carefully removed from Page's cherished Virginia culture the surface-level horror story may be, the underlying tale cuts considerably closer to home for purveyors of plantation myth. In the course of the story, Page reveals that abolitionists had been discovered in the area—"several emissaries of the underground railway, or—as they were universally considered in that country—of the devil" (171). Most of the slaves they help to escape are captured, but one evades his pursuers. He comes from the lower Mississippi, and again, he seems alien and unique: "He was of a type rarely found among our negroes. . . . [He] was of immense size, and he possessed the features and expression of a Congo desperado. . . . He was alike without their amiability and docility, and was as fearless as he was brutal" (172). This slave, of course, is the dark figure that the narrator encounters in the plantation house—Page mentions that he has taken to stealing and slaughtering pigs, which accounts for the "dark mass" he carries with him. His exotic appearance and unusual mannerisms explain the strange cursing that heralds his arrival. Ironically, though, the natural explanation for the narrator's ghostly encounter is far more troubling in its implications for Page's Virginia society than an otherworldly occurrence could ever be.

While the horrors of "No Haid Pawn" seem easily enough contained, the threat represented by the abolitionists is considerably more pervasive. Page makes their dangers abundantly clear: "It was as if the foundations of the whole social fabric were undermined. . . . Whatever the right and wrong of slavery might have been, its existence demanded that no outside interference with it should be tolerated. So much was certain; self-preservation required this" (174). The presence of the abolitionists, and the looming reminder of the escaped slave in the swamp, present a considerably more powerful and practical threat than walking ghosts or moaning spirits. When we take this narrative into account, the careful quarantining of No Haid Pawn and its sinister swamp, and of the horrors that led to their current condition, threatens to break down. While it seems at first to insulate idyllic Virginia from criticism, the very alienness of the owner and escaped slave may also represent a kind of haunting of its own. As Rubin points out, "It is important that the owner had not been from the neighborhood, but was from the West Indies, where slave revolts had wiped out the French planters, and that the fugitive slave was from the lower Mississippi. For whatever slavery might have been in Virginia, however much it may have been gentled there, nevertheless in the deep South it was something very horrible and brutal, with little of the mitigating mildness that, as Page so often insisted in his other stories, characterized it in Virginia" (*Edge of the Swamp* 98). This subtle sense of collective guilt is not the only subversive element in "No Haid Pawn." Viewed with the abolitionists and escaped slave in mind, the entire tale takes on new possibilities. The dark boatman does, after all, call out as he approaches the house, suggesting that he may have accomplices. However happy and contented the Virginia slaves may seem, there is at least a suggestion that they may be helping this man evade capture. If this is the case, the initial tales about the swamp—the terrified warnings about its supernatural dangers, the insistence of the slaves that the pestilence connected with the swamp bore a "peculiar" relationship to No Haid Pawn—could all be part of a broader, subversive strategy to discourage the whites from approaching the place of sanctuary, this junglelike retreat for the escaped slave.

All of this, of course, is only subtly suggested in Page's story, as is the true identity of the monstrous apparition. The tale becomes a study in contrasts, layering its truly troubling and subversive subtext in layers of removal, even as Kennedy does in *Swallow Barn*'s Goblin Swamp episode. He exiles the terrors in the darkest of swamps, assigns blame to mysterious outsiders, and even has the place blasted out of existence and reclaimed by the swamp's waters at the close of his tale. If he follows Kennedy in his strategy of exile, though, he also follows Poe in the potential ramifications of his coded cultural critique. It is as if Page, in the midst of a collection devoted to presenting the South as a lost Eden, takes a single, uncharacteristic tale to plunge into the murky ambiguities of guilt and anxiety—the swamp at the edge of the pastoral garden.

Emerging as unique voices during the literary culture war that was determining the image of the American South in the national consciousness, George Washington Cable and Sidney Lanier present visions of the Southern swamps as distinct from those of their contemporaries as they are from each other. While Cable made use of the swamp's tropic significance to argue for social reform, and for a new vision of Southern culture that left little room for the ideology of the old, Lanier moved toward separating landscape and culture entirely, representing the swamp as a creation of the individual, rather than collective or cultural, imagination. Taken together, the works of these two authors indicate the extent to which swamp discourses were transformed in the decades after the Civil War and provide hints of the direction that conceptions of the swamp would take in the early twentieth century and beyond.

It is in some ways ironic, in some ways inevitable, that the part of the South that produced the most enduring literature during the Reconstruction period was New Orleans—a place more literally and figuratively linked with the swamp than any other major Southern city. Louisiana, only joining the United States in 1809, has always had a peculiar relationship to the rest of the South. In some ways, it epitomizes Southernness in the American mind; in others, notably its mix of cultures and stubbornly distinct codes of law, it has always stood apart from the other Southern states. As early as 1873, King remarked on Louisiana's situation as emblematic of the larger struggle that was happening, to a greater or lesser extent, throughout the Reconstruction-era South: "Louisiana today is Paradise Lost. In twenty years it may be Paradise Regained. . . . [I]t is the battle of race with race, of the picturesque and unjust civilization of the past with the prosaic and leveling civilization of the present" (199). New Orleans, the cultural and economic center of the state throughout the nineteenth century, distilled both the typically Southern and the subversive and exotic elements of Louisiana. Characterized by strict social categories and lax moral codes, by jealously defended bloodlines and by the unique and vital cultural mix brought about by its status as the South's major port city, and arguably as the first truly urban center in the South, New Orleans, like the swamp itself, remained both inextricably part of the South and unassimilably alien to it.

New Orleans was naturally conducive to a thriving literary scene in the late nineteenth century. If Northern readers sought picturesque tales of unfamiliar cultures through local-color literature, there could be no more fruitful ground for them than America's most exotic city. As Lewis Simpson has pointed out in "New Orleans as Literary Center: Some Problems" (1992), the flowering of New Orleans literature was peculiarly bound up in the South's defeat: "Had the South won the war, the city might never have developed an appreciable literary image. But after the surrender . . . the aura of a never-never-land exoticism began to spread over the land of the Lost Cause—New Orleans in the guise of *Old* New Orleans became the leading presence of that form of nineteenth-century exoticism known as local color" (80). Though the most enduring New Orleans writers of the late nineteenth century combined their quaint portrayals of cultural oddities and picturesque renderings of the city's exotics with insightful cultural commentary and compelling social arguments, the city's otherness, its compelling air of difference even within the South of which it became the most conspicuous literary image, clearly made its status as a literary hub possible.

New Orleans is particularly important to this study not so much because of its centrality to late-nineteenth-century Southern letters, but more because that centrality occurred in a place so profoundly linked, both physically and meta-phorically, with the swamp. First and foremost, the city itself was constructed on an uneven patch of relatively high ground in the midst of a vast swamp, stretching from the Mississippi River to the shores of Lake Pontchartrain. Efforts to drain the city dominate early New Orleans history and continue into the present day: even now, as Donald W. Davis points out in his article "Historical Perspective on Crevasses, Levees, and the Mississippi River" (2000), "Twenty-two drainage-pumping stations drain New Orleans. Several are con-sidered to be the world's largest, with the pumping capacity to empty a ten-square-mile lake, 13.5 feet deep, every twenty-four hours" (89). This drainage system, instituted in the late nineteenth century and maintained in only slightly altered form today, is one of a very few factors separating urban New Orleans from the surrounding swamps. Much of New Orleans's history can be seen as a continuing battle with the swamp, both in its literal dimensions and in its superstitious overtones. The swamp became linked in New Orleans with physical disease and with moral turpitude, even as the city itself took on those associations for the rest of the South and the nation: New Orleans, through both natural environment and culture, became a powerful exemplar of the aesthetic of ruin that informed Northern perspectives on the South.

Throughout the nineteenth century, and arguably still today, New Orleans carried a distinct aura of moral decadence and a reputation as a hotbed of gambling and prostitution. Even as the city walls tenuously separated the urban center from the surrounding swamps, a different kind of swamp coalesced in the walls' shadow: in the 1820s, a certain area in the "back of town" was more or less designated for prostitution and other illicit activity and was given the nickname "The Swamp" by both locals and visitors. By midcentury, the area called Greater Tremé, "part of the vast swampy area outside city fortifications," became the infamous red-light district known as Storyville. The undeveloped land became a place for activities outside the strictly delineated cultural stan-dards of Victorian Southern manhood and began the longstanding association of New Orleans with lax morality and indulgence of vice. This association would produce a central tropic character in Southern literature—the dissolute, mysterious, dark young New Orleanian who carries a vague air of menace and hint of racial indeterminacy.

Thus, the rise to literary prominence of New Orleans ran directly counter to myths of the grand Old South and emphasized an aesthetic of ruin writ upon the human body. The postwar literary ascendancy of New Orleans brought to the forefront the very elements of the swamp that the antebellum South, and the postwar romanticizers of plantation life, sought to suppress. Racial purity had been key in sanctifying Confederate heroes. Works of the era presented the conflict as one of white Southern gentlemen battling polyglot hordes of Yankee hirelings: as one representative text of the time states the case, "The Confederate soldier . . . fought the trained army officers and the regular troops of the United States army, assisted by . . . swarms of men, the refuse of the earth—Portuguese, Spanish, Italian, German, Irish, Scotch, English, French, Chinese, Japanese—white, black, olive, brown[,] . . . who died for pay, mourned by no one, loved by no one" (qtd. in Gray 85). New Orleans, a racial and cultural polyglot, contradicted the impulse to guard cherished myths of Southern purity. This was a place of literal, moral, and racial contagion, of ruin and degeneracy, a place rapidly becoming representative of a South that had constructed itself according to rules and codes that the city itself seemed to flaunt.

It is fitting, then, that the most noted New Orleans writer of the late nineteenth century is George Washington Cable, a vocal critic of mythologized Southern culture. Generally regarded as political reformer first, writer of fiction second, Cable was singularly devoted to political reform, particularly in matters of race, and crusaded against paranoia about racial contamination, as well as against the cultural stagnation he perceived in the South as a whole. Cable's defenders hold him forth as the first Southern realist: his most enduring work, especially his stories of Old New Orleans in *Old Creole Days* and his novel *The Grandissimes*, troubles racial categories and critiques the cultural conventions he believed impeded the progress of the South in general and New Orleans in particular. Taking the ornate, inflexible, and ultimately insubstantial social and racial codes of New Orleans as a synecdochic metaphor for the codes that still influenced the entire South, Cable became one of the most influential critics of Southern life of the Reconstruction era.

Though Cable was a New Orleans native, and an avid chronicler of the culture he observed around him, the political and cultural criticism suffusing his work marked him as an outsider in New Orleans society, and eventually in the South as a whole. Fred Hobson sums up Cable's literary mission in *Tell about the South* (1983): "It was not Cable's primary purpose . . . to remember, defend, preserve, or even appreciate the South. His purpose was to improve it" (108). Cable can only problematically be considered a Southern writer—of Northern parentage and certainly out of line with mainstream Southern thought, he saw the South as a festering wound in an otherwise vital and vibrant nation: as he claims in an 1890 essay for *Book-News Monthly*, "This country of ours . . . is a giant with one arm in a sling. That arm is the South. The whole country knows that because of something wrong in the South, the whole country, great, rich, free, and progressive as it is, is immeasurably less than it ought to be. . . . [H]alf the thought given to the betterment of the economic and civic conditions of our country is taken up with the problems of how to establish a full share of our national vigor, freedom, enlightenment, and wealth in this crippled, bleeding, and aching arm" (qtd. in Hobson 109). By inclination as well as biographical fact, Cable resists the label of Southern writer, although he may well have been the most broadly known and respected such writer of his day. His career as a writer of fiction began in earnest when he was "discovered" by King in 1873, while Cable was at work on the short stories that would eventually be anthologized in *Old Creole Days*; he worked primarily with Northern publishers and spent most of his career living in New Hampshire, New York, and Massachusetts.

He met with considerable success outside the South, even taking part in a celebrated tour of literary luminaries alongside Mark Twain; however, Cable met with little acceptance in the land of his birth. Cable's fictional critiques of the Creole people, though often glazed with a patina of romanticism, shone through in *Old Creole Days* and *The Grandissimes*; his overtly political pieces, especially 1884's "The Convict Lease System in the Southern States" and 1885's "The Freedman's Case in Equity," had no camouflage for their condemnation of Southern political practices and racial attitudes. He made throngs of enemies among the people of New Orleans and of the South as a whole. As Alice Hall Petry points out, the French-Creole community, who were particular targets of Cable's critiques, perceived that he "had betrayed New Orleans by insinuating to alien readers that its residents were degenerate, that Creoles, true to the etymology of their name, had the dreaded 'taint of Negro blood,' and that theirs was a town of violence, gunrunning, and circuses in which beasts battled with only slightly less beastly New Orleanians" (2). Cable's more direct challenging of racial boundaries earned him equal antipathy elsewhere in the South: when in Nashville in 1889 he dined with a black family, the Nashville *American* offered a withering commentary: "In the South . . . a man must choose the race with which he associates and Mr. Cable having signified his preference for the negro race over his own should be left undisturbed to his choice. We do not mean to say that Cable lowered himself by accepting the hospitalities of Mr. Napier, colored; on the contrary we think he found his proper level" (qtd. in Ladd 40). As a kind of exile by choice who met with considerable literary success and fame throughout the rest of the nation, Cable contributed to the broad national perception of New Orleans as a stagnant, decaying, and dangerously polluted racial swamp. His influence, in fact, extended beyond his own work, if in camouflaged form: as W. Magruder Drake points out in his introduction to the 1972 edition of *The Great South*, Edward King, Cable's literary "discoverer," relied on Cable for much of his information about Louisiana and New Orleans in particular (xxx n30). Indeed, King's ironic and decidedly unromantic depiction of the city's early history bears marks of Cable's critical assessment of the city's nobility: "[T]all grasses grew up to the doors of the houses, and the hoarse chant of myriads of frogs mingled with the vesper songs of the colonists. . . . [A]mong the reeds of the city thitherward always harked a host of criminals . . . and airy gentlemen and stately dames promenaded in this queer, swamp-surrounded, river-endangered fortress, with Parisian grace and ease" (22). King's observations of New Orleans "types" also bear the marks of Cable's interest in the city's mulattoes—aspects of society that the white Creole class would prefer to de-emphasize. King observes "[t]he rich savage face in which the struggle of congo with French or Spanish blood is still going on," as well as "a mulatto girl hardly less fair than the brown maid [one] saw at Sorrento, or in the vine-covered cottage at the little mountain town near Rome"(47). King's emphasis on these types may, of course, merely indicate that the white Creole class's desire to downplay them was merely a flat denial of reality, but the voice, or at least the enthusiastic assent, of Cable seems clear in these passages.

A great deal of work has been done on the problem of race in Cable's work: such luminaries as Louis Rubin and Lewis Simpson, and more recently Barbara Ladd, in her excellent study *Nationalism and the Color Line in George W. Cable, Mark Twain, and William Faulkner* (1996), have examined and reexamined his troubling of racial categories and efforts to undermine racial essentialism. To retrace those steps here risks redundancy. Taking Cable's emphasis on undermining strict racial categorization as a critically established given, I will focus, instead, on his use of landscape—particularly the swampy qualities of the New Orleans environs—in a representative tale from his early collection *Old Creole Days*, "Jean-ah Poquelin," and in his depictions of Old New Orleans in *The Grandissimes* to underscore and develop his critiques of

New Orleans culture. Cable avoids the "aesthetic of ruin," which colors King's work and influences many depictions of the swamp-ridden South of his era. Instead, Cable puts the swamp to mercurial uses in crafting his literary art and in promulgating his social philosophy, at times echoing tropes of the past and at times anticipating visions of the future.

In *Old Creole Days*, a collection of the short stories that first made his literary reputation, Cable began to explore the potential of the swampy New Orleans environment as symbol and rhetorical tool. In these stories, Cable follows Poe in rendering a landscape shaped by, and reflective of, the moral and ethical flaws of its inhabitants. The stories in which the swampy environment of New Orleans figures most prominently present a kind of empathic and moral landscape offering its own judgment on the lives and values of the Creole people. *Old Creole Days* represents perhaps the most even balance between Cable the writer of local-color fiction and Cable the political and moral crusader: less overtly political than Cable's later works, it is a collection of portraits, vignettes, and pseudo folktales. Even in avoiding the direct sermonizing of his later work, Cable weaves unmistakable cultural critique into his quaint portraits of Creole life.

One story in particular makes specific use of the unique environment of New Orleans as a city on a swamp to critique Creole culture: "Jean-Ah Poquelin," which centers on a once rich plantation that decays into a foul, unhealthy marsh. All over the South, rice and indigo plantations, left untended after the Civil War, were being subsumed back into the wild swamps from which they had only partially been separated. The story's setting reflects a larger change in swamp representation, echoing what we have seen in King's work: here, the swamp is not a primordial space outside the control of society but a chaos born of a civilization's necrotic decay. This tale features Cable's most direct rhetorical use of the swamp as reflective of old sins, and as embodiment of Creole society's resistance to progress.

The story's plot can be briefly summarized. Jean Poquelin was an indigo planter of an apparently exalted line (his father is buried beneath St. Louis Cathedral) and a "bold, frank, impetuous, chivalric adventurer" (134). After falling on difficult times due to a general agricultural failure, Jean and his younger brother Jacques become slave traders. After an extended absence, he returns home, apparently alone, and becomes a hermit. His house and land revert to a hideous swamp to the extent that Poquelin and the house itself become the stuff of local folklore: "The name of Jean Marie Poquelin became a symbol of witchery, devilish crime, and hideous nursery fictions" (136), while credulous neighbors claim to see the *feu follett* rise from the swamp and race through the house at midnight and claim that beneath the house is a bottomless pit. As modernization transforms the city, and the government wants to build a road through Poquelin's marsh, he stubbornly resists. Finally, even as a mob threatens to descend on the old house, Jean Poquelin dies. As his funeral processes, as if set free by his death, the secret of his house appears—his brother, long thought dead, stricken by leprosy during the pair's travels as slave traders, emerges from the house accompanied by the African mute who had served the brothers. Before the eyes of the incredulous crowd, the two figures disappear into the swamp at the edge of the ancient city.

From the story's beginning, Cable makes clear that his criticisms of the central character, Jean Poquelin, can be applied broadly to a reactionary Creole society as a whole: he establishes his setting as the first decade of the nineteenth century, "when the newly established American government was the most hateful thing in Louisiana—when the Creoles were still kicking at such vile innovations as trial by jury, American dances, anti-smuggling laws, and the printing of the governor's proclamation in English" (133). The first depiction of Jean Poquelin's ruined house, following directly on the heels of his characterization of an overall stagnant Creole mindset, leaves little doubt that Poquelin's story is an extreme distillation of generalized Creole recalcitrance. His ruined house, as Cable describes it, "stood aloof from civilization, the tracts that had once been its indigo fields given over to their first noxious wildness, and grown up into one of the horridest marshes within a circuit of fifty miles" (133). Swamp imagery pervades the story, becoming a central and none-too-subtle metaphor for the necrotic disease inherent in the Poquelin brothers' old sin: "Two lone forest trees, dead cypresses, stood in the center of the marsh, dotted with roosting vultures" (134). Cable, following Poe, employs morbidly picturesque visions of a wasted landscape as direct reflections of the racial sin that prevents the Poquelins—and, by extension, a Creole society resistant to the Americanization and progress that Cable held as a self-evident good—from moving beyond putrid stagnation.

Poquelin's marsh becomes a clear signifier of racial guilt; it becomes, like the disease that causes its growth, a punishment, not only for the dwellers within, who engaged in the morally reprehensible practice of slave trading, but for the community that once rewarded their endeavors and now seeks to move beyond. Cable underscores the marsh's connection to the brothers' sins against Africans throughout: at one point, the narrator exclaims, "What wonder the marsh grew as wild as Africa!" (137). Somewhat more subtle, though, is the mysterious, mute African servant, the silent giant who, like a grim vision of Charon, rows Poquelin through his dark swamp with downcast eyes, equal parts, as we discover, servant and jailor. The story's close leaves little doubt as to the story's racial overtones: the diseased Jacques Poquelin, turned "white as snow" by his affliction, accompanied by the great black mute, embodiment of silent guilt, vanishes into a swampy Land of Nod: "For a moment more the mute and the leper stood in sight. . . . [T]hen, without one backward glance upon the unkind human world, turning their faces toward the ridge in the depths of the swamp known as the Leper's Land, they stepped into the jungle, disappeared, and were never seen again" (154). Whatever pathos and sympathy Cable introduces into his coda, the story makes clear that purging the Poquelins is a necessary and positive step in the evolution of New Orleans. Cable links the essence and tenacity of the marsh not only to the slave traders' initial sins but to the stubborn refusal of Poquelin—and, by extension, Creoles resistant to cultural change—to let go of tainted traditions and cultural legacies. In the governor's office, Poquelin mounts his resistance to the development of his land based on two seemingly contradictory impulses: first, he points out that "the marass is too unhealth' for peopl' to live"; then, when told that they plan to drain the marsh, he insists that "the canal is private" (139). However putrid and diseased, the land is Poquelin's own, and he refuses to see it changed, despite the governor's claim that its value will increase tenfold.

Progress toward urbanization and the reclamation of the swamp are figured throughout in unequivocally positive terms: even as Creole culture's hegemony is challenged by a flood of "alien races pouring in," progress seems irresistible: "Fields became roads, roads streets. Everywhere the leveler was peering through his glass, roadsmen were whacking their way through willow braces and rose hedges, and the sweating Irishmen tossed the blue clay up with their long-handed shovels" (137). The canals built to drain Poquelin's marsh effect a dramatic and beneficial transformation: "Lilies and the flower-de-luce sprang up in the place of reeds; smilax and poison oak gave way to the purple-plumed ironweed and pink spiderwort. . . . Over all these came a sweet, dry smell of salubrity which the place had not known since the sediments of the Mississippi first lifted it from the sea" (141). Cable's progressive impulse here overcomes any impulse to aestheticize ruin: too invested in the improvement of New Orleans culture and Southern culture in general to find beauty in decay, Cable inscribes his progressive agenda upon a revived and rejuvenated landscape, product both of the flood of immigrants who transform both land and stagnant culture and of the work they perform to exorcize the old demons at the heart of the morass.

In order for the physical and cultural rebirth to take place, however, the old evils must be purged. In a sense, the grotesque pair of the leper Jacques Poquelin and the nameless African mute become communal scapegoats. Unfortunate embodiments of Creole society's guilty past, laden with the old bad ways that yoke them like the mute servant's "heavy burden," the two vanish into a swamp now firmly outside the boundaries of the burgeoning city—a swamp that becomes, to borrow Rod Giblett's fanciful phrase, "more scape-land than landscape, the geographical equivalent of the scapegoat on which communal sins are heaped" (13). The exile of the two, before a mob-turned-funeral that consists of younger Creoles as well as representatives of a newly multicultural New Orleans, becomes an intriguing inversion of the kind of purgation ceremony Mary Douglas describes—only for Cable, the true impurity comes from the misbegotten belief in cultural superiority that enabled the slave trade.

The Grandissimes is Cable's best known and most fully realized work. First appearing in installment form beginning in 1879, it made considerable impact on release; changing critical trends and the passage of time have amplified its significance. Rubin credits it as the first Southern novel to "attempt to deal honestly with the complexity of Southern racial experience" ("Division" 27). Cable's aim in the novel is to trouble the entrenched and categorical ways of thinking about race that so troubled him. As Suzanne Jones puts it in her introduction to the 1988 edition, "Cable used The Grandissimes not only to examine the problems of reconstruction but to challenge his readers' own assumptions. To this end, he deliberately confused his audience with masked balls, mistaken identities, and unexplained behavior, trying to break readers—both northern and southern—of customary modes of thinking" (vi). The novel's swamp imagery mirrors and enhances the complexity of its racial and cultural commentary. The earliest descriptions of the New Orleans landscape, from the perspective of the outsider Frowenfield as he first approaches the city, add to the idea of New Orleans as a place of contradictions, containing both otherworldly beauty and ominous darkness: "[T]he funereal swamps slowly shut out again the horizon. How sweet the soft breezes off the moist prairies! How weird, how very near, the crimson and green and black and yellow sunsets! How dream-like the land and the great, whispering river!" (9). As the ambivalence and inscrutability ascribed to the landscape itself suggest, categories, borders between black and white, aristocrat and commoner, fragrant prairies and "funereal swamps," will be uncertain throughout the novel. Shortly on the heels of the swamp description, Frowenfield is introduced to New Orleans society by Doctor Keene's story of the interloping quadroon being slapped for daring to appear at a Creole ball—a tale that mirrors the mysterious and puzzling nature of the swamp landscape: "[H]is narrative, when it was done, was little more than a thick mist of strange names, places and events; yet there shone a light of romance upon it that filled it with color and populated it with phantoms. Frowenfield's interest rose—was allured into this mist—and there was left befogged" (15). Very early on, Cable troubles the distinction between the strange and inscrutable landscape and the supposedly clearly stratified Creole society.

At times in the novel, racial purity seems unambiguous. Cable says of Honore Grandissime that "[h]is whole appearance was a dazzling contradiction of the notion that a Creole is a person of mixed blood" (38). The De Grandissime girls, as well, evince racial purity, marked by "transparency of flesh and classic beauty of feature" (22). At other times, though, racial and cultural identity seems profoundly troubled and unclear: Honore f.m.c. (free man of color) is a puzzling blend of racial and cultural traits, possessing "manners Castilian, with a gravity almost oriental" (41), while the mulatto Palmyre paradoxically bears "that rarest of gifts in one of her tincture, the purity of true womanhood" (60). Palmyre in particular, with purity that lies outside strictly racial definitions of the term, frightens Agricole: as Doctor Keene observes, "he tolerates her even though she does not present herself in the 'strictly menial capacity.' Reason why—*he's afraid of her*" (60). These figures become troublesome to Creole society because they cannot be classified according to Fusilier's purportedly self-evident system.

The story of the origins of both the Fusilier and Grandissime families similarly troubles the traditional Southern narrative of gentlemanly conquest of wilderness and of cherished racial purity. Both Epimanondas Fusilier and Zephyr Grandissime, breaking off from D'Iberville's expedition, are lost and dying in the swamps before the Indian Lufki-Humma, "The Diana of the Tchoupitoulas ranging the magnolia groves with bow and quiver" (21), rescues them in a peculiar blending of classical imagery with description of a racial other. Epimanondas Fusilier—progenitor of Agricola Fusilier, the most immovable figure in the novel on matters of race, who claims to Frowenfield that "[t]he non-mention of color always implies pure white; and whatever is not pure white is to all intents and purposes pure black" (59)—wins the Indian bride who rescued him from the swamps in a dice game. This fact undercuts Agricola's pretensions to familial and racial purity while exposing the capricious nature of officially sanctioned family pedigree in colonial New Orleans: "Thus, while the pilgrim fathers of the Mississippi Delta with Gallic recklessness were taking wives and moot-wives from the ill specimens of three races, arose, with the church's benediction, the royal house of the Fusiliers in Louisiana" (22). Cable's ironic description of Louisiana's settlement by indiscriminately marrying and breeding French in a wilderness that often vexes their imperial efforts sets the tone for his critiques of an artificial system of classification.

Throughout the novel, comments on New Orleans society and particularly on its treatment of African Americans—the "Shadow of the Ethiopian"— echo Cable's initial figuration of the landscape as a combination of beauty and the looming darkness of the swamps. Honore's comments on that shadow evoke and echo descriptions of the swamp: "Ah! My-de'-seh, when I try sometimes to stand outside and look at it, I am *ama-aze* at the length, the blackness of that shadow! . . . It is the *Nemesis* w'ich, instead of coming afteh, glides along by the side of this morhal, political, commercial, social mistake! It blanches, My-de'-seh, ow whole civilization! It drhags us a centurhy behind the rhes' of the world! It retahds and poisons everhy industrhy we got!—mos' of all our-h immense aghricultu'e! It bhreeds a thousan's cusses that nevva leave home but jus' flutter-h up an rhoost, my-de'-seh, on ow *heads*; an' we nevva know it!—yes, sometimes some of us know it" (156). The images of racial injustice as an obstacle to civilization's progress, as a source of pollution and poison as well as of supernatural curses, erode the clear boundaries between the traditional representations of the surrounding swamps and the stubbornly stagnant culture of New Orleans.

The story of Bras-Coupé, which haunts the entire novel and serves, as Rubin puts it, as the novel's "physical and moral center," indicates the swamp's significance most clearly. From his earliest introduction, long before we know his full story, Bras-Coupé's presence haunts the seemingly uninhabitable swamp. Frowenfield's discussion with an unnamed passenger on the boat that takes him to the city establishes both the swamp's connection to blackness as well as the continued looming shadow of Bras-Coupé:

But he was assured that to live in those swamps was not entirely impossible to man—"if one may call a negro a man." Runaway slaves were not so rare in them as one—a lost hunter, for example—might wish. His informant was a new passenger, taken aboard at the fort. He spoke English.

"Yes, sir! Didn' I had to run from Bras-Coupé in de haidge of de swamp be'ine de 'abitation of my cousin Honore, one time? You can hask 'oo you like!" (10).

The haunting, inchoate specter of Bras-Coupé finally takes definite form when Frowenfield hears his full story. The image of the escaped slave establishing his own dark kingdom in the depths of the swamp reflects a terrible freedom:

Bras-Coupé was practically declaring his independence on a slight rise of ground hardly sixty feet in circumference and lifted scarce above the water in the inmost depths of the swamp.

And what surroundings! Endless colonnades of cypresses; long, motionless drapings of gray moss; broad sheets of noisome waters, pitchy black, resting on bottomless ooze; cypress knees studding the surface; patches of floating green, gleaming brilliantly here and there. . . .

The pack of Cuban hounds that howl from Don Jose's kennels cannot snuff the trail of the stolen canoe that glides through the sombre blue vapors or the African's fastnesses. His arrows send no tell-tale reverberations to the distant clearing. (182)

Before his return and grisly dismemberment and execution, the liberty and protection the swamp affords Bras-Coupé carry a strange and terrible power. From its shelter, he engenders chaos, as his curse makes the land itself rebel against Don Jose, destroying his crops and covering his fields in intractable weeds. The supernatural victim of racial oppression extends the swamp's chaos to undermine plantation order.

As terrible and frightening as Bras-Coupé's swamp fortress is, Cable repeatedly compares the slave's situation favorably to the conditions of the novel's victims of class, race, and familial prejudice. Frowenfield, confronting Honore f.m.c. about the state of the quadroon in Creole society, claims that "I would rather be a runaway in the swamps than content myself with such a freedom" (196). Somewhat later, Aurora Nancanou makes a more explicit and disparaging comparison of the social order to Bras-Coupé's swamp: "There are many people who ought to have their rights. There was Bras-Coupé; indeed, he got them—found them in the swamp. Maybe Clotilde and I shall find ours in the street" (260). Cable's most compelling employment of the swamp's tropic signification comes in these references, tying the comparatively subtle racial and cultural injustices of an inflexible and cruel New Orleans society to the vivid and grisly tale of Bras-Coupé. Cable goes beyond the disparaging linkages between New Orleans society and the swamp, both implicit in race thinking of the time and explicit in literature indulging the aesthetic of ruin: he offers the swamp, as terrifying as it might be, as a more moral environment than New Orleans society itself. There is no picturesque romanticization here: Cable foregrounds the swamp's horrors, only to emphasize the greater horrors that face Creole society's dispossessed.

Even as the beginning of the Grandissimes' and Fusiliers' lineage comes with an ironic commentary on "civilization's conquest" of the swamp, late in the novel Cable offers a similar dark satire of the traditional figuration of the white Southerner as chivalric knight venturing into a racialized wilderness. As Captain Jean-Baptiste Grandissime lays a trap in the wilds for the black Clemence, who will lead him to the "voudou queen" Palmyre, Cable scornfully presents him as a parody of an armored crusader: "[U]nder his clothing, he was encased from head to foot in a complete suit of mail. Of steel? No. Of brass? No. It was all one piece—*a white skin*; and on his head he wore an invisible helmet—the name of Grandissime" (311). The fruits of his quest, which leads to an inglorious victory in a lawless lynching, are no more noble: "Some rods within the edge of the swamp . . . the younger and some of the harsher senior members of the Grandissime family were sitting or standing about, in an irregular circle whose centre was a big and singularly misshapen water-willow. At the base of this tree sat Clemence, motionless and silent, a wan, sickly color in her face, and that vacant look in her large, white-balled, brown-veined eyes, with which hope-forsaken cowardice waits for death" (321). Cable's scene seems a degraded re-creation of Simms's swamp, the domain of brave gentlemen warriors who impose their will upon the forbidding landscape. These knights' quest is pathetic, their victory over the helpless Clemence singularly inglorious.

Perhaps the clearest image of the deteriorating boundaries between the swamp's chaos and New Orleans society comes as the sick and suicidal Doctor Keene wanders at the northern boundary of the city: "Down the empty street or road, which stretched with arrow-like straightness toward the north-west, the draining-canal that gave it its name tapered away between occasional overhanging willows and beside broken ranks of rotting palisades, its foul, crawling waters blushing and gliding and purpling under the swiftly waning light, and ending suddenly in the black shadow of the swamp. . . . As his eye passed them slowly over and swept back again around the dreary view, he sighed heavily and said: 'Dissolution,' and then again—'Dissolution! Order of the day—' " (263–64). Doctor Keene's delirious commentary, coming at one place in the city where "one could think aloud . . . with impunity," suggests a creeping, continuous process of erosion, of social and cultural decay, leading the city with "arrow-like straightness" into the swamp's darkness. In the context of Cable's critique, the questions becomes whether swamp infects civilization or vice versa. Cable's use of the swamp in *The Grandissimes* both echoes and undermines old tropes, presenting the swamp in all its horrors, but breaking down the cultural bulwarks that supposedly hold it at bay, suggesting that it, and the inherited guilt that it signifies, might reach out and infect the civilization it borders—or worse, that civilization itself breeds its own infection and the swamps merely reflect culture-deep corruption.

One of the most celebrated poets of the late nineteenth century, Sidney Lanier stood firmly against the encroachment of the industrial world on the South of his birth—however, he always did so for reasons more in line with Thoreau than with George Fitzhugh or even Edmund Ruffin. Lanier wrote about the swamps in a manner increasingly, and eventually near totally, divorced from the concerns and considerations of Southern culture, both old and new. As such, he represents a figure both crucial to modern depictions of the Southern swamp and curiously removed from them. Lanier not only follows Thoreau in imbuing the swamps with an air of purity and positive cultural removal as no Southern author had yet done but takes them beyond Thoreauvian concepts of purity and rejuvenation to render them spaces of indefinite and mercurial significations, presenting them as creations not of culture but of the individual mind.

As Lucinda MacKethan makes clear, Lanier's appreciation and literary treatment of the swamp environment was divorced from any Old South pastoral nostalgia: she calls Lanier "one of the first Southern writers of pastoral intent yet also one of the very few such writers before the twentieth century who did not exploit the plantation tradition to develop and convey his major themes" (20). Lanier did not fit the conventional mold of the Southern writer of his era; however, his early work shows a marked drive to defend elements of his South from the Northern journalistic imperialism then in vogue. Though his work in some ways reflected the enthusiasm of his era for the picturesque and escapist in Southern literature, Lanier resisted the trend of marketing the South for tourists with trivializing and shallow travelogues. Best known for his poetry, which will be considered momentarily, Lanier also entered the booming field of Southern travel writing with an 1875 book entitled *Florida: Its Scenery, Climate and History*. Lanier was deeply critical of the superficiality of most tourist writing; he makes his unique perspective and agenda clear in his introduction: "[I]t is not in clever newspaper paragraphs; it is not in chatty magazine papers; it is not in guide-books written while the cars are running, that the enormous phenomenon of Florida is to be disposed of. There are at least claims here which reach into some of the deepest needs of modern life. . . . The question of Florida is a question of an indefinite enlargement of many people's pleasures and of many people's existences as against that universal killing ague of modern life—the fever of the unrest of trade throbbing through the long chill of a seven-months' winter" (13). Lanier's distaste for common representations of Florida might be expected of a Southerner seeing his region spoken for by a popular Northern press; his reaction, however, looks to the future rather than nostalgically echoing Simms and speaking for his culture in a defense whose very terms concede present defeat, as so many of his contemporaries did. Lanier's Florida is a place of infinite possibility: emphatically not the economic possibility that industrialists and developers were beginning to perceive and seize but spiritual possibility as an ameliorative to that very drive. In this sense, Lanier becomes an important transitional figure in bridging the considerable gap between the majority of postwar Southern fiction and the profound revisions of Southern modernism, which will be considered in the next chapter.

The swamp descriptions in Lanier's Florida book escape from the tropes that generally bind swamp description—or, rather, present such a dizzying array of tropes, each supplanting the last, that they can scarcely be regarded as rote repetitions of conventional responses to swamp vistas:

At first, like an unending procession of nuns disposed along the aisle of a church these vine-figures stand. But presently, as one journeys, this nun-imagery fades out of one's mind, and a thousand other fancies float with ever-new vine-shapes into one's eyes. One sees repeated all the forms one has ever known, in grotesque juxtaposition. Look! Here is a great troop of girls, with arms reached over their heads, dancing down into the water; here are high velvet arm-chairs and lovely green fauteuils of divers pattern and of softest cushionment. . . . Yonder is a bizarre congress—Una on her lion, Angelo's Moses, two elephants with howdahs, the Laocoon group, Arthur and Lancelot with great brands extended aloft in combat. Adam bent with love and grief leading Eve out of Paradise. . . . It is a green dance of all things and times. (28)

Lanier is stubbornly atypical here in his perception of the swamp as a constantly shifting playground of significations: instead of stagnation, he sees in its depths a constant becoming. Free of overdetermined trope and cultural convention, Lanier's swamps are spaces ripe for reinterpretation, apart from history and the numbing march of progress. Even as they stood apart from Southern cultural determination, they remain, at least momentarily, apart from modern commodification, free from the burdens of past and future in "a green dance of all things and times." Alongside the swamps' infinite possibilities is their persistent resistance to containment within a single signification—a resistance to conceptual colonization that would inspire later Southern writers in a variety of ways.

Lanier was not, at least early in his career, completely silent on issues pertaining to the future of Southern life and culture. Poems such as "Corn" (1874) dealt directly with the problems facing the yeoman farmer, and Lanier was earnest in his advocacy of small-scale agriculture as the moral and economic future of his region. His 1880 essay "The New South," perhaps his most direct statement about the future of specifically Southern life, earnestly predicted a regional future in line with what the agrarians would nostalgically evoke decades later in *I'll Take My Stand*: in it he claims, unproblematically, that "the new South means small farming" (334). The essay, though, mingles throughout a sense of stubborn denial of reality and an attendant aesthetic idealization of history. Prerequisite for understanding his argument, Lanier claims, is "stop[ping] our ears to the noisy child's play of current politics" (337) in favor of a recognition of a universal and eternal dialectic that he envisions as governing human history. At one pole of the dialectic is "the spirit of control"; at the other, "the spirit of independence": for Lanier, these two are embodied in contemporary America by the large business or corporation as the former and the small farmer as the latter. In keeping with his aesthetic design, the controlling corporations are firmly entrenched in the Northwest—thus, for the sake of a self-evident and undeniable balance, the independent small farmers must inevitably maintain their hold on the Southeast (338). Lanier's vision relies far less on observations of what was actually occurring in the South of his day—the increasing and seemingly undeniable industrialization that characterized improvement for progressives such as King and Cable—than on a philosophical and even metaphysical theory of balance which he presents as inevitable. Although his ideals were categorically different, Lanier's efforts to depict his region and to construct its future hearken back to the antebellum South, when a society based upon fundamentally literary, aesthetic, and linguistic creation, even in blatant contradiction of objective fact, was more tenable. In a region no longer in command of its own destiny, such attempts at creation could only be naive denial.

"The New South," written relatively late in Lanier's career, was an uncharacteristically "Southern" work for that time in the poet's life. Lanier's turn to the swamps in his later years represented a more practicable escape from social and cultural reality than did his aestheticized visions of the South's future. Jean S. Gabin, in her 1985 book *A Living Minstrelsy: The Poetry and Music of Sidney Lanier*, charts Lanier's artistic development in terms of his distance from the South of his birth: she describes his life as "an odyssey from a small Southern city to the great cultural centers of the nation" and thus "from an aesthetically restrictive tradition to a life fully imbued with the arts" (1). As MacKethan indicates, the more Lanier dedicated himself to swamp topics, the further he moved from specific cultural identification: "Lanier was already condemning, by 1868, 'the habit of regarding our literature as Southern literature, our poetry as Southern poetry, our pictures as Southern pictures.' . . . In his last years, when he was writing his marshland verses, he seemed to have been moving into new areas of concern that were even less specifically southern than his early interests" (21). Seizing on the element in the Southern landscape that had always resisted and still did resist inclusion in the culture and civilization that surrounded it, Lanier infused his swamp poetry with a Thoreauvian spirit of escape. While in some ways his marsh poems reflect the recreational trend toward the swamps that characterized his era, Lanier was no tourist—in the swamps he sought spiritual regeneration and solace rather than diversion. In poems such as "The Marshes of Glynn" (1878), Lanier presents a purely romantic vision of the swampland, painting a portrait of inner calm and moral quietude evoked by the pure landscape. Beginning with a simple tribute to the swamp's natural beauty—

Glooms of live-oaks, beautiful-braided and woven
With intricate shades of the vines that myriad-cloven
Clamber the forks of the multiform boughs,—

Emerald twilights,—
Virginal shy lights,
Wrought of the leaves to allure to the whisper of vows. (lines 1–6)

—Lanier goes on to posit the marsh as a place that frees the soul from complication and moral dilemma:

Somehow my soul seems suddenly free
From the weighing of fate and the sad discussion of sin,
By the length and the breadth and the sweep of the marshes of Glynn. (62–66)

While Lanier's poem presages modernist treatments of the swamp as a wilderness place of moral purity, and thus foreshadows what will become a prevailing twentieth-century swamp trope, it is emphatically and purposely removed from cultural or political involvement. As MacKethan puts it, "This is Lanier's answer to materialism and to time—a love of nature so complete that it triumphs over all" (31). Poems like "The Marshes of Glynn" show a level of detachment from the world, a studious uninvolvement with his age, that aptly characterizes much of Southern literature of the Reconstruction era.

Later, as such detachment became a central issue in Southern literature of the modern era, Lanier's work would prove profoundly significant. Lanier stands as the first Southern writer of note to present the swamps as something other than spaces of culturally determined meaning. His swamps are neither lurking threats to Southern culture, nor sympathetic manifestations of that culture's moral failings. As Gabin points out, the swamps, "signifying an embodiment of God's infinite plan, show him the paradox of experience: There is ultimate good in everything. The marshes are made 'to suffer the sea and the rains and the sun,' but they are yet beautiful and steadfast, symbolizing the 'good out of infinite pain' and 'sight out of blindness' that come with faith" (161). Lanier presents the swamps as *enduring*, steadfastly resisting the forces of culture that threaten them. Though he clearly imparts moral value to the swamps, he removes them from Southern swamp rhetoric, underscoring their distance from culture as its own kind of purity. In this sense, Lanier is more "modern" than the Southern modernists: his nature is less a fact embedded in culture than it is a place of sensuous and synaesthetic response, and of genuine freedom. It is this formulation of the Southern swamps that modern Southern authors will appropriate and interrogate in the decades to come.

The future of Southern swamp writing, though, would prove considerably more connected to history and to culture than are Lanier's fluid and protean swampscapes. While his removal of the swamps from their culturally determined context anticipates a sea change in Southern understanding of the wetlands, the events of the subsequent decades would lead the next great waves of response to the Southern swamp—those of the Southern and Harlem Renaissances—to maintain a profound and necessary grounding in a troubled, developing culture. For all its removal from culture, though, Lanier's treatment of the swamps becomes important in that it opens swamp discourses to a multiplicity of significations: the swamps were no longer simply sites of pure innocence, places of uncontrolled menace, or mirrors of cultural sin or decay. While Southern swamp discourses would, for the most part, focus again on cultural critique, they would do so in nontraditional and radically revisionist ways in the twentieth century.

Chapter Three

THE SWAMP IN THE TWENTIETH-CENTURY SOUTH

Even as the South was being redefined in the eyes of the nation by the "literary imperialism" of Northern travelogues, articles, and other depictions, a wave of economic imperialism was beginning to transform the landscape and, in turn, the culture of the South. At the time Edward King was writing *The Great South*, Northern industrialists were just beginning to realize the potential profits to be had by harvesting the timber-rich Southern wetlands. King himself perceived virtually limitless wealth to be had from the timber-rich South and perceived no threat to the natural beauty of the landscape from even the most aggressive reaping of timber resources. His description of Southwestern Louisiana in *The Great South* indicates his general perspective: immediately after attesting that, "save in the final disruption of the world, there is no end to the fairy beauty and fertility of the bayou lands, or to the luxuriant vegetation of the vast plains" (84), he provides a more practical assessment of the area's economic potential: "In the parishes which comprise South-western Louisiana, there are more than 3,000,000 acres of land of almost inexhaustible fertility. The giant cypresses along the lakes and bayous are abundant enough to last for a century. Employment to hundreds of mills and thousands of workmen could readily be furnished, the lumber being easily floated down the innumerable bayous and along the lakes to market" (84). Once developers discovered the wealth to be had, though, they moved to reap it with remarkable speed, creating a dizzying flurry of logging activity that transformed the economies of wetland areas, swelled their populations with stunning speed, then left a wasteland in its wake as the "inexhaustible" timber supply was, by the mid-1920s, all but exhausted.

What cannot be ignored, on the one hand, is the Southern complicity in harvesting the swamps to exhaustion. On the other hand, nor can the Southern welcome for the Northern timber barons be attributed to mere avarice or economic opportunism. The South's general poverty throughout the late nineteenth and early twentieth centuries is well documented and led to Southern support for the influx of Northern industry; still, a more particularized and specifically swamp-related problem also led to the South's complicity in its own deforestation. Wetland flooding, particularly in areas near the lower Mississippi, was becoming an ever greater problem in the latter half of the nineteenth century, and the postwar South had little money for flood control. Ann Vileisis emphasizes the ways that undrained swamplands remained a practical problem for the lower Mississippi in the 1870s: "For decades, residents of the lower Mississippi sat like ducks before a loaded gun as the river repeatedly discharged its floodwaters. The numerous floodplain swamps could not be effectively drained without first controlling the overflow waters. Swamp drainage and flood control were essentially two sides of the same coin" (78). Flooding and the intractable swamps bred a general sense of hopelessness: "By the late 1870s, it seemed that there was little hope of containing and controlling the Mississippi River, let alone draining the swamps along its banks. . . . Despite persistent efforts, spending over $11 million and building over 22 million cubic yards of levee, flood control plans had failed miserably. To top it all off, an epidemic of yellow fever, which people still attributed to miasma, swept through the valley in 1878" (82). While Northern writers explored swamps as fascinating tourist attractions, many Southerners struggled with their intractability and with what they still perceived as swamp-borne pestilence. In winter of 1849, as a response to extensive flooding of the Mississippi and inundation of the surrounding lands, delegates from Louisiana and Mississippi proposed the Swamp Land Act, the first official, federally endorsed plan for draining swamps. The Swamp Land Act stated that wetlands that were subject to severe flooding would be made property of their individual states by the federal government. The land could then be sold, and the money used for improved drainage and levee construction—thus making the swampland timber industry possible. In its initial form, the act applied only to Louisiana, but was extended in 1850 to include fourteen more states—primarily in the South. As Donald W. Davis explains, the initial goal was to make the drained lands "fit for cultivation and settlement" (97). The results of the Swamp Land Acts were wide-ranging: as James A. Schmid recounts in his 2000 article "Wetlands as Conserved Land-scapes in the U.S," between the 1850s and the 1920s, "sixty-four million acres were transferred from public domain to the states for the specific purpose of conversion into private farmland" (135).

The earliest results of the Swamp Land Acts were limited by the same factors that limited antebellum Southern efforts to transform swamps into productive land—the technology of the age, as Albert Cowdrey explains in his 1983 study *This Land, This South: An Environmental History*, was simply not adequate to the task (93). The attitudes and practices of those who sought to capitalize on the Swamp Land Acts even in the pre–Civil War era gave a clear indication of what was to come when technology inevitably surmounted the swamp's stubborn defenses. Cowdrey describes the fraud-riddled feeding frenzy that erupted in response to the Swamp Land Acts and indicates how from the very beginning efforts at wetland reclamation and flood control were tied to industrial profiteering: "As a result of the federal Swamp Land Acts of 1849–1850, expanses of the best cypress land in the valleys of the Mississippi, Red, and Atchafalaya Rivers passed via frauds by state agents and surveyors to men of political influence. . . . Efforts by the state[s] to prevent illegal cutting apparently had little effect, as did Federal efforts" (93). A combination of the federal government's ignorance about the realities of the Southern landscape and the laissez-faire attitude that ruled the general application of the Swamp Land Acts led to massive fraud and misrepresentation of the kind of land that changed hands. Actual reclamation of swampland for the purposes of flood control was negligible during the first decades following the acts' passage. The Swamp Land Acts allowed states to supply their own evidence, without federal survey or review, that the land granted and sold via the Swamp Land Acts was in fact wetland. As Cowdrey recounts, a great deal of the granted land "was not wetland at all. Appointing their own surveyors and commissioners, the states presided over a process by which useful land passed into the hands of influential individuals and lumber, railroad, canal, and drainage companies. . . . [L]ittle reclamation was carried out anywhere" (98).

Although the Swamp Land Acts met with limited success in the initial four decades after their inception, they enabled the timber industry boom of the 1880s. Further, the opportunism and profiteering inaugurated by those acts set the tone for the nature of industry to come once technology could conquer the swamps. Tempted by accounts such as King's of unending forests of rich cypress, Northern entrepreneurs began to set their sights on the rich resources of a defeated and economically depressed South. Southerners, the agricultural base of their prewar economy grievously weakened by abolition, optimistically welcomed the timber barons: as Vileisis puts it, "Because the extensive bottomland forests were the region's most readily available resource, Southerners looked to these big trees as the foundation for future economic and industrial growth" (117). In short, Southerners elected to follow the path of the Great Dismal Swamp Company more than a century before—where agriculture failed, perhaps a nascent timber industry would not.

Jack Kirby has pointed out the paradoxical catch-22 inherent in slaves working for the timber industry before the Civil War—in harvesting swamp timber, the slave laborers were destroying the very region that gave them a measure of freedom and independence in their work (161). The early part of the twentieth century saw Kirby's paradox writ large to encompass the entirety of a depressed Southern region. The Southern states were only too happy to sell the swamplands that had meant little but trouble to developers, who would then inherit the problems of draining them while pouring desperately needed funds into flood prevention.

Northern businessmen were eager to reap this untapped Southern wealth. Books such as Chicago author William H. Harrison's *How to Get Rich in the South* echoed King's claim that Southern timber was inexhaustible; undaunted by the fact that a very large portion of Southern timber lay in the swamps, the areas least likely to have been cleared for agricultural cultivation, Northern industrialists bought up swamplands at an astounding rate in the 1880s (T. Clark 14). As Vileisis recounts, in Louisiana alone "northern purchasers secured the deeds to well over 1 million acres between 1880 and 1888" (112).

The rage for Southern timber radically altered the demographics and economies of swamp areas. Timber towns sprang up, fueled by Northern capital and technology, throughout the Atchafalaya basin: "New workers, including immigrants and former slaves, flocked to the Louisiana swamps to partake in the cut. As a result, the population of the Atchafalaya Basin grew ten percent between 1890 and 1900" (Vileisis 120). An intense spirit of optimism about the enterprise of draining wetlands and harvesting timber reigned among both Northern investors and Southern state governments between 1880 and the early 1920s. Enabled by rapid advances in logging and railroad technology, the visions of William Byrd II, Edmund Ruffin, and the Great Dismal Swamp

Company seemed newly practicable, and the swamps, still more problem than boon despite the burgeoning tourist trade to the pretimber South, seemed key to a Southern economic renaissance. Zeal for wetland reclamation began to spread beyond harvesting of timber, as Southern companies resuscitated dreams of using converted swamplands for agriculture: the Louisiana Meadows Investment Company, for example, mounted a public relations campaign in the North around 1915 entitled *Making Rich Black Farms from Louisiana's Wet Lands*. As Vileisis points out, a new rhetoric began to be developed by Southern land salesmen surrounding the fecundity of the swamps: "Persuasive pamphlets boasted of alluvial black soils 'rich as the bottomlands of the Nile.' Comparing swamp and bottomland fertility to that of the world-renowned Nile became a cliché widely used by salesmen to invest familiar value into the unknown wetlands" (132).

Despite the explosion in wetland sales and development, the swamp was not quite ready to give up the ghost in the late nineteenth century. In some places wetland reclamation still proved incredibly difficult, and the promise of easy money for the clever investor proved premature and hollow. The case of developer Hamilton Disston indicates that the swamps retained a measure of their initial power to thwart exploitation. Disston, drawn to Florida initially as a tourist during the late-nineteenth-century swamp vogue, perceived enormous profit potential in the vast Everglades. After inheriting a great deal of wealth, Disston bought vast tracts of swampland granted to Florida by the Swamp Land Acts—somewhere between ten and twelve million acres. Disston's was a high profile endeavor: the *New York Times* took notice, lauding the entrepreneur in its February 18, 1881, issue for potentially "reclaiming from ten to twelve million acres of the richest land in the world" (qtd. in Vileisis 135). Disston's fame quickly turned to scandal, however, as his 1883 reports of having drained two million acres were proven false by a special committee, who charged that by 1887 only 50,000 acres had actually been drained. Disston's investors began to pull out, his land sales dropped off, and he ultimately shot himself in 1896 (Vileisis 133–36).

Disston's tale not only indicates the lingering intractability of the swamp, but also emphasizes the rapidity of technological progress between the 1890s and 1920s. The new wave of enthusiasm for draining and exploiting swamplands may have run ahead of technological capability, as Disston's tragedy makes poignantly clear, but it did not run far ahead. By the early 1920s, the South had not yet been drastically transformed—it remained largely rural and agricultural. By the beginning of that decade, the brief and artificial boom brought about by a wartime swell in crop prices had passed, and the South was once again vulnerable to economic depression. Roger Biles, in *The South and the New Deal* (1994), describes a "promotional orgy," resulting from the vast expansion of railroads and the collective results of draining and wetland reclamation in the early decades of the twentieth century that erupted in the early to middle 1920s. The swamp-laden South was no longer just a tourist attraction but a place for outsiders to settle and, ostensibly, to prosper: "The 'Dixie Highway' from Michigan to Miami opened in 1925, and the suddenly ubiquitous automobile made Florida's inviting climate accessible as never before. . . . [A] frantic race for quick riches spawned overnight subdivisions" (6).

In the 1920s, the industrial colonization of the South begun by the timber industry around the turn of the century was joined by an influx of residential settlers, now drawn by a climate rehabilitated in the public eye by the swamp vogue of the late nineteenth century. And yet, the swamp, even in the face of ever-increasing development and colonization, retained some measure of subversive potential—but in a crucially different form than it had previously. Biles describes a transformation of the swamp's subversion by commodification and subsumption into the burgeoning real estate economy of 1920s Florida: "Before the speculative mania ended with a destructive hurricane in 1926, many out-of-state investors arrived to find their suburban havens located in mangrove swamps" (6).

By the mid-1920s, the infinite expanses of unclaimed swamp had begun to look distinctly finite. The Atchafalaya basin in Louisiana was an early casualty; as Vileisis recounts, "By the mid-1920s old-growth trees were all cut. Timber scouts from the eastern portion of the Atchafalaya Basin combing the area for suitable timber began meeting scouts from the western part of that enormous swamp, which people had long thought inexhaustible" (121). The wildfire enthusiasm for swamp development took a rapid and dramatic toll on the Southern wetlands. The new technology that could not conquer the Everglades in Hamilton Disston's day by the 1920s worked too well, and the swamps could not sustain an industry grown out of control. Schmid puts the effects of the industrial invasion of the Southern wetlands in perspective: "By the mid-twentieth century, the extant wetland in the nation had been reduced by half, with more than 182,000 square miles converted into various uses" (136). The greatest losses, predictably, were in Louisiana, Florida, and Texas. The economic revolution that many Southerners had envisioned as the region's future failed to provide the long-term prosperity the South so desperately needed. The timber barons moved in, took what they could, and, inevitably, moved out. As Vileisis puts it, "As in all extractive industries, the economic benefits lasted only as long as the natural resource lasted. Because the capital for timber investment came mostly from outside the region, businesses had little interest in sustaining the industry over the long term. The timber barons simply moved on, taking their money with them" (122). The result of what literary and cultural critic Lawrence Buell has since dubbed the "cut and get out" phase of the Deep South timber industry was a profoundly different Southern landscape. The timber barons left behind a transformed but still impoverished South, stripped of its most valuable natural resource and, as writers of the next few decades would discover, curiously culturally diminished.

The urban and industrial transformation of the South jeopardized the wetlands by more than direct reclamation and harvest. The solutions urban centers developed to the recurring problem of river flooding often came at the expense both of wetlands and their inhabitants—the rural poor not yet assimilated into the progressive South. The most dramatic example of this victimization came in New Orleans, in response to the Mississippi River flood of 1927. The city's response to the impending flood represents, as Gay Gomez puts it in her article "Perspective, Power, and Priorities: New Orleans and the Mississippi River Flood of 1927" (2000), "a confrontation between urban and rural perspectives and priorities—a clash that echoes across time and place" (109). The clash Gomez describes was between the urban center of New Orleans and the swamp community of St. Bernard Parish, which lay downriver. New Orleans had grown and prospered in the years since Cable rendered it so vividly, and had prospered particularly during the preceding decade, as "the city's economy boomed along with its newly renovated port, strengthening New Orleans's linkages with the American Midwest and Latin America" (Gomez 109). Technological advances had vastly improved drainage in the city, which was shaking off the trappings of picturesque ruin that had so long characterized it and was moving into the national and even global economy. As the city progressed in this direction, the ties its inhabitants felt to their immediate environs and local culture weakened considerably: as Gomez puts it, "[T]he progressive climate of the 1920s . . . reinforced New Orleanians' superior attitudes toward their rural neighbors, people they apparently neither depended upon nor thought highly of" (110).

Gomez's claims, while probably accurate, present only part of the picture. As Pete Daniel points out in *Deep'n as it Come: The 1927 Mississippi River Flood,* the disastrous losses caused by the flood may have resulted as much from hubris as from cultural chauvinism: "Perhaps the Army Corps of Engineers had been lulled into overconfidence by the technological accomplishments of the era. . . . America exuded confidence, and doubtless the engineers were only parroting this spirit when they claimed that levees could 'prevent the destructive effects of floods'" (8). The 1927 flood, caused, in part, by what Daniel calls "the cumulative tinkering of humans" (7) as well as by unexpectedly torrential rains, has become a mythologized symbol for the limitations of science. The flood itself is often personified as a bestial, uncontrollable force in accounts of survivors: "Indeed, some observers reported that when the levees gave way and the water burst through, it *did* roar like a beast; people who heard it compared the sound to a tornado, a strong wind, Niagara Falls, a deep animal growl" (9). The flood waters transformed towns into veritable swamps: a Greenville, Tennessee, resident describes how "[h]is sister had continual fights with crayfish in the rooms where water remained, while frogs, cockroaches, and water bugs made themselves at home" (qtd. in P. Daniel 129). Snakes filled the streets of many towns along the river, and the Memphis *Commercial Appeal* on May 6 said of Clarendon Arkansas that "[t]he stench in Clarendon is unbearable. Mud and slime fill the streets" (qtd. in P. Daniel 129). Within a shockingly brief span of time, towns along the Mississippi returned to waterlogged wilderness.

Whatever the root causes of the flood, the poor and powerless bore the brunt of the damage. New Orleans's rural neighbors were, by necessity, swamp folk—due both to the region's landscape and to the water and waste shunted their way by the titanic pumps that kept the city from inundation. When city officials learned that, due to prolonged heavy rains, a major flood of the Mississippi was imminent, there was little contest in their minds about whether the urban center or the fishing and trapping communities of the St. Bernard Parish swamps should bear the brunt. Governor O. H. Simpson made the decision to cut the levee downriver from the city, sparing the urban center and more developed outlying areas upriver and unleashing the flood's full brunt on the rural swamps, destroying the marsh dwellers' homes and livelihood. A passage from the April 28, 1927, edition of the *New Orleans Times Picayune* reflects the general urban attitude regarding the decision and the subsequent evacuation of the local population—sympathetic yet patronizing, and confident in the inherent rightness of preserving the urban center at the expense of the rural communities: "Simple souls and primitive, bittered with the loss of their homes, their gardens and their fisheries, they are, nevertheless, resigned at last to fate and secure in their faith in a rich neighbor which has turned to them in its hour of danger" (qtd. in Gomez 114–15). The trappers and fishermen had little choice but to comply, and little ground for argument, as they all depended on the city for a market for their catches. The culture and economy of St. Bernard Parish were virtually destroyed by the flood, which killed or washed out a large portion of the muskrat population sustaining the fur trade. The event had considerable impact on Louisiana's perception of urbanization and of its state and local governments, and was memorialized in the 1980s in Randy Newman's song "Louisiana 1927."

The story of the flood of 1927 is only a vivid example of the general trend in the early-twentieth-century South toward privileging the urban over the rural, and toward the ready sacrifice not only of physical swamplands but of rural ways of life in the name of urbanization and of progress. It also provides a cautionary tale of the limitations of that progress, and the perilous effects it was having on the Southern landscape. The inexorable and rapid progress of the timber industry; the entry of Southern urban centers like New Orleans into the national and global markets, facilitated by advancements in transportation technologies; and the burgeoning attitude within the South itself that "Northern" progressive capitalism represented the region's only viable future formed a different kind of flood, seemingly no less inexorable in destroying the Southern wetlands. Granted, not all of the impetus behind draining and reclaiming wetlands can be classified as "Northernist" or even as motivated by a pervasive urban prejudice. As Nelson Manfred Blake points out in his study *Land into Water, Water into Land* (1980), the drive to drain the Florida Everglades in the late nineteenth and early twentieth centuries had essentially populist origins: "[T]he politicians who authorized the digging of an ambitious system of canals and ditches saw themselves as champions of the people redeeming millions of acres of soil from wealthy monopolists and transforming these swampy tracts into an agricultural paradise for small farmers" (88). Still, whether at the behest of, or in defiance of, Northern land barons, swamp reclamation, at last fueled by technology more than equal to the task, had begun to take a serious toll on the Southern wetlands, and a few Southerners began to take notice.

Donald Hey and Nancy Philippi report that much of the early impetus behind a Southern environmental movement came from Southern hunters: "It was only after sportsmen and wildlife enthusiasts noticed the diminishing numbers of migratory waterfowl traversing the flyways that they connected this decrease with lost wetland habitat" (2). Small, grassroots efforts began to form in response to swamp drainage. John V. Dennis, in *The Great Cypress Swamps* (1988), describes a very early local campaign for swamp preservation in west Tennessee known as the "Night Riders' War." As Dennis describes it, "Local residents banded together to prevent a group of entrepreneurs from draining Reelfoot Lake. After several years of bitterness, the disturbance came to an end in 1908 with a complete victory for the residents" (1). Small-scale resistance began to spread and develop into more codified philosophy and stronger organization. The late 1920s and early 1930s saw the first faltering emergence of a conservation movement in response to the widespread destruction of Southern forested wetlands, as personal and local concerns began to translate into wide-ranging critiques of the effects of large-scale environmental policy. Hey and Philippi report that "[t]he first national awareness of the interrelatedness of the different features in a watershed came in the late nineteenth century with the notion that the loss of forests, at the hands of the timber barons, was resulting in increasing floods and reduced water supply" (45). The response to this realization, to an age devoted to industry and not yet concerned with conservation, was the imposition of artificial flood controls—levees, drainage, and other man-made efforts to tame the rivers without compromising the profit potential of the timber-rich wetlands. By the late 1920s, though, the limitations of those efforts were becoming painfully apparent. Hey and Philippi report that "water resources planners asked why flood damages were increasing along the nation's major rivers, no matter how many flood control works had been installed, realizing too late that the wetlands that had once captured and then slowly released the heavy flood flows had been cut off from river channels by navigation and flood control projects" (2). The answer, which would become apparent gradually and would not be widely and institutionally accepted until the early 1970s, was that the wetlands themselves, used as bartering chips for flood prevention funds, performed many of the functions that states had sought to fund through their clearing and exploitation. Vileisis explains that the broad efforts supported by the Swamp Land Acts and pursued by both state agencies and eventually by the federal government were destructive as they drained lands crucial to ecological balance and ultimately made more work and expenditure for the draining agencies necessary: "By retarding runoff and allowing water to seep back into the ground, many wetlands have played a crucial role in recharging the aquifers that people rely on for agricultural and domestic water supplies. With their spongelike capacities, the wetlands have absorbed and stored water, providing natural flood control along many rivers. Wetlands have also preserved water quality by filtering excess nutrients and pollutants. But clearing, draining, and development have compromised these services, resulting in the 'need' for costly dams, levees, and water treatment plants" (4). In a 1928 issue of *Ecology*, Percy Viosca presented one of the first compelling critiques of the large-scale destruction and alteration of the wetlands in southern Louisiana, as well as one of the first arguments for the swamp's inherent value, in his article "Louisiana Wetlands and the Value of their Wildlife and Fishery Resource": "Reclamation experts and real estate promoters have been killing the goose that laid the golden egg. . . . [O]ur future conservation policy should be restoration of those natural conditions best suited to an abundant marsh, swamp, and aquatic fauna" (217). Viosca's observation represents environmental science's belated recognition of the problems created by an industrial science that far outstripped any clear understanding of the natural world.

Observations like Viosca's would not be completely lost on the local and federal governments; however, since the passage of the Swamp Land Act in 1850, those governments had been heavily involved with subsidizing and encouraging efforts to drain and reclaim the swamps. The official response, at state and federal levels, to swamp reclamation and preservation was a marked ambivalence that would continue, some would argue, until the present day. The federal ambivalence about wetlands in an era of ever-increasing national-ization provides an interesting context in which to view Southern depictions of, and responses to, the swamps that dwindled around them.

The New Deal era saw the beginnings of a schizophrenic and paradoxical approach to wetland development and conservation. In the early 1930s Franklin Roosevelt created agencies such as the Civilian Conservation Corps (CCC), which would work on "forestry, the prosecution of soil erosion, flood control and similar projects" (qtd. in Hey and Philippi 45). Roosevelt limited the group's focus to working on flood control across large regions rather than working on individual (and privately owned) plots of land—still, his vision revealed a con-sciousness of the value of wooded wetlands in preventing floods. Morris Cooke, administrator of the Rural Electrification Administration (REA) and an influen-tial advisor to Roosevelt, championed a study by H. S. Person entitled *Little Waters: Their Use and Relations to the Land*, which argued that wetland losses along river basins had great impact in causing disastrous floods. Cooke's view-point changed the way many Americans thought about flood control (Hey and Philippi 45).

And yet, for every effort or agency devoted to wetland conservation, another government initiative led to increased draining of swamps in efforts to ameliorate economic depression. The United States Department of Agriculture (USDA) in the early 1930s encouraged swamp drainage as a way to jumpstart the agricultural economy in response to the Great Depression. In 1936, national legislation for the first time recognized that flood control was a responsibility of the federal government and gave the responsibility to the Army Corps of Engineers. As a result, Hey and Philippi point out, "large tracts of riverine wetlands were destroyed by the flood control activities of this branch of the Army subsequently, as thousands of miles of agricultural and urban levees were constructed to protect residential and commercial development and to allow the pumping, draining, and production of agricultural crops on riverine wetlands" (50). Further, in 1944 the Agricultural Conservation Program (ACP) was formed and both funded and oversaw wetland drainage: "Between 1940 and 1980, nearly 57 million acres of wet farmland . . . were drained with ACP funds" (47). Even as some branches of the New Deal and post–New Deal government recognized the benefits of swampland and sought to protect wetlands, other branches continued clearing, draining, and cultivating them. The government's ambivalent attitude would continue until the late 1970s, when Jimmy Carter's Executive Order 11990 made federal agencies across the board "take action to minimize the destruction, loss, or degradation of wetlands" (qtd. in Hey and Philippi 47).

In the South, concerns about development and industrialization in the early part of the twentieth century sprang much more from a desire to preserve an assailed Southern culture than to preserve the swamps that had never been a part of its mainstream. Industrialization, coupled with ever harsher Northern critiques of Southern culture in the wake of national embarrassments like the Scopes trial, in which Southerners were represented as uneducated reactionaries, prompted a cultural, as well as scientific, backlash; a conservative as well as conservationist response. This backlash was directed not just against Northern ideological imperialism but also against the economic transformation of Southern landscape and culture to fit Northern industrial models. The South felt compelled to defend its way of life, whether actual or ideal, and did so in dramatically different ways.

The most disturbing response and reaction against change came in the resurgence of the Ku Klux Klan in the early twentieth century. Initially established in 1866 as a fraternal order of Confederate veterans, the Klan swiftly metamorphosed into a terrorist organization devoted to preserving the old Southern ways of life by intimidating and often murdering blacks and liberal whites during the Reconstruction era. One of the most articulate voices in expressing the Klan's philosophy and goals was the novelist Thomas Dixon, who contributed to paranoia about race mixing and did much to fuel fears of free blacks, whom he characterized with the specter of "the roving criminal Negro." In *The Leopard's Spots* (1902), Dixon advances some of his most reactionary ideas about the future of the white race, transforming the threat of the free black man into an all-consuming, supernatural menace: "[T]his towering figure of the freed Negro had been growing more and more ominous, until its menace overshadowed the poverty, the hunger, the sorrows and the devastation of the South, throwing the blight of its shadow over future generations, a veritable Black Death for the land and its people" (33). Dixon is utterly unambiguous in expressing his beliefs that freedom for African Americans would lead (and was leading) to retrogression to savagery and that the freed slaves carried on a campaign of terror that included the "almost daily" rape of white women. The majority of *The Leopard's Spots* consists of the kind of reactionary racist rhetoric that has become all too familiar now, and recounting it at length seems somewhat perverse. Still, its cultural impact cannot be denied— with sales rivaling those of *Uncle Tom's Cabin*, the novel had a major impact on the American consciousness—so much so that D. W. Griffith based his infamous *Birth of a Nation*, which glorified and romanticized Klan activities, on Dixon's work. To a Northern citizenry whose racial progressiveness often tended to be exaggerated (Dixon had a wide Northern readership and was favorably reviewed in many Northern newspapers), works like Dixon's contributed powerfully to the image of a chaotic, intractable South.

Dixon's fixation on the evils of miscegenation is perhaps his novels' most significant contribution to the Southern literary drive to guard racial purity as key to the maintenance of identity. Again and again, Dixon's protagonist, the political hopeful Charles Gaston, recalls the words of Reverend Durham, to the point that they become a kind of mantra: "*My boy, the future American must be an Anglo-Saxon or a mulatto! . . . This Republic can have no future if racial lines are broken, and its proud citizenship sinks to the level of a mongrel breed of mulattoes. The South must fight this battle to a finish. Two thousand years look down upon the struggle, and two thousand years of the future bend low to catch the message of life or death!*" (198). This perception of the South's potential mongrelization inspired Klan violence in its early-1870s heyday, before the advent of Redeemer governments pushed it into comparative dormancy (in part by codifying some of the Klan's ideals as law). In the 1920s, the Klan reemerged in response to more dramatic challenges to traditional white Southern life after World War I. As Biles explains, "The Klan's popularity in the 1920s reflected the fear and mistrust with which so many Southerners viewed the rapid changes after the war" (10); accordingly, the Klan expanded its crusade beyond the prevention of miscegenation and the "control" of free blacks to a larger base of enemies representative of an influx of new peoples and perspectives in the South—their nemeses would now include "Catholics, Jews, Communists, and other 'non-Americans'" (10). The Klan represented the most violent and desperate reaction of the South to inevitable change. Kenneth Jackson, in his 1967 study *The Ku Klux Klan in the City, 1915–1930*, explains the impetus behind the increased urban presence and general popularity of the Klan: "Fear of change, not vindictiveness or cruelty, was the basic motivation of the urban Klansman. . . . Sensing that the traditional values, religion, and way of life of an older America were in danger, he donated ten dollars to a hypocritical secret society in a vague attempt to halt the forces of time" (242–43). The Klan's efforts were aimed at stemming the irresistible tide of progress; their victims casualties of a desperate nostalgia. Though the threats to tradition were far more varied than they had been in the 1870s, and the Klan's violence was less focused and more broadly based, the looming specter of a perverted chivalry justified their efforts in their minds. The irrational fear of black rape, of adulteration of that last bastion of Southern purity, the Southern woman, remained the persistent if generally inaccurate rationale for their violence: as Biles puts it, "Although the NAACP reported that only one out of six victims of lynch mobs had been accused of rape, the paeans to chivalry persisted as lynching's primary defense" (8).

A less frightening but equally powerful form of popular reaction to change can be seen in the surge in religious fundamentalism in the South after World War I. Dramatically and embarrassingly brought to light in the Scopes trial fiasco of 1925, when John Scopes of Dayton, Tennessee, was tried for violating a state law against teaching evolution. The fundamentalist position, logically indefensible in being faith based and torn very publicly to shreds by attorney Clarence Darrow for the defense, contributed much to the nation's vision of the South as backward and benighted. Journalist H. L. Mencken, who had blasted the South previously in a 1917 essay entitled "The Sahara of the Bozart" as an intellectual and cultural backwater, was responsible for much of the newspaper coverage of the legal circus and painted the South once again as an intellectual wasteland. The trial and its blistering media coverage served primarily to entrench the beliefs and values of Southern fundamentalists more firmly than ever, evincing stubborn resistance to ambiguity and change.

The Southern conservative reaction was not confined to terrorists and zealots. At the forefront of the intellectual response to economic and cultural imperialism were the Fugitive Agrarians, a group of Southern scholars centered at Vanderbilt University. Shortly after the public embarrassments described above, and largely in response to them, the Agrarians formulated what Will Brantley has called "one of the most clearly articulated movements in American conservatism" (8). The release of *I'll Take My Stand* in 1930 marked the most celebrated and conspicuous response to the fading essence of Southern culture in the wake of Northern economic and cultural influence. *I'll Take My Stand* is generally regarded as a kind of Southern manifesto, a statement of Southern values and a blueprint for the ideal Southern society. Though in some ways bitterly divided, especially on the subject of race, where the most opposite poles were the reactionary Donald Davidson and the then cautiously progressive Robert Penn Warren, the Agrarians agreed that the South's culture and future must be codified and set forth in a constitution built on a bedrock assumption of common values, perspectives, and faith. As we shall see, in its own way, this idea posed as real a threat to the figurative modern swamp, a liminal space of ambiguity and retreat from an overbearing if wounded culture, as the encroaching "Northern" force of industrialization posed to the dwindling literal swamps.

The view of *I'll Take My Stand* as a unified manifesto is misleading when applied to the text as a whole; it is, in fact, a collection of essays presenting twelve largely disparate and often oppositional voices. As Paul Conkin points out in "The South in Southern Agrarianism" (1998), *I'll Take My Stand* in fact "proved infinitely confusing, for it spoke with several voices" (133). It has come, though, to be regarded as largely univocal and represented almost entirely by its introductory "Statement of Principles," authored by John Crowe Ransom. Today, only the introduction and occasionally Ransom's essay "Reconstructed but Unregenerate" are generally anthologized. Further, as Lewis Simpson points out in *The Fable of the Southern Writer* (1987), Ransom's introduction is the only element of the text that can be considered anything like a manifesto (18). Thus, in large part, the voice of the Agrarians is the voice of John Crowe Ransom.

In some ways, Ransom's vision of the South was built upon respect for the natural world: as Conkin puts it, "Central to Ransom's argument, one shared with Marxists, was the primacy of productive arrangements in determining all facets of a culture. Thus, an agrarian economy fostered a respect for nature, a flowering of the arts of good living, and an openness to religious myth, all either precluded or distorted by industrialism" (133). Further, the Agrarian emphasis on the small farmer, rather than on the plantation system, as central to Southern culture and identity implies a certain populist perspective. However, the Agrarian ideal as conceived and expressed by Ransom expressed a devotion to idea over reality, to intellectual and ideological system over practical program. "Nature," in the Agrarian context, must have a particularized definition: Ransom's nature is nature conceived theologically, in service to culture rather than independent of it. Also, concern for the Southern people and the physical region is secondary to concern for a way of interpreting, conceiving, and describing the South that was threatened with transformation by industrialization. As Michael Kreyling argues in *Inventing Southern Literature* (1998), what is being defended in *I'll Take My Stand* is not so much "the South" and a Southern way of life as it is the South as imagined by an intellectual and cultural elite: "It was not so much 'the South' that triggered *I'll Take My Stand* as the presence in the cultural/historical arena of competing 'orders' of cultural power that threatened to imagine the South in other ways, ways that would have disenfranchised the agrarian elite. And they fought back" (6).

Although the Agrarians were not wholly confined to ivory tower speculation and wishful imaginings and cannot rightly be called elitists in an economic sense—Conkin points out that they "joined in antimonopoly crusades, in attacks on concentrated wealth, in support of vigorous antitrust enforcement, local handicrafts and folk arts, and openly discriminatory taxes against great wealth, or in any measures that would help decentralize production and bring it back as close as possible to the household or proprietary ideal, even if it meant some loss in efficiency" (136)—they had at the heart of their "manifesto" an essential ideal that imposed intellectual and spiritual order on a specialized conception of history, virtually ignoring issues of gender and race, that foreclosed on any opposing viewpoints and zealously battled against ambiguity. The Agrarians were clear about holding forth not the South as it actually was as a cultural ideal but the South as it should have been—in other words, the South of literary construction, of chivalry, washed clean of its flaws and its racial guilt as if those elements were excisable from the whole. The ideal became more spiritual than actual, particularly in Ransom's rhetoric. Kreyling describes a key element in Ransom's ideology as "the assertion that the South as cultural ideal is apprehended with the same human faculties with which religion is acknowledged and the notion that intellectual, critical thought proceeds through binary oppositions. The idea is that only two positions are possible in any moment of debate or inquiry—the one you hold and its opposite. Compromise is bad faith, or 'impurity,' to return to anthropologist Mary Douglas's terminology" (11). Simpson further explores the strict limits of the Agrarian worldview in describing the new gentlemanly ideal, here transferred from the planter to the man of letters, called for by Ransom's program: "[T]he Southern man of letters must function not only as poet, novelist, and literary critic but as cultural theorist and social prophet—as an eminently self-conscious interpreter and guardian of values of social order to be secured through the restoration and perpetuation of the traditional Western amalgam of classical-Hebraic-Christian values" (*Fable* 19). The Agrarians' idea that the South should be conceived in the context of a program that united the "social, philosophical, literary, economic, and religious," coupled with Ransom's binary perspective that, as Kreyling puts it, "leaves no middle ground, no site for the miscegenation of ideas" (12), ran directly counter to developing currents in modern Southern literature.

Southern writers generally identified with the literary flowering known as the Southern Renaissance in the early to middle twentieth century, as well as Southern African American writers connected with the slightly earlier but roughly contemporaneous Harlem Renaissance centered in New York, used the swamp as a locus for precisely the "miscegenation of ideas" that Kreyling evokes—a unique space removed from both old and new, a space that encouraged and enabled texts that expressed ambivalence, that foregrounded ideas of transition and responded to them ambiguously. The swamp became the liminal foundation for two-pronged protest, aimed both at the guilty traditions of Old Southern culture and at the industrial development that threatened to destroy it. While many of the most significant works that explore and make use of the swamp can be viewed as in part reactionary, critical of the industrialization sweeping the South even as the Agrarians were, a significant part of their reaction was directed at Southern culture itself—both at its complicity in its own perceived impending demise and at the values and social strictures that flawed the Old Southern traditions. Voices that had formerly not engaged the swamp landscape outside of prescribed forms and tropes embraced the swamp as a place that encouraged and enabled new, more complex symbologies. Many of these voices understandably embraced the changes against which the South fought so stubbornly. Male authors who identified more fully but no longer unquestioningly with Southern culture and Southernness regarded the natural world and the aging systems that repudiated it, as well as the fading traditions that embraced it, with new eyes. These authors exploited the swamp's status as removed from mainstream culture, as fundamentally liminal, and as endangered. It often represented a fading remnant of a fading culture, but a remnant of a different culture than the Agrarians and, more disturbingly, the Klan, defended. In opposition to cultural efforts to proclaim and defend racial purity and to the Agrarians' efforts to impose a single cultural ideal rooted in the values of the white Christian gentleman, modern writers emphasized the swamp's connection to racial mixture, often making literal miscegenation the vehicle for the "miscegenation of ideas" that made their texts essentially oppositional. This chapter considers key swamp-centered texts by Zora Neale Hurston, Lillian Smith, and William Faulkner in tracing the ways that changes in both the empirical swamp and in swamp imagery reflected and influenced the evolution of a threatened, drastically changing, yet paradoxically revitalized South.

A few words about the problematic yet compelling term "modernism" as it applies to the South between the world wars are instructive about the broad reinterpretation of the swamp in the literature of that era. Modernism itself, in sharp contrast to the Victorian philosophies that, as we have seen, led to the swamp's demonization, is best defined by contradictions. Some critics and theorists, notably Irving Howe and Daniel Bell, see at its heart a mercurial and unclassifiable melange of ideas linked solely by a rage to rebel against order; Marshall Berman, in his 1988 book *All That is Solid Melts into Air: The Experience of Modernity* offers a definition of the modernist "movement" as one that defies definition: as a "family of artistic and intellectual movements that have been radically experimental, spiritually turbulent and militant, iconoclastic to the point of nihilism, apocalyptic in their hopes and fantasies, savagely destructive to one another—and often to themselves as well—yet capable of recurrent self-renewal" (16). This relatively chaotic interpretation of modernism runs alongside the undeniable view, put forth by theorists such as Peter Gay in *Freud, Jews, and Other Germans: Masters and Victims in Modernist Culture* (1978), that modernism was a pervasive aesthetic, philosophical, and social revolution of which the inchoate clash of ideas that Berman describes is only the surface: "Its bursting of boundaries did not imply hostility to discipline; its vigorous aesthetic criticism did not involve a yielding to depression; its profound exploration of unreason was not a celebration of irrationality"

(70–71). The general critical trend of the last two decades has been a kind of necessary capitulation—a recognition that modernism was many things, without concrete boundaries of beginning and end, neither chaotic and disjointed nor fully and holistically comprehensible. Peter Nicholls's 1995 study *Modernisms: A Literary Guide* admirably articulates this perspective—as the title suggests, it moves toward a consideration of modernism as defined by its plurality—an amalgam of movements addressing central questions about the human condition, neither formless nor monolithically unified.

Southern modernism must be considered, then, in this context—as a particularized and problematic facet of the whole. A key work in understanding the origins, nature, and dynamics of Southern modernism is Daniel Singal's *The War Within* (1982). Singal begins by recognizing the difficulty of interpreting modernism as any kind of unified movement, attesting that there is "considerable doubt as to whether [stock] formulations will ever be possible in twentieth-century intellectual history" (xi). Though Singal rightly resists accounting for the changes in Southern thought and literature during the modern era in terms of sweeping intellectual trends and generalizable movements, focusing instead on individual "wars within" key writers and thinkers of the time as they dealt with and adapted to cultural change, he raises some commonalities among most modern Southern thinkers that help explain the dramatic shift in attitude about Southern culture reflected in changing conceptions and representations of the Southern swamp.

Singal observes the general trend that "southern intellectuals . . . moved toward a new mode of culture largely by way of rebelling against the culture they had inherited. It was their deep dissatisfaction with traditional values and assumptions, and not social realities per se, that brought them to their best work" (xiii). Though Singal is correct in attributing the change in Southern literature between the wars to a rebellion against tradition, his separation of such a rebellion from social realities rings false, particularly in light of the voices outside the white male canon that emerged during the era he describes. That the inherited Victorian culture of the South—however literarily conceived and disconnected from actual Southern life—had tangible and lamentable implications for "social realities" can be seen in the chivalric justifications employed to excuse and explain Klan violence, to choose the most dramatic of many examples. Even if industrialization—with the key exception, as we have seen, of the timber industry—would not radically transform the South until after World War II, the influx of immigrants, the new communities of free blacks, and the undeniably changing economy that itself forced the South into a desperate return to agriculture in response to the Depression were effecting their own transformations of Southern culture. While Singal's antideterministic view of Southern modernism as the result of individuals grappling with history's legacy is hardly undermined by the reintroduction of social reality as a driving force, it is limited in its dismissal of the changing social, economic, and natural Southern landscape as a primary trigger for philosophical change.

Singal perceptively cites a shift in the social class of the most prominent Southern writers as one force behind the paradigmatic shift in understanding Southern culture between World War I and the midcentury. A democratized vision of Southern experience, articulated from perspectives previously excluded save through slave narratives or more or less genre-bound works by antebellum women that admitted only the most subtle subversion, emerged during this period. It is significant that the two female authors who will be treated here, Hurston and Smith, have traditionally resisted classification in terms of either of the two major renaissances—Harlem and Southern—that might be expected to embrace them, respectively. Will Brantley, in *Feminine Sense in Southern Memoir* (1993), notes their absence in many of the cornerstone books about Southern modernism—Singal's *The War Within*, Michael O'Brien's *The Idea of the South* (1978), and Richard King's *A Southern Renaissance* (1980), for example. Brantley sums up both writers' outsider status by illustrating the difficulty in classifying them in terms of larger sociopolitical trends in literature: "Lillian Smith was not accepted by most of her white southern male colleagues because they believed she was obsessed with race; by contrast, Zora Neale Hurston was rejected by most of the black male intellectuals of her day—both from the South and the North—because she was not obsessed with the issue of race" (33). What becomes intriguing is the way that these (until recently) noncanonical Southern writers and perhaps the most canonical of Southern writers, William Faulkner, all used the swamp's betweenness, its status as a landscape that both evoked transition and was itself transforming, and its historical exile from the carefully and oppressively constructed Cavalier South, as a means of exploring the nature and possibilities of the South's slow but inevitable transition into the modern world.

Although the works explored in this chapter were written before the rise to prominence of anything that can accurately be called an environmentalist movement—and ecological consciousness has always been a bit slower to evolve in the South, whose agricultural tradition connects the landscape more

directly with profit and livelihood and thus renders it less likely to be preserved for its own sake than in other parts of the country—all are united by
a sense that the swamp, or at least its power over Southern culture, is fading.
From the antebellum era through Reconstruction, as we have seen, the swamp
in the Southern mind was largely demonized but indomitable, endless and
impenetrable, a region that posed a genuine threat to Southern order. But
even as Hurston and the other Harlem Renaissance writers reclaimed the
swamp as a site of spiritual race-memory, they recognized the inevitable passing of the region they invested with religious and cultural significance. Smith's
invocation of the swamp as signifier of subversive ambiguity in *Strange Fruit*
(1944) presents subversion as a losing battle, as the town of Maxwell purges
potential disruption through violence and fire at the novel's close. Faulkner,
most emphatically, recognizes the vanishing of the swamp and of its traditions
in his 1942 novel *Go Down, Moses* and even, I will argue, undermines the
redemptive power inherent in the swamp-centered, countercultural tradition
of the hunt even before the encroachment of industry and modernity on the
formerly inviolate bottomland. Modern treatments of the swamp embody
both rebellion against the Southern traditions reinforced by Southern conservatism and consciousness that the power of the swamp as an alternative space
within the overarching structure of Southern culture is as fragile as the vanishing swamps themselves.

Perhaps the most significant and dramatic literary revisionings of the swamp
came from those who had been most thoroughly excluded from the Southern
culture that traditionally demonized the swamp and who historically found
solace and protection, however imperfect, within its borders. Although African
American writers, generally in slave narratives, had provided alternative visions
of the swamp since the mid-nineteenth century, the literary and cultural awakening of the Harlem Renaissance brought with it an unprecedented celebration
of the swamps and their subversive import for those who had been slaves.
Though the Harlem Renaissance is generally regarded as a northern phenomenon, and came about due to the increased freedom and mobility that allowed
African Americans to leave oppressive surroundings behind and seek new
opportunities and cultural communities outside the South, the reexamination of
African American cultural roots that it enabled provided an alternative interpretation of Southern experience, removed from the carefully constructed literary
narrative that described the idealized white South. The most prominent figures
of the Harlem Renaissance, known during its 1920s apex as the "New Negro

Renaissance," were primarily and programmatically forward looking: Alain Locke's keystone anthology *The New Negro* (1925) was devoted to reshaping the identity of the archetypal African American from a rural and uneducated subaltern to a sophisticated, progressive urban being. Further, as Cheryl Wall points out in her 1995 study *Women of the Harlem Renaissance*, "Although Harlem was 'a magnet' for Negro intellectuals, as Langston Hughes put it, few of them were migrants from the rural South" (5). Nevertheless, African American writers, even some who were most adamant in casting off the degrading traditions that bound their race in the South, recognized the significance of the swamp as a space beyond white cultural domination. They found and expressed a profound sense of cultural history, divinity, and even a kind of purity in the swamps that had sheltered escaped slaves and served as daunting but liberating natural churches for the remnants of African religion.

The Harlem Renaissance authors were not the first African American writers to posit a connection between the landscape and African American culture. As Jeffrey Myers ably demonstrates in his 2003 article "Other Nature: Resistance to Ecological Hegemony in Charles W. Chesnutt's *The Conjure Woman*," Charles Chesnutt draws significant links between the Carolina pine forests and the African Americans who lived among them throughout his collection of stories and even invests his tales with a nascent ecological consciousness. W. E. B. DuBois's *Souls of Black Folk* (1903), written well before the Harlem Renaissance but considered a seminal and influential work in laying the groundwork for its philosophies, contains an early expression of a rehabilitation and recognition of the Southern swamp landscape as a locus of self-determination and defiance for racial others in a rigidly white-dominated society. Introduced in the context of DuBois's central metaphor of the Veil, the omnipresent divide between the segregated realms of black and white experience, DuBois's brief but poignant characterization of the swamps of southern Georgia gives insight into the clouded but empowering nature of the region. DuBois acknowledges the threatening aura of the swamps—"Below Macon the world grows darker; for now we reach the Black Belt, that strange land of shadows, at which even slaves paled in the past, and whence come now only faint and half-intelligible murmurs to the world beyond" (667)—but also the swamps' strange aesthetic appeal: "The shadow of an old plantation lies at its edge, forlorn and dark. Then comes the pool; pendent gray moss and brackish waters appear, and forests filled with wild-fowl. In one place the wood is on fire, smouldering in dull red anger; but nobody minds. Then the swamp grows beautiful; a raised road built by chained

Negro convicts, dips down into it, and forms a way walled and almost covered in living green. Spreading trees spring from a prodigal luxuriance of under-growth; great dark green shadows fade into the black background, until all is one mass of tangled semi-tropical foliage, marvelous in its weird savage splen-dor" (122). DuBois's musings are not confined to mere appreciation of the nat-ural landscape and its departure from the regimentation of the Southern social and agricultural design. His aesthetic response quickly becomes linked to a remembrance of resistance to the white imperial order, as he recalls the rise of Osceola in the Florida swamps as a battle for righteous vengeance: "In yonder shadows a dark and hideously painted warrior glided stealthily on,—another and another, until three hundred had crept into the treacherous swamp. . . . Waist-deep, they fought beneath the tall trees, until the war-cry was hushed and the Indians glided back into the west. Small wonder the wood is red" (122–23). Dubois's imaginative reminiscence marks the swamp as a place of opposition to the white order; doomed opposition, perhaps, but nevertheless testament to the "savage splendor" that set the swamp apart from encroaching Anglo civilization. DuBois's reclamation of the swamp from traditional white tropes linking it with hell is underscored by his discussion of the ordered and prosperous plantations just beyond the swamps: he points out the richness and beauty of the plantations but reflects that it was all built upon the suffering of black laborers: " 'This land was a little Hell,' said a ragged, brown, and grave-faced man to me. . . . 'I've seen niggers drop dead in the furrow, but they were kicked aside, and the plough never stopped. And down in the guardhouse, there's where the blood ran' " (123–24). By juxtaposing his description of the swamp and the heroic battles waged there with the hidden "Hell" that the idyl-lic plantation represented for the slaves who worked its carefully ordered fields, DuBois inverts the traditional antebellum construction presented most clearly in Kennedy's *Swallow Barn*. The dichotomy of the "Goblin Swamp," home to the devil and capricious nemesis of cultural order, is reversed as DuBois pres-ents it from an avowedly representative black perspective. To the Southern African American, DuBois claims, the plantation is Hell, and the swamps the remnant of a noble but fading culture.

Another, more emphatic exaltation of the swamp's significance to Southern African American culture would come in 1923, in Jean Toomer's *Cane*, the genre-defying work often hailed as the crowning masterpiece of the Harlem Renaissance. While I will not venture a verdict on that claim, the significance that it imparts to Toomer's work indicates the resonance of

Toomer's figurations of Southern black experience. *Cane*, which owes a clear formal debt to DuBois's *Souls of Black Folk* as a work that resists generic classification, combines poetry with prose and drama to chronicle the transformation of black American culture from its rural Southern beginnings to an urban Northern present: in so doing, it presents aspects of the African American slave experience previously unexplored in literature. Two poems from the first section of *Cane*, which deals with black experience in the rural South, reveal Toomer's perspective on African American spirituality and his positing of the swamp as a haven for a pure divinity. The poems "Georgia Dusk" and "Conversion" reveal an alternative vision of spirituality, outside the white Christian orthodoxy that governed the plantation South and would govern, in the Agrarians' worldview, a revived, idealized South.

Although it follows after "Georgia Dusk" in the larger work, "Conversion" provides a pointed engagement with a theme that the earlier poem addresses less directly. "Conversion" condemns the adulteration of traditional African religion by what Toomer clearly perceives as a degraded and degrading white Christian tradition:

> *African Guardian of Souls,*
> *Drunk with rum,*
> *Feasting on a strange cassava,*
> *Yielding to new words and a weak palabra*
> *Of a white-faced sardonic God—*
> *Grins, cries*
> *Amen,*
> *Shouts hosanna. (28)*

Toomer's vision of African spirituality compromised and transformed by a condescending white religion acknowledges the dilemma facing the Southern African American in the late nineteenth and early twentieth centuries that Hurston explores in *The Sanctified Church*. As Hurston explains, the African American, confronted by a rapidly changing world and in many ways actively dissociating him- or herself from oppressive tradition, found his or her central ways of understanding God and religion additionally challenged by the encroachment of orthodox Christian views on traditional African spirituality, creating a central dynamic of "the older forms of Negro religious expression asserting themselves against the new" (103). Toomer perceived this dynamic acutely, scorning the imposition of a degraded form of white religion on slaves and former slaves and exploring, in later parts of *Cane* such as the prose piece "Box Seat," the possibilities of a new and redemptive urban Christ in African American spiritual life. In his autobiography, Toomer's description of a trip to rural Georgia expresses his conception of a fading spiritualized landscape approaching the bittersweet transformation of modernity: "The setting was crude in a way, but strangely rich and beautiful. . . . I realized with deep regret, that the spirituals, meeting ridicule, would be certain to die out. . . . The folk-spirit was walking in to die on the modern desert. That spirit was so beautiful. Its death was so tragic. Just this seemed to sum life for me" (123–24). Toomer's regret at the transition from a traditional, racialized spirituality of memory to a spiritually denuded modernity is refined and linked powerfully to the vanishing swamp landscape in the poem "Georgia Dusk."

"Georgia Dusk," initially published in *The Liberator* in 1922, begins with an image of a feast held in the midst of a landscape in transition, as workers at a sawmill pause to celebrate in "an orgy for some genius of the South." The sawmill, an agent in the landscape's change, stops, "and silence breaks the bud of knoll and hill," clearing the air for the songs of celebration. In the poem's center, Toomer links the transformed landscape with the vestiges and memories of African and Afro-Caribbean culture, resurrected in the music as the workers make "folk-songs from soul sounds." The fourth and fifth stanzas work together to evoke a resurrection of a dying landscape and of traditions that are now only memories:

> *Smoke from the pyramidal sawdust pile*
> *Curls up, blue ghosts of trees, tarrying low*
> *Where only chips and stumps are left to show*
> *The solid proof of former domicile.*
> *Meanwhile, the men, with vestiges of pomp,*
> *Race memories of king and caravan,*
> *High-priests, an ostrich, and a juju-man,*
> *Go singing through the footpaths of the swamp. (Cane 15)*

Black men, in a landscape destroyed by industry, seek out the swamp as the locus of "race memories," the space set apart for evocations of a holy and exalted past which they can access only through memory and song. Toomer

underscores the connection between the men's songs and the swamp landscape, as the trees themselves join the chorus:

> [T]he pine trees are guitars,
> Strumming, pine-needles fall like sheets of rain . . .
> Their voices rise . . . the chorus of the cane
> Is caroling a vesper to the stars. (15)

The men's spiritual connection to the swamp, and the race memories evoked in
the part that has not yet been leveled by the sawmill that employs them, introduces a new nostalgia, categorically removed from Agrarian nostalgia for an
idealized South. Toomer recognizes an alternative divinity—still touched by
Christianity, as he exhorts in the poem's final line that the singers "[b]ring
dreams of Christ to dusky cane-lipped throngs," but steeped in an exclusively
African American experience. Although Toomer's vision is thoroughly progressive—he would even, after the publication of *Cane*, disavow his connection to
the black race and claim to be a new breed of man, solely American—he clearly
perceives the vanishing of an old, pre–American African culture, linked to and
doomed by the vanishing landscape, as a significant loss.

Toomer's poems are instructive here in their introduction of issues that
Hurston would treat more fully in her first novel, the frequently overlooked
Jonah's Gourd Vine (1934). Foremost among those who examined the swamp
and its significance for African American folklife, Hurston was a profoundly
atypical writer of the Harlem Renaissance era and one of the very few who
chose to remain in the South for most of her life. As a Southerner who often
chose to embrace rather than to repudiate Southern African American culture,
Hurston fit imperfectly into the model of the New Negro which became the
Renaissance's central icon. *Jonah's Gourd Vine* examines the promise and peril
facing the "New Negro" in the American South at the beginning of the twentieth century: in essence, Hurston uses the novel, and the swamp within it in
particular, to capture a transitional moment for the Southern African American,
crystallized between the promise of travel, industry, and liberation on the one
hand and the rich spiritual traditions and paradoxical, alternative freedoms
offered by the old ways of life on the other.

The novel tells the story of John Pearson, a mulatto exiled from the virtual
slave community of his birth, who encounters the modern world, organized
religion, and the possibilities and pitfalls of a rapidly transforming South.

Hurston's novel, like much of her work, is heavily influenced by her own experience: John and Lucy are based loosely on her own parents. Further, the novel shows the marked influence of Hurston's childhood in the "frontier town" of Eatonville in Florida. Ann R. Morris and Margaret M. Dunn, in "Flora and Fauna in Hurston's Florida Novels" (1991), point out that Hurston "grew up unconsciously absorbing impressions about Florida's flora and fauna" (6). Hurston's own account of the town of Eatonville casts little doubt on that assertion. Eatonville, an all-black town five miles from Orlando which had been incorporated for only fifteen years in 1901, the putative year of Hurston's birth, was a town that, as Hurston describes it in her autobiography *Dust Tracks on a Road* (1942), had only been partially reclaimed from the surrounding swamps. In her neighborhood, "bears and alligators raided hog-pens, wildcats fought with dogs in people's yards, rattlesnakes as long as a man and as thick as a man's forearm were found around back doors" (33). Further, as Robert Hemenway points out in *Zora Neale Hurston: A Literary Biography* (1980), Hurston's extensive anthropological fieldwork in search of black folktales in the 1920s brought her into contact with swamp gangs whom she followed and interviewed as they worked, despite the looming danger of being "snake-bit" or "gator-swallowed" (38–39). Hurston was intimately familiar with the swamp and its dangers but also with the elements of African American culture that survived there, preserved in swamp communities largely untouched by either white plantation culture or by the spiritually leveling force of modernity: she cheerfully endured the swamps' dangers for access to cultural memory. They represented, for her, spiritual and cultural traditions that she devoted much of her life to cataloguing and preserving.

For Hurston, ever a proponent of an almost primitivistic "pure art" of the folk against the politicized "propaganda" of Locke, DuBois, and the New Negro, the "progress" of modernist philosophical and intellectual understanding was always deeply suspect, representing at least as much loss as gain to African American culture, identity, spirituality, and true self-expression. In *Jonah's Gourd Vine*, Hurston examines the loss of cultural and spiritual identity that comes with the encroachment of modernity upon a small black community at the edge of the swamp. The novel is a study in betweenness, ambivalent in balancing nostalgia and elevation of folk traditions with the opportunities for empowerment and self-actualization that modernity meant for African Americans. John Pearson, the mulatto protagonist, becomes a kind of African American Everyman, a signifier of a race and culture in transition. Hurston devotes little attention to John's parentage, beyond the strong suggestion that he was fathered by the white landowner Alf Pearson; instead, his mixed-race status, and the light skin that marks him as a "yaller god," serve to emphasize his lack of stable belonging in either the traditional community on one side of the swamp or in the modern world beyond it. The novel in fact engages questions of race and of white culture very little: Hurston focuses on a black past and black future, and the critiques inherent in the novel rarely touch upon the specter of oppression that informs the majority of both contemporaneous African American and Southern fiction. In part, the swamp becomes Hurston's vehicle for her own reaction against the negative aspects of modernity unrecognized by promulgators of the New Negro ideal—the challenges to black spirituality and subjectivity that paradoxically accompanied the new age. Through the course of the novel, John encounters two major disruptive forces, each emblematic of modernity's challenges to traditional African American spirituality: first, the mingling of African religion with Lucy's orthodox Christianity, which imposes strictures on John's sexuality and subjectivity even as it empowers him and "makes him a man"; and second, the encroachment of the outside world, the enabling of travel, and the destruction of community embodied in the symbol of the train. Each new force calls for a new kind of understanding: John finds himself compelled to learn language to express his new spirituality as his newly Christian God moves from the physical and natural world around him into a rarefied and hitherto inaccessible realm of words. Further, as he encounters the fascinating, terrifying train for the first time, John must decipher the language he insists lies beneath the impersonal clamor the other men hear: " 'Naw, it say some words too. Ahm comin' heah plenty mo' times and den Ah tell yuh whut it say" (16). Each new force is its own distinct intellectual challenge—each demands a new form of understanding and the mastery of a new language. In leaving the swamps, the region that defied linguistic and literary colonization in the Old South and thus sustained a kind of freedom from language for the black victims of that colonization, John sacrifices a spiritual subjectivity that he will never fully regain.

At the beginning of the novel, John lives in a community sequestered from modernity and change by a swamp, divided by an intervening creek. Hurston's depiction of John's early community is too complex for the Edenic imagery she weaves through her narrative to be completely effective: the heavy legacy of slavery and Ned's resentment and abuse mitigate against the easy formulation of John as African American Adam exiled from the Garden. Rather, Hurston presents this community in an ambivalent manner that reflects both the residual African proximity to natural divinity and the lingering specter of slavery. John embodies this dual characterization: profoundly physical, powerful, and beautiful, he is marked by a light coloration that attests to his plantation owner father and leads the cruel and resentful Ned to designate him a "yaller god" (3). As Alan Brown points out in his 1991 article " 'De Beast' Within: The Role of Nature in *Jonah's Gourd Vine*," Hurston throughout her writings "makes the point that people living in rural Florida had to become tough—that is, more animalistic—in order to surmount the same obstacles that the creatures of the swamp had to cope with every day" (76). Banished from Ned's household after a fight, John becomes symbolically linked to the traditional swamp in multiple senses—he is a mulatto, an exile. However, when he enters the swamp itself, he finds not a twisted morass of immorality that mirrors his stunted soul, as Stowe's Dred does, but an Eden in its own right, to which he unquestionably belongs. John is a conscious and active participant in the music of nature before he crosses over into a more modern world: "John plunged on down to the creek, singing a new song and stomping the beats. The big creek thundered among its rocks and whirled on down. So John sat on the foot-log and made some words to go with the drums of the creek. . . . The hound dog's lyric crescendo lifted over and above the tree tops" (12).

Music is a central theme in Hurston's novel. John's plantation community makes music that is all drums and rhythm, its lyrics wholly subordinate to the transcendent rhythms that invoke an intuitive connection to community and to deity, embodied in Hurston's evocation of "Kata-Kumba, . . . [t]he drum with the man-skin." In crossing the liminal space of the creek bed, John enters into a hybrid community, still steeped, to an extent, in African tradition, but in which the music comes from the Church: this music, all treble rather than bass, depends on lyrics and voice rather than on drums and body. In the swamp, though, John marries the two in his own music. John's subjectivity, as evinced in his rebellion against Ned's cruelty and his satisfaction in solitude, is more secure and uncomplicated in the swamp, before he enters the creek, than at any other point in the novel. Though he will later puzzle over the "words" of the train, agonize over his inadequate vocabulary in wooing Lucy, and disavow any personal responsibility in speaking as God's conduit from the altar, John unselfconsciously makes his own words to accompany the creek's drum and the ambient music of the surrounding swamp. In this sense, Hurston revives the trope of the swamp as the domain of the mulatto and of the exile, but she imbues it with its own purity, turning it from a mirror of internal corruption into an idealized, prelapsarian space—an alternative, Africanized muse, outside the classical Agrarian aesthetic ideal.

The easy coexistence of John's linguistic self-expression and the natural, physical world around him at this stage in his development is essential to understanding the relationship between language, body, and spirit that Hurston posits in John's initial community. John's return to his mother, Amy, and to the rest of his family on Pearson's plantation after their initial separation occasions Hurston's stunning evocation of traditional African survivals in African American culture, embodied in the music of the drum: "[T]he voice of Kata-Kumba, the great drum, lifted itself within them and they heard it. The great drum that is made by priests and sits in majesty in the juju house. The drum with the man skin that is dressed with human blood, that is beaten with a human shin-bone and speaks to gods as a man and to men as a God" (29). Hurston's descriptions evoke Toomer's "Georgia Dusk," as race memories emerge in swamp celebration. Here, Hurston strongly asserts a link between John's early community at the swamp's edge and the spiritual community of an African tribe. In *The Power of Black Music* (1995), Samuel Floyd interprets a strikingly similar ceremony and explains its significance to African religious tradition: "Dance, drum, and song was inseparable from the traditional communities in which it existed—communities in which social and cultural conformity and egalitarianism prevailed, in which . . . the failure to live up to one's social obligations [was] interpreted as hostility toward the community" (33). In the context of *Jonah's Gourd Vine*, dance, drum, and song are important not only in their role in the cohesion of John's initial, traditional community but in their inherent eroticism as well. The sacred music that the community creates celebrates the physical; it comes directly from their bodies, with no intermediary instruments or other artifacts interposed between the worshipper and prayer: "They called for the instrument they had brought to America in their skins—the drum—and they played upon it" (29). As Floyd says, "African song in general is erotic because fertility and sexual prowess are central values in African life; African dances are designed to educate boys and girls for their adult sexual roles in a polygynous world" (27). Further, Floyd points out that, although African communities have a vivid and complex idea of the afterlife, "salvation and redemption are not part of the African religious conception" (18). Sin—particularly sexual sin—as a discrete, predefined act, is alien to African religion as Floyd describes it. At this stage, then, John's theology carries with it no conception of adulterous sin. His sexuality is central, not antithetical, to his identity and membership in the community. John's youthful lack of any idea of sexuality as sinful becomes clearest late in the novel, as a shamed, fallen John ruefully tells Hambone, "Don't it look funny, dat all mah ole pleasures done got tuh be new sins? . . . Havin' women didn't useter be no sin. Jus' got sinful since Ah got ole" (169). Sin becomes a function of John's distance from the community of his youth. This youthful, prelapsarian spiritual stage, characterized by dance, drum, and song in the sheltering swamp environs, finds John at his most powerful, self-assured, and innocent.

The swamp is not a pervasive trope in Hurston's novel—primarily because its ephemerality is key to its rhetorical power. The remainder of the novel following John's initial scene of spiritual and natural transcendence concerns the breakdown of the spiritual wholeness that the swamp, and its removal from culture, provided. In his efforts to master the cognitive understanding necessary to assert himself in a world he is initially ill equipped to understand, John sacrifices the prelapsarian intuitive wholeness, the idealized and ultimately unsustainable marriage of nature and self-generated language, of instinct and intellect, that he finds in the moment of transition as he sits in the swamp and joins in its music. Karl Marx claimed in his 1856 "Speech at the Anniversary of the *People's Paper*" that "the victories of art seem bought by the loss of character. At the same pace that mankind masters nature, man seems to become enslaved to other men or to his own infamy" (577). The protagonist of Hurston's novel embodies the dilemma that Marx describes: in joining the inevitable struggle to master his world, John loses his essential sanctity—the intuitive wholeness that Hurston presents as true divinity inevitably shatters. In leaving the sanctified swamp, always in defiance of categories, itself unclassifiable, John becomes vulnerable to the divisions of body, mind, and soul that become his undoing.

When John emerges from the swamp and encounters Lucy, a crucial and ultimately tragic bifurcation begins in his understanding of his physical and spiritual selves. Despite her abiding religious faith, Lucy in many ways signifies modernity. Hurston aligns her early on with education and financial success, and at their first meeting she shames John for the apparent backwardness of the life he has led: "He felt ashamed of his bare feet for the first time in his life. How was he to know that there were colored folks that went around with their feet cramped up like white folks" (14). Shoes become an important signifier in Hurston's heavily biblical symbology: John's community over the creek, where people go unshod, resonates with biblical descriptions of "hallowed ground," while John's arrival on the far side of the creek indicates a removal from an inherently sanctified space. Further, with John's first encounter with Lucy comes his first discomfort with his own body—in this new world, the body becomes something to conceal and to contain. His association of this behavior with "white folks" indicates its separation from the cultural practices John knows and follows—in her disdain Lucy interposes herself between John and his body and between John and his culture. The "yaller god" that Hurston presents in the novel's first chapter will soon understand himself as an uneasy and irreconcilable mixture of man and beast.

Although Lucy becomes in one sense the catalyst for John's dissolution, Hurston certainly does not condemn her. Admittedly, in later essays Hurston endorses more purely African and Afro-Caribbean forms of spirituality over the artificial overlay of Christianity that occludes them in African American society, but *Jonah's Gourd Vine's* autobiographical dimension complicates its theological dimension. Loyalty to her mother may keep Hurston from a whole-hearted endorsement of old religion over new: in his literary biography of Hurston, Hemenway relates that, on her deathbed, Hurston's mother requested that no one perform the traditional rituals that accompanied death in her community—taking the pillow from under her head and covering the mirror and hourglass with cloth. However, ignoring the nine-year-old Zora's demands that they stop, the elders carried out the ritual: "Her father held her, and despite her protests the mourners softened dying by removing the pillow and turning the bed to the East (so it would not be crossways of the world), while the hooded clock and mirror preserved the good fortune of the household" (16). In spite of her own developing theories of theology and spirituality, Hurston's maternal loyalty produces a more complex relationship between African tradition and Christianity in her first novel than she, in later days, could be expected to endorse. Further, Lucy's status as essentially faultless martyr only underscores the mechanistic, fatalistic vision of John's moral and actual destruction that Hurston creates: the "world-historical forces" are at work, and the individual has little power to resist them.

Early on, Hurston conflates John's relationship with Lucy and his relationship with the church, and hence with a new vision of the spiritual. They develop their relationship in church, singing in the choir and passing surreptitious notes in their hymnals. Well before their marriage, John realizes that his love for Lucy occupies a spiritual plane far removed from his dalliances with other women—as he tells Mehaley, "Ah tastes her wid mah sould, but if Ah didn't take holt uh you ah'd might soon fuhgit al about you" (81). With Lucy, John develops a sense of love detached from the physical, and thus a sense of the Christian duality of body and soul that comes to torment him.

Even as Lucy empowers John by helping him to find the "voice" he has lost since first emerging from the swamp into the town, she also threatens his agency by alienating his spiritual self from his physical body. Lucy's church community, in contrast to John's plantation community, lives by a more restrictive set of values that target and demonize sexual expression. Just as it made him ashamed of his bare feet upon first crossing over from the swamp, Lucy's community singles out and condemns another seemingly natural element of John's self: his sexuality. John comes to understand sexual sin through Lucy; as John Lowe says, "his infidelity in some way seems a rebellion against both [Lucy's] authority and her charity, which forms an analogue with that of the church he serves" (88). Further, although Lucy empowers John to preach and thus brings about his greatest moments of triumph, John feels an acute separation between the man who speaks so powerfully from the pulpit and his true self—his speech is something outside himself that he channels and disseminates but does not truly own: "When Ah speak tuh yuh from dis pulpit, dat ain't me talkin', dat's de voice uh God speakin' thru me. When de voice is thew, Ah jus' uhnother one uh God's crumblin' clods. . . . Ahm uh natchel man but look lak some uh y'all is dumb tuh de fack" (122). The preacher cannot be a "natchel man": in Lucy's church, sanctity and nature must remain mutually exclusive.

The uncomplicated spiritual communion with nature that John experiences in the swamp, underscored by the ease with which he dispatches the snake that threatens Lucy, will prove irretrievable. The division between John's spiritual life, as evinced by his sermons, and the truth of his character echoes an aspect of modernism that Berman describes as connected chiefly with theorists such as Roland Barthes and artists such as Clement Greenberg—the idea of the work of art as autotelic, removed from modern life: "Modernism thus appeared as a great attempt to free modern artists from the impurities, the vulgarities of modern life" (30). Indeed, John reveals an acute consciousness that his linguistic creation is profoundly removed from his status as a "natchel man": sacred speech has little to do with base action, and, for all Lucy's efforts, John's preaching cannot effect the change in his behavior she so earnestly desires. This moment, then, clearly reveals the sharp division in

John's self that his immersion in the modern world has wrought: the linguistic John and the physical John exist on separate and irreconcilable planes.

Late in the novel, Hurston diverges from her central narrative to set aside a discrete chapter devoted entirely to an impressionistic rendering of modernity's effects on Southern African Americans. She foregrounds her image with a deistic characterization of a world whose progress is very similar to that of a locomotive: "The Lord of the wheel that turns on itself slept, but the world kept spinning, and the troubled years sped on" (141). With the train comes an impulse to the younger members of John's church to travel North, to abandon the Southern spiritual community: "And black men's feet learned roads. . . . The wind said North. Trains said North. The tides and tongues said North, and men moved like great herds before the glaciers" (148). While Hurston clearly recognizes that progress, as embodied in the train and played out in the Great Migration, has filled John and Lucy's world with far more possibilities than Ned and Amy enjoyed, her complex pastoral remains ambivalent.

Earlier, Hurston has hinted at a tension between political progress for African Americans in the South and the sanctified community embodied in the church. When presented by the politically progressive preacher, Reverend Cozy, who defines himself as "a race man," two of the elder women sit unconvinced, passing judgment with the simple, condemnatory phrase, "Ah ain't heard whut de tex' wuz" (158). If sacred words are the "man-making" instruments of the church, the elder women's dismissal of Cozy's speech as a lecture rather than a sermon attests to the inadequacy of political speech in building their paradigm of spiritual manhood. The final effect of political progress and the new migration is troublingly clear in Hambone's lament near the chapter's close that the church "done lost two hund'ed members in three months" (149). Hurston's characterization of the travelers as "great herds" underscores their distance from the "man-making" institution of the church: with progress and possibility comes an implicit loss of spirituality and thus humanity. John's eventual decline and self-destruction are in fact tied, a bit overbearingly, to the train that has become modernization's clearest signifier. Done in by sexual sin and guilt, John is ultimately destroyed by the embodiment of the once natural, now bestial impulses within him, of the alienation of his physical self from the spirituality it now betrays. While in the swamp John had effortlessly defeated the serpent who threatened Lucy, he finds himself robbed of agency by the mechanized serpent of what in his sermons he has called "The Damnation Train."

In *Jonah's Gourd Vine*, Hurston contrasts the swamp, and the spiritual community it enables and preserves, not with white civilization, as tradition would dictate, but with African American progress. It is a contrast she views with suitable ambivalence: while she would clearly not wish John to stay in the plantation-like surroundings of his birth, she conveys a clear sense of something lost, something tied inextricably to a fading natural world. The novel is not so much critique as observation, withholding judgement on the culture it examines even as it withholds judgement on John, whom she assesses at the novel's close to be just "a man" (202). Nevertheless, Hurston's first novel provides a clear indication of a shift in literary representations of the swamp. She presents not only the culturally untouched swamp that initially embraces John but also the imperfectly modern community of Eatonville, itself a city in a swamp populated and governed entirely by African Americans, with a wistful acknowledgment of the swamp's inevitable demise that recalls Kennedy's tone in *Swallow Barn*. Hurston uses the swamp and swamp communities to evoke an alternative nostalgia, in defiance both of the linguistic and literary construction that white tradition propounded as the Old South and of the arch denigration of folk culture implicit in the New Negro Renaissance.

Even as DuBois, Toomer, and Hurston examined the role of the swamp in shaping a rapidly changing African American culture, white Southern writers as disparate as Lillian Smith and William Faulkner explored the possibilities that the same subversive space offered for a more contemporary escape from a monolithic and constricting cultural history that, however besieged and critiqued by the rest of America, still asserted powerful control over Southern life. Although their agendas and perspectives on race relations were profoundly different, both Smith and Faulkner, in *Strange Fruit* (1944) and *Go Down, Moses* (1942), respectively, use the swamp as a place of potential escape from rigid social codes and from collective racial and cultural sin; in the final analysis, each ultimately concludes that such an escape is impossible. Framed tragically, each novel describes a final, ironic victory of Southern culture and society over the now diminishing swamps that once defied them.

Another author who, like Hurston, resists classification, Lillian Smith was, as Beth Harrison observes, at least as renowned for her politics as for her art. This was true both in Smith's own time, when former Georgia Governor Eugene Talmadge blasted her 1944 novel *Strange Fruit*'s social message, claiming that it depicted interracial romance "in such glamor" that it would "make courtships between negroes and white appear attractive" (qtd. in Harrison 18), and in contemporary criticism, as critics such as J. P. Payne call her "a dedicated human rights activist who challenged the categories of race, class, gender, *and* sexual orientation with a progressive, if not radical, zeal" (8). Although Smith at times complained that the political furor created by her works occluded their appreciation as literature, she clearly foregrounded social and political critique in her life and work. Will Brantley calls Smith "the sharpest disruption of a conservative discourse and a narrow set of assumptions that until the late seventies were generally taken as adequate explanations of the origin and direction of a major body of 20th Century writing" (193).

Smith, as a white, at least nominally Christian, Southern lady who also evinced strong criticism of the Southern racial order as well as at least ambivalence about her own sexuality, was a living disruption of the categories that the conservative South held to ever more fervently as Southern identity threatened to slip away. She was a strong and outspoken critic of the Agrarian conception of the South, pointing out the realities that their admittedly idealized evocation of Southern history ignored: "The basic weakness of the Fugitives' stand, as I see it, lay in their failure to recognize the massive dehumanization which had resulted from slavery and its progeny, sharecropping and segregation, and the values that permitted these brutalities of spirit" (qtd. in Biles 15). While the Agrarians agreed with near unanimity that the largest question facing the South in the modern era was "the Negro Problem," and addressed it with widely varying degrees of progressiveness and reaction, Smith rejected the very terms on which they discussed the issue. In her 1944 essay "Humans in Bondage," Smith shifted the blame for what was commonly called "The Negro Problem" firmly onto the shoulders of white society: "There is a problem facing each of us, black and white, but it is not the 'Negro Problem.' It is the problem, for Negroes, of finding some way to live with white people. It is the problem, for whites, of learning to live with themselves" (*Winner* 38). Smith called for an end to the clearest institutionalized reinforcement of Southern social order, segregation, when most liberal Southerners would only speak of ameliorating the race problem within the bounds of that system. Further, Smith openly attacked the Southern intellectual tendency to elevate the mythic past in place of progressing toward a redemptive future and critiqued the adherence to dead systems in place of faith in humanity. As she puts it in the closing chapter of her memoir *Killers of the Dream*, "The years go by. We are still fighting false battles or dead ones. We are still defending old worn-out systems, pitting them against each other. We know, our minds know, that the Twentieth Century dialogue has to do with relationships not systems; but we have not confessed it. Nor are we basing plans for the future on this knowledge. It is as if we cannot bridge the chasm between the past and what lies ahead" (233). Smith's central plea in *Killers of the Dream*, as Wynn Cherry points out in "William Faulkner and Lillian Smith: Two Distinct Journeys" (1997), is that her readers "bridge mythic and rational mind . . . to connect our childhood with the present and the past with the future" (21)—a profoundly anti-Agrarian sentiment. The Fugitives' recognition that the South they evoked was divorced from the South as it actually was only compounds what Smith viewed as the South's central problem: the rigid adherence to mythic and idealized codes of behavior that have little relation to human lives and relationships.

Set in the post–World War I South of Smith's youth, *Strange Fruit* is her most fully realized fictional critique of the rigidity of Southern codes and their effects on people compelled to live by them. Smith's novel eschews a single narrative perspective: as J. P. Payne puts it, "There is no main plot, theme, or character; instead there are many different ones as well as multiple narrative perspectives which reveal many different sides of the story" (9). Throughout the novel, Smith employs images of the swamp in a variety of significations, representing it in different ways in the minds of different characters and in relation to different institutions and ideas. Rather than seizing on a single swamp trope, Smith evokes multiple traditional iconographic significations for the swamp: at various times it represents miscegenation, in the case of Nonnie's pregnancy; purity, in the freedom from social mores that Nonnie and Tracy find in the swamp; female sexuality, as Tracy's imagination links Nonnie's sexuality with the swamp to which she feels an intuitive connection; masculine escape from feminine social rules, in the broad tradition of American wilderness literature; and fear of that escape for the white women of Maxwell. Ultimately, Smith presents the swamp at various times as any ambiguity, any element that troubles the carefully constructed social and moral order of Maxwell.

Smith has acknowledged the swamp's significance in her own life as emblematic of a lurking, subversive ambiguity. Biographer Anne C. Loveland recounts of Smith's childhood in the north Florida town of Jasper, upon which she modeled Maxwell, Georgia, the setting of *Strange Fruit*, "she was fascinated by the swampy areas that extended like fingers from the great Okefenokee Swamp in Georgia. The Indians called them 'trembling earth' because of the sink holes and quicksand and bottomless ponds, and to Lillian, even as a child, they seemed symbolic of the uncertainty and mystery of life" (3). In *Killers of the Dream*, Smith includes a section called "The Trembling Earth," evoking the Indian term for the Okefenokee in the context of the restrictive and often contradictory, fear-based religious instruction that served as her indoctrination into the Southern codes she attacks throughout the book. At the close of the section, she describes the significance of the swamp at the edge of town to her child's mind and to her development:

> *The physical setting for [our] tangled dreams and anxieties, the place we lived, was a backdrop to our Deep South childhood that seemed no more than a giant reflection of our own hearts. Back of our little town was the swamp, tangled green, oozing snakes and alligators and water lilies and sweet-blooming bays, weaving light and shadow into awful and tender designs, splotching our lives with brightness and terror. . . . This is the South I knew as a child. Swamp and palmetto and "sinks" and endless stretches of pines. . . . Our lessons were learned against this backdrop which rubbed on the senses day in, day out, confirming all that our feelings told us was true in life.*
> *Here also, we unlearned our lessons.* (112–13)

The swamp in *Strange Fruit* echoes that of Smith's childhood in undermining cultural strictures and enabling ambiguity. For each of the central characters in Smith's novel, the swamp takes on a different set of significations, determined by that character's position in, and dedication to, the ideals of white Southern society.

The relationship between Tracy Deen and Nonnie foregrounds the interplay of differing understandings of the swamp in determining the ways that both characters conceive of each other and of their relationship. Smith once described the characters in the novel as "shaped and twisted by their learning as if their personalities had been placed in a steel frame within which they could grow, but only according to the limits defined by the rigid design of the frame" (qtd. in Loveland 63). Although Tracy regards his relationship with Nonnie as an escape from the codes that govern the rest of his life, Nonnie and Tracy's relationship can only grow to the extent that the frame will let it. Nonnie, the character least bound by societal codes and categories in the novel, is thus the character with the most intimate and intuitive connection with the swamp. Even as a child, we discover, Nonnie has "notions about swamp sounds." Her initial encounter with Tracy Deen introduces her empathy with the swamp, and Tracy's inability to understand it:

> He spat and studied her face. "What you do in that swamp?"
> "Nothing just goes." She paused. "It says, 'come here, come here, come here.'"
> He squinted his eyes.
> "You hear it?" She whispered.
> "Nope. Nothing but frogs croaking, and dogs." (4–5)

Both Nonnie and Tracy conceive of their relationship in terms of the swamp, but in crucially different ways. Nonnie's connection to the swamp is intuitive, independent of social determination; the purity of that connection underscores her conception of her and Tracy's relationship. Neither is bound by trope or cliché; neither is constructed according to preconception. Her perception of the swamp to which she feels an almost supernatural connection is mercurial, mirroring her emotional response to her relationship with Tracy: "All her life she had been . . . afraid of the swamp and the night, or their loneliness. And yet they were a part of her, as was no living creature, except Tracy. . . . Thinking of him now made the distance greater, as if something were pulling him away and she could only stand and watch his going. She was cold and afraid. The swamp behind her, the night, were ugly and threatening" (122). Nonnie's understanding of the swamp admits complexity: as compelling as she finds it, she never simply idealizes the swamp any more than she does her relationship with Tracy. Nonnie's visions of nature and of romance exist outside the social codes that seek to dominate both; she and the swamp are set apart from culture in that both admit ambiguity.

Rejection of ambiguity is, of course, the governing trait of Maxwell's white society. The preacher, spiritual center and chief advocate of Maxwell's prejudices in codified form, expresses the drive for racial and gender separation most vehemently. He warns Tracy against the perils of miscegenation: "You see, Deen, you have to keep pushing them back across that nigger line. Keep pushing! . . . Kind of like it is with a dog. You have a dog, seems right human. More sense than most men. . . . But he's still a dog. You don't forget that. And you don't forget the other. . . . [I]t's the same" (88). The preacher is similarly adamant about the importance of separating men's and women's worlds: "[W]hen a man gets over into a woman's world, he gets into bad trouble. He don't belong there. . . . God wants your soul where it belongs, for then He'll be surer of getting it than if it was on the other side—where some woman'll get it all. . . . Too much love makes you soft. No-count! Tying you to a woman's apron strings!" (90).

Confronted with these rigid, theologically enforced categories, Tracy, who has "pushed the South from him as he went through it, pushed everything he had ever known or feared or hated or believed in, away from him" during his time in the military, sees Nonnie as his escape to a world beyond the race line: when he is with her he feels "glad to be back in a world where nothing was ordered as in white Maxwell" (135).

Tracy envisions Nonnie as antithetical not only to the overarching race and gender divisions that govern Maxwell but to the seemingly sexless white women who seem to him to control his destiny in a rigid and resented matriarchy. White women, for Smith, epitomize the old Southern order that simultaneously worshiped and repressed them. Tracy's mother, Alma, becomes an archetype of the sexless, smothering mother: "She had been a good wife to Tut, submitting to his embraces quietly, without protest—though that part of marriage seemed to Alma a little unclean and definitely uncomfortable" (77). Alma exemplifies the rigid categories that the preacher describes in her relationships with her children. She recalls beating Tracy for "playing Africa" with Henry as a child, outraged at his nakedness, his race-play, and his "stubborn silence, his refusal to admit her rightness" (70). Further, her aversion to sexuality becomes particularly pronounced as she finds her daughter Laura's clay figure, sculpted under the tutelage of the woman with whom Laura has a vague lesbian relationship. Smith's description of the moment of discovery brings together several troublesome ambiguities and outrages to Alma's sensibilities: "She found it in Laura's drawer, wrapped in a wet cloth. Uncovered, it lay in her hand, urgent, damp, like something in gestation. A lump of wet dirt" (67). While Alma's discomfort at the sexualized "lump of wet dirt" evokes the swamp's symbolic mixture of water and land in its own right, the more telling detail is her connection of the sculpture with "something in gestation," not only evoking a general nascent subversion in the still-maturing Laura but undeniably conjuring an image of the baby growing in Nonnie's womb, the embodiment of transgression of racial and sexual boundaries, a gestating anathema to the Maxwell status quo. Smith underscores Alma's conflation of Laura's troublesome, emerging sexuality with Tracy's own actions: "And now as she sat in Laura's room, holding the little clay torso, a hideous thought swept through her mind. *Tracy is destroying Laura*" (70). Alma's compulsive, violent reaction strikes out at both of her children's threat to her obsessively maintained ideal of order. In destroying the clay torso, Alma performs a symbolic abortion, destroying the fetal sculpture even as the town would destroy the tangible expression of Tracy's transgression. Having carried out this prescient purgation, Alma collects herself—"carefully adjust[ing] her broad-brimmed white hat, carefully powder[ing] her nose, smooth[ing] her heavy black eyebrows while gray eyes looked steadily back at her from the mirror" (71)—and goes immediately to church.

The church becomes the center of the white female matriarchy that Tracy perceives as "ruling the town. White goddesses" (195). And yet it also becomes, in the revival scene, the chief element that fans the flames of their fear of losing control. The traditional sheltering of white women from the "man's world" has taken root in Alma and the other white women in Maxwell as a willful ignorance, a tacit denial of facts beyond their control. As the preacher addresses his all-female congregation in the revival tent, Smith underscores the connection of the swamp with all that lies beyond the easy and unexamined categories that govern the women's intentionally limited perception of their world. He asks the women where their husbands, their sons are—where they go at night, and the women's unease clearly evokes the surrounding swamps: "In the quick stillness the croak of frogs came through the tent, bringing the night. Darkness fell on the hearts of the women of Maxwell. Dread of knowledge seeped about their ignorance of their men's lives like cold swamp water, straining complacency, chilling sheltered spirits. And they were afraid. Where were they tonight? They did not know. They had never known. Like their knowledge of the Nigger Quarters, they knew of their men's lives only that which came into their homes. They did not want to know more" (309). The swamp, for the white women of Maxwell, evokes all that lies outside their intentionally circumscribed female world—an idea that governs, with tragic results, Tracy Deen's understanding both of the swamp and of his relationship with Nonnie.

Tracy's tendency to essentialize Nonnie's sexuality as primal, visceral, and uncomplicated has clear roots in an earlier trend in modern Southern literary depictions of African American women. The foremost examples of this trend lie in the novels of Julia Peterkin, a white Southern woman who presented primitivist depictions of Southern black folk culture in a series of novels, the most famous of which is the Pulitzer Prize–winning *Scarlet Sister Mary* (1928). Peterkin, by her own admission, lived vicariously through the sexually open and polygamous black women she observed. As Susan Millar Williams says in *A Devil and a Good Woman, Too: The Lives of Julia Peterkin* (1997), "The black women Peterkin knew pursued their lovers openly and changed them at will. . . . They spoke openly about their feelings of lust, jealousy, and betrayal, subjects forbidden to genteel white women" (xii). She wrote to Mencken in 1921 that "I envy them, and I guess as I cannot be them, I seek satisfaction in trying to record them" (qtd. in Williams xii).

Scarlet Sister Mary tells the story of a young black girl on a plantation who exults in her body and emergent sexuality but struggles with ideas of sin. Mary becomes pregnant by her fiancé and is accused by her relatives of "scarlet sin"—the novel's title reflects the contradictory forces of that sin and her membership in the church. Mary's husband leaves her, and she is thrown out of the church, and eventually she rejects the church's values and has eight more children by different fathers with the help of a voodoo love charm. Peterkin clearly situates the vibrant, fertile, and sexual Mary as more viscerally alive, more in tune with nature than the members of the church she rejects as she returns, pregnant again, to face the church members: "Face to face with that group of failing black women, some of them fat, some of them shriveled, she felt young, firm-bodied, a part of the fresh outside day. The church was cold with a damp chilly smell, but the blood in her veins rippled warm now. Life burned bright within her, making her feel young, strong, and light on her feet in spite of the troublesome burden she carried" (255). At the novel's close, Mary has a moment of revelation and redemption, in which she prays to God to forgive her for each of her babies born in sin, presented as scarlet streaks on a white cloth that fade one by one as she prays over them. She returns to the church and receives a second baptism but will not surrender her love charm: "I'll lend em to you when you need em, Daddy, but I couldn' gi way my love-charm. E's all I got now to keep me young" (345). Peterkin represents Mary's sexuality as fundamental and life giving, free of the artificial restrictions of the church and without real consequence: Mary's ever-growing family is rarely the source of any trouble for the impoverished single mother. Peterkin's widely read and praised novel presents Southern black female sexuality as simple, naive, and life affirming, essential and elemental.

Though Peterkin conceived of *Scarlet Sister Mary* as a vicarious means of empowerment through free and open sexuality, Smith examines the detrimental dimension of the stereotype of the sexually free and insatiable African American woman when transferred from Peterkin's all black world into the racially mixed American South. Tracy Deen, in his intermingled associations of the swamp and Nonnie's sexuality, is tempted by the same kinds of assumptions that drive

Peterkin's text. Tracy's conception of the swamp embodies the novel's central, ironic tragedy: in imagining that Nonnie represents pure escape from the social order he so resents, he only underscores the system of easy categorization that he so violently rejects in the white South. He conflates Nonnie and the swamp repeatedly as the novel progresses. While he undeniably loves her, after a fashion, he turns to her most often in frustrated response to the culture he wants to escape, and thus inevitably conceives of her in terms determined by that culture. For all his fervent desire to escape the categorical thinking that binds Southern society, Tracy's inability to escape his training becomes clear early on, as he reacts powerfully to the disruption of cherished racial lines after a conversation with a black reverend and his wife: "In the old world, that would have been all. They would have gone on to Negro Quarters, to be forgotten, and he would have stayed in White Town, forgetting. . . . But that was not all. As they stood there, between the speaking and the turning away, Tracy felt as if the blood were draining from his veins" (59). The abrupt reassertion of categorical thinking, even very early in the novel, threatens to ruin his relationship with Nonnie: "All he knew was that thirty minutes ago he had been with the woman he loved. Now there was a colored girl named Nonnie. That was all there was to it" (59).

As the novel progresses, Tracy's understanding of his relationship with Nonnie vacillates between the "woman's world" of love and affection and the masculine drive to escape the categories of a feminized church and culture. The swamp in turn vacillates between a place of intuitive connection, as it is for Nonnie, and a space for sexual rebellion, as it is for the women in the revival tent. The times that Tracy most explicitly conceives of Nonnie in terms of the swamp come in response to his frustrated rage toward white Southern womanhood, embodied most acutely in Dottie, his eventual fiancée, a woman with "beliefs as defined as a row of little upright wires" (46). Dottie represents for Tracy the antithesis of Nonnie, whom he idealizes as free from the rigidity of white Southern culture. He imagines Dottie "in her bed, cool, clean, composed, all of her life completely contained in the rigid little box which shut the right way to do things away from the wrong. . . . Yes, she knew the rules and wanted them kept. Simple to her as a recipe for making cake or peach pickle, and to be followed as carefully" (42–43). Tracy's derision toward Dottie expands, as the novel progresses, to encompass white women in general—"all the white women in the world. Yeah, they tie their love around you like a little thin wire and pull, keep pulling until they cut you in two. That's what they do. . . . Pure as snow—dole out a little of their body to you—just

a little—see—it's poison—you can't take but a few drops—don't be greedy—
do as I tell you" (195). Rigid, sexless, and controlling, white women come to
embody all that Tracy wants to rebel against.

Tracy's conception of Nonnie's sexuality comes as a clear response to his
resentment of white women. He conceives of her less as a person than as an
antidote to Southern gentility. He muses that "whatever he wanted she would
give him. That was Non. Her body—or a drink of water. It'd all be the same.
And she'd give it like a swamp bay lets you smell its sweetness. Just as simply"
(147). He is struck by Nonnie's apparent connection with nature, by the
untroubled way that she interacts with it: "A piece of moss had fallen from the
limb above them on her breast, and she had let it rest there. Any other girl
would have jumped or exclaimed or thrown it off. But Nonnie let it rest there.
Easy" (92). Tracy essentializes Nonnie, evoking the tropic image of the swamp
as a place of escape and of luxurious bounty. Her importance for him becomes
all that she is not. While white women control, Nonnie does not; she serves.
While white women withhold sexuality, Nonnie does not; she gives freely. While
white women are frigid, Nonnie is not; she is passionate. Nonnie's understanding links their relationship to the swamp in its compelling allure and its troubling uncertainty; Tracy sees Nonnie as a sweet swamp bay into which he can
escape, alluring primarily on the terms of the society that imparts its subversive
identity.

The nature of Nonnie and Tracy's relationship becomes clear as the two
make love on the bluff, overlooking the water at the edge of the swamp. The
bluff's surroundings are steeped in the beauty of the swamp, and Tracy imagines them in a romanticized, uncivilized space that delivers them from oppress-
ing cultural categories—"brown water swirling below you, sky paled out by the
moon above you, great oaks with sagging moss draping your nakedness, hiding
you from the world, you could think that word [negro] without getting sick at
your stomach. You could say it, say Nonnie's name after it, and still believe in
her and yourself. The world's wrong, you could say. Dead wrong" (95). And yet,
the escape from social categories in this quasi-wild space is illusory. The bluff,
a lime cliff overlooking the river and the swamp beyond, "belonged to white
folks and every nigger in the county knew it" (95). The bluff mirrors Tracy's
relationship with Nonnie: it is a place of temporary escape, a sheltered region
that provides a view of the swamp's beauty from a slight remove but remains
firmly designated as a white-owned space. Much as Tracy might wish to characterize his bringing Nonnie there as a transgression, he is ultimately exercising

his culturally given prerogative as a privileged white man—a role that he eventually assumes more thoroughly with fatal results.

The novel's close, with the burning of Henry as brutal ceremonial restoration of order after Tracy's murder, is Smith's testament to the failure of the swamp in all its forms in the face of a still-determined Southern culture. Henry's execution, like Alma's earlier burning of Laura's art book, is a cleansing by fire of the element that upset the town's order. Even as Tracy's act of "giving" Nonnie to Henry heralds the destruction of the swamp as a place of escape from Southern culture by the cruel reassertion of old cultural categories, Henry's execution exorcizes the ambiguity—the "cold swamp water"—inherent in the racial outrage of a white man's murder. The novel's closing passage communicates Nonnie's perception of the town in the aftermath of the violence: "The swamp was in deep shadow behind them. . . . Around the curve of the cemetery, past Miss Ada's old house, the town lay. The streets would be in full sunshine by the time they got to their kitchen doors. And Dan would be delivering ice. . . . Everything would be the same—as it always was" (371). The novel ends with the victory of tradition over ambiguity, the restoration of order that throws the subversive swamp into deep shadow.

Though *Strange Fruit* met with great success outside the South, becoming a bestseller and attaining sufficient notoriety to be banned in Boston, subsequent Southern and national reaction against Smith's more directly polemical later nonfiction work *Killers of the Dream* (1949) led to a swift drop-off in popularity and critical attention that, as Margaret Rose Gladney claims, led to Smith's being "effectively silenced as a writer" (4). As Joel Williamson points out, the response to Smith in her community evinced a similar drive to maintain pure categories by purging anomaly. Smith's radical views about race and sexuality, as well as the "obscenity" seized upon by some critics as the novel's central flaw (a position that Smith regarded as a "smoke screen" for the novel's real issues), were "very frustrating to the racially conservative South because Lillian Smith was so very much and undeniably Southern, and a Southern Christian lady at that" (138). So, Williamson says, the dominant white Southern culture found an alternative way to disarm her disruption of the accepted order and to assimilate her into their paradigm: "The Southern white mind did what it always does when forced to cope with a persistent irritant; it lacquered her over as the oyster does the intruding grain of sand and made of her a pearl. The pearl is alien to the body, but it is made smooth and round and beautiful . . . and, other than being there and occupying a space, it has nothing to do with the body.

The rhetoric ran that 'Miss Lil' was a 'deeply Christian woman,' a fine lady, and the book was something that the Yankees made. Really, people meant, she didn't do it, and it had never happened" (138). By isolating Smith's works from Smith herself, the dominant "Southern white mind" was able to quarantine the hazardous elements in Smith's character while preserving the myth of Southern Christian white womanhood. The process evokes Mary Douglas's description of the first cultural method of dealing with the problem of ambiguity threatening cherished cultural divisions—declaring them sufficiently rare and uncharacteristic that they pose no actual threat. Smith's novel and, in a sense, her life indicate that however threatened Southern culture may have been in midcentury, the swamp's ambiguity had lost much of its power. The swamp and all its tropes had ceased to be unassimilable elements; Smith's *Strange Fruit* ultimately attests to the ways that any ambiguity could and must be ritualistically purged from traditional white Southern society.

As the widely acknowledged exemplar of modern Southern canonicity, William Faulkner clearly stands apart from the "problematic Southernness" of Hurston and Smith; however, his late work *Go Down, Moses* (1942) centers on exactly the question that each of those authors treats: the viability of the swamp as a space for life outside the shaping forces of culture. Like Hurston and Smith, Faulkner interrogates in *Go Down, Moses* the surviving status of the mythic and actual swamp as a place resistant to, and free of, Southern culture—the survival of the tropic nineteenth-century swamp in the modern era. Faulkner depicts the swamp, both as the broad region he calls the Mississippi bottomland and as a specific, mystical space within, as part of an alternative Southern culture, removed to some uncertain degree from white plantation culture. There, the heirs of Southern gentility concede their status to mixed-race societal outcasts, and the rigid Southern caste structure seems to fade in the face of the alternative, sacred lineage of the hunt. The wilderness, the parts of the Southern landscape that have more or less escaped inclusion in Southern society, seems to offer the protagonist Ike McCaslin the possibility of moral regeneration, of freedom from the "original sin" of land ownership and the family legacy that haunts him. Ultimately, Faulkner deconstructs the swamp's mythic potential, both in the traditional sense that held it as always beyond the reach of Southern society and in the more modern formulation that posited it as a corrective to cultural sin and escape from social order. For Faulkner, the swamp is a myth that does not so much die with the land that is "deswamped and denuded and derivered in two generations" (347) as it meets with the revelation that it was never really fact but a noble, self-deluding, Quixotic fiction.

More directly than Hurston or Smith, Faulkner addresses the physical transformation of the Southern landscape and intersects somewhat with the environmental consciousness nascent at the time he composed *Go Down, Moses*. For this reason, two great temptations confront the critic who considers any questions of nature and culture in the novel, both of which stem partially from a conflation of Ike McCaslin's perspective and voice with Faulkner's.

The first, and most recent, temptation is to use the elevation of nature in *Go Down, Moses* to paint Faulkner as a protoenvironmentalist—a claim that Judith Wittenberg explores perceptively in "*Go Down, Moses* and the Discourse of Environmentalism" (1996). Wittenberg situates the novel as protoecological by pointing out its resonances with Thoreau's *Walden*: "Central elements of *Walden* occur, *mutatis mutandis*, in *Go Down, Moses*: the concepts that in the wilderness one confronts 'only the essential facts of life' and is able to respond simply and meaningfully; that ownership of property is a deleterious, and 'imprisoning' state" (54). To Wittenberg's credit, these elements are all undeniably present in Faulkner's novel. She further compares the perspectives on nature in *Go Down, Moses* to those in environmentalist pioneer Aldo Leopold's 1948 work, *A Sand County Almanac*. stating that both "evolved from a more general and increasingly well articulated discussion of environmental issues" and that Faulkner's work parallels that of ecologists like Leopold in that both embrace the idea of "the network"—a proto-poststructuralist idea, evident in the works of theorists such as Lacan, Derrida, and Foucault, that "[critiques] the dominant structures of Western culture such as the idea of an authoritative locus of hierarchical meaning or of the human being as either central or centered" (52–53). In other words, *Go Down, Moses*, in Ike's rejection of concepts of man's dominion over nature and of the fundamental idea of land ownership, shifts the focus from man in nature to man as a part—and perhaps a peripheral part—of a larger biotic community. However, unlike his predecessor Thoreau and his contemporary Leopold, who claimed that land could survive only if we "see land as a community to which we belong" and "begin to use it with love and respect" (xviii–xix), Faulkner tells an essentially fatalistic tale—his wilderness is doomed, as are human efforts to find refuge within from cultural determinism. Further, as Wittenberg does acknowledge, Faulkner was more concerned with society and culture—with human relationships and racial interaction—than he was with what she calls the "biotic community." While Faulkner's clear and acute consciousness of the ecological tragedy that the South was undergoing is evident throughout *Go Down, Moses*, one cannot read the story of Ike McCaslin as an earnest vehicle for ecological protest, or as primarily an endorsement of a less human-centered conception of the natural world. Rather, Faulkner uses Ike and his developing, tortured philosophy to depict the impossibility of a redemptive, wilderness-centered fiction as a viable alternative to a morally flawed Southern culture. Ike's perspective, not Faulkner's, conflates Thoreau and Leopold to essay a relationship with nature free of cultural influence: *Go Down, Moses*, in large part, is about the impossibility of nature outside of culture in the South.

The older of the two critical temptations can be used to illuminate the flaws of the newer: the common reading of the "core" of *Go Down, Moses*—"The Old People," "The Bear," and "Delta Autumn"—as a "Romance of the American wilderness after the manner of Cooper, Hawthorne, and Melville," as John Pilkington puts it in his 1977 article "Nature's Legacy to William Faulkner" (104). In claiming the novel's place in this tradition, Pilkington points to the theme of initiation, the elevation of the Indian, the general mythologization of the wilderness, and the sympathy for its end that run through that section of the novel. All of these characteristics are undeniably present in *Go Down, Moses*, and acutely so in "The Bear" when read alone as short story—particularly if one excises section 4, as Faulkner himself advised for those reading it that way. Even so, when one steps back from Ike's perspective and considers the novel as a whole, each of these factors is eventually compromised. Although Faulkner is clearly sympathetic to the process of mythmaking that carries the trappings of traditional American wilderness romance, *Go Down, Moses,* as I will show, is finally about the recognition of that myth's falsity, of the failure of Ike's and Sam Fathers's attempts to purge the tainted blood of their heredity and to replace it with the sanctified blood of the wilderness. Faulkner's representations of the wilderness are indeed, as Lawrence Buell points out in "Faulkner and the Claims of the Natural World" (1996), always filtered through the literary—"[s]tock romantic imagery of pastoral retreat from Andrew Marvell to A. E. Houseman, American masculinist wilderness narrative from Cooper to Melville and Twain" (3)—but not unconsciously or haphazardly so. Faulkner constructs his narrative around the interplay of idealizing fictions and unromantic reality, displaying an acute consciousness not only of the conventions he evokes but of their ultimate inadequacy in enabling Ike to forge a new identity. Thus, *Go Down, Moses* is less about the destruction of the physical swamp than it is about the possibility or impossibility of a nature imbued with fictional significance as corrective to the South's "original sin."

Donald Kartiganer's discussion of the place for consideration of nature within larger modernist movements puts Faulkner's evocations of the natural world in clearer perspective. In his introduction to *Faulkner and the Natural World* (1996), Kartiganer explains that consideration of nature as physical fact runs counter to the modernist project as conceived under the influence of the French Symbolists, who believed that "the task of art is not to record and report a merely visible reality, but to discover a reality normally inaccessible to us: one we can reach, presumably, only by freeing ourselves from what is palpably before us" (viii). Kartiganer builds on this assertion in discussing the New Criticism and its role in promulgating Symbolist tenets and claims that "for a criticism preoccupied with the contextual production not only of meaning but being, any naturalist attempt to entertain an 'essentialist' reality is little less than high treason. . . . Every imaginative conception of nature is just that, an *imagined* perspective that cannot help but reflect the culturally informed mind that is its source" (xx). Though Kartiganer offers this conclusion in foregrounding the complexity and problems of considering the place of physical nature in Faulkner's essentially modernist work, the latter part—the assertion that any imagined conceptions of nature "cannot help but reflect the culturally informed mind that is its source"—can just as easily serve as an epitaph for Ike's idealistic quest to redefine himself and his world in a manner that both tangibly and intangibly rebukes his lineage.

David Evans correctly asserts in his essay " 'The Bear' and the Incarnation of America" (1996) that the story "is really about the *invention* of nature or, more accurately, about the way in which the principal character, Ike McCaslin, defines a natural world in order to invest it with a special significance" (180). Adding that Ike believes that nature is not so much the place of good as the place of *truth*, Evans argues that Ike's viewpoint reflects a trend in American imagination of seeking truth in places ostensibly untouched by the "fictions" of culture. I will show that "The Bear" and *Go Down, Moses* in general critique this exact trend in a Southern context. Faulkner presents us with a regenerated swamp, in much the same way that Hurston does—to Ike, at least, it is a place outside of time, of respite from both past and future. Ultimately, though, Faulkner reveals that both are inevitable, and that Ike's imaginative construction of the swamp—his own manifestation of the modernist approach to nature—must ultimately give way to an unromantic, postmodern iconoclasm.

The characteristics of American literary convention in the novel's depiction of the wilderness that Pilkington observes—elevation of the Indian, sacred initiation, and mythologization—all become profoundly troubled and undermined as Ike's story progresses. Faulkner's construction of the wilderness in general, and the swamp in particular, ultimately anticipates Jean Baudrillard more than it echoes Mallarmé—particularly at the central moment of Old Ben's death, when the Immortal Spirit of the Wilderness is revealed as a surprisingly small, crippled bear. Baudrillard warns in *Simulacra and Simulation* (1981) that "it is dangerous to unmask images, since they dissimulate the fact that there is nothing behind them" (5)—a statement that embodies the essence of Ike's hunt in "The Bear."

In *Simulacra and Simulation*, Baudrillard poses an essential question about the nature of spirituality in a world of simulacra: "[W]hat if God himself can be simulated, that is to say can be reduced to the signs that constitute faith? Then the whole system becomes weightless, it is no longer itself anything but a gigantic simulacrum—not unreal, but a simulacrum, that is to say never exchanged for the real, but exchanged for itself, in an uninterrupted circuit without reference or circumference" (5–6). This, ultimately, is the fate of the hunt, the "yearly pageant-rite of the bear's furious immortality," once that very immortality is proven spurious and the sanctity of the hunt its own self-perpetuating creation. *Go Down, Moses*, in a sense, moves from a modernist to a postmodernist perspective, revealing Ike's conceptions of the wilderness as the locus of purity and truth as artifacts, created images revealed in their emptiness, stripping the mythologized swamp of significance even as industry destroys its empirical counterpart.

In this context, the swamp, though not referred to as such except in a few key instances, becomes crucial to Faulkner's project. As Vileisis recounts, the fledgling environmentalist movement in the mid-twentieth century recognized the need for new nomenclature in arguing for wetland preservation as ecological consciousness began to outstrip superstition: "In the 1950s, ecologists coined the term *wetland* to replace the imprecise and value-laden *swamp*" (7). Faulkner shows similar motivations in describing the Mississippi wilderness as "bottomland"; still, his descriptions of the camp "set on stilts above the spring high water," of the "earth which never completely dried" (197), and of the "swampers" whose claim to be present at the eventual bear hunt seems more valid than that of the later spectators leaves little doubt that we are in the swamp. Faulkner takes full advantage of the swamp's status as virtually the only element of the Southern landscape that historically defied inclusion in the Southern narrative of identity and interrogates the survival of that renegade status and its implicit potential for personal redefinition. Faulkner's rehabilitation of the swamp follows that of Hurston in that he posits it, certainly in Ike's myth-centered mind but also on his own terms, not as a source of corruption or pollution but as a place that has itself been corrupted by white Southern society. He has elsewhere described a "[g]host of ravishment that lingers in the land" and claimed that "the land is inimical to the white man because of the unjust way in which it was taken from [the Indians]" (*Faulkner in the University* 43). This injustice is the central "sin" against which both Sam Fathers and Ike strive in attempting to redefine their lineage, and thus identity, by a kind of metaphysical transfusion, replacing the tainted blood in their veins with the ostensibly pure blood of the wilderness.

The problem of heredity, and more specifically of blood, runs throughout the "core" of *Go Down, Moses*—the thematically unified stories "The Old People," "The Bear," and "Delta Autumn." I will focus on these stories throughout my discussion, in part because they deal most directly with Faulkner's use of the swamp and in part because I follow John T. Matthews's claim in *The Play of Faulkner's Language* (1982) that the first three stories are a kind of parodic prelude that "contaminates the rituals of the wilderness so as to demystify their content and emphasize their structure as statements" (218–19). Sam Fathers, whose mixed blood and intuitive understanding of the wilderness form an analogue with John Pearson, another racially mixed character who finds brief but doomed sanctuary in the swamp, becomes Ike's spiritual guide in his search for moral regeneration and for an alternative lineage outside of Southern civilization—however, as "The Old People" reveals, he is a troublesome guide. McCaslin Edmonds tells Ike that Sam "was born in a cage and has been in it all his life," imprisoned by the fact that he was "betrayed, the blood of the warriors and chiefs had been betrayed. . . . Not betrayed by the black blood and not willfully betrayed by his mother, but betrayed by her all the same, who bequeathed him not only the blood of slaves but even a little of the very blood which had enslaved it; himself his own battleground, the scene of his own vanquishment and the mausoleum of his defeat" (161–62). That Sam Fathers, imprisoned in a cage of tainted blood, performs Ike's symbolic baptism in the ways of the wilderness, "[marking] his face with the hot blood which he had spilled and he ceased to be a child and became a hunter and a man" (171), provides an ironic foreshadowing of the inescapable flaw that undermines both men's attempts to replace the blood of their fathers with the blood of the wilderness. Ike's new catechism is corrupt from the outset, his "novitiate to the true wilderness" undermined by the inescapable legacies carried by both teacher and pupil.

Faulkner's only direct, significant evocation of the swamp as a specific, value-laden term comes at the apex of Ike's mythic creation of a sanctified and deified wilderness. Ike's most dramatic spiritual experience, his face-to-face encounter with Old Ben in the heart of the wilderness, a space that he can only find after leaving the physical tools of mapping and mastering time, place, and the wilderness—his watch, compass, and gun—is also the only time that Faulkner makes significant use of specific swamp terminology and swamp terrain: "[A]nd beyond the log a little swamp, a seepage of moisture somewhere between earth and water, and he did what Sam had coached and drilled him as the next and the last, seeing as he sat down on the log the crooked print, the warped indentation in the wet ground which while he looked at it continued to fill with water until it was level full and the water began to overflow and the sides of the print began to dissolve away" (200). In this scene, and in Ike's subsequent encounter with a strangely mystical and inchoate vision of Old Ben, "dimensionless against the dappled obscurity" (200), Faulkner makes full use of the rhetorical clout with which centuries of Southern literature and folklore have invested the swamp: it is a place of uncertainty, of indefinite mixture of water and land, a place where tracks vanish through force of the land itself, and where Old Ben himself seemingly vanishes after their brief and silent meeting. This center of the wild, the swamp, is the place where Ike's goal of renouncing society and entering into a new, spiritual lineage seems most attainable—the space least touched by humanity and its conventions. And yet, Faulkner effectively evokes the swamp's liminality at the same time, undercutting the truth and permanence that Old Ben is supposed to exemplify, as first his tracks and then the bear himself fade almost as soon as Ike perceives them. The swamp as mystic, untouchable space embodies the heart of the myth that Ike and Sam Fathers want so desperately to adopt—and yet, the permanence and transcendence they imagine it holds are doomed to fade, not in the mythic, fatalistic end to the grand pageant-rite that Ike imagines but with an abrupt and ugly vanishing that belies that they ever truly existed.

The final hunt for Old Ben represents a gradual deconstruction of the almost sacramental experience that Ike and Sam Fathers anticipate it will be. Ike has come to understand and justify his part in what his mythic symbology has built up to be the destruction of the "wild immortal spirit" of the wilderness as part of an inevitable and almost holy plan to be carried out by archetypal figures whose roles are preordained: he and Sam Fathers know immediately that the mongrel Lion will be the dog who brings down Old Ben, and the entire endeavor, once the hunt has moved from a "pageant-rite of the old bear's furious immortality" (186) into its final progression toward Old Ben's death, becomes to Ike "like the last act on a set stage" (216)—a tale already written that his initiation has made him worthy to witness in humility and pride.

From the time that Ike expresses this literary vision of its end, the hunt begins slowly to degrade. Ike's trip into town with Boon marks the beginning of the hunt's demystification. Frustrated with the drunken Boon, Ike decides that he must have no part in Old Ben's death: "It would not be Boon. He had never hit anything bigger than a squirrel that anybody ever knew, except the negro woman that day when he was shooting at the negro man" (225). Faulkner underscores Boon's unworthiness as he imagines a trivialized, domesticated spectacle in place of the supposedly mystical hunt to come: "Then they would take the first train back to camp, get Lion and come back to the zoo where, he said, the bears were fed on ice cream and lady fingers and he would match Lion against them all" (225). Boon's sacrilegious vision, though, represents only the logical end of the spectacle that the hunt has already threatened to become. Spectators, drawn by news of Lion, have already begun to join the hunting party. The first among them have some claim in Ike's understanding: they are "swampers: gaunt, malaria-ridden men appearing from nowhere," part, in a sense, of the same mythic wilderness that Old Ben embodies—Major DeSpain even concedes that "[h]e's more your bear than ours" (213). The very act of DeSpain's granting the men permission to shoot the bear if they encounter him, though, begins a domestication of the hunt, imposing a hierarchy of permissor and permitted that runs sharply counter to Ike's idealistic conception of the wilderness as beyond rules of ownership and social order. Following this first invitation, other guests, far less justifiable by Ike's mythic understanding of the hunt's significance, come to the camp: "a dozen strangers . . . not all swampers this time. Some of them were townsmen, from other county seats like Jefferson, who had heard about Lion and Old Ben and had come to watch the great blue dog keep his yearly rendezvous with the old two-toed bear. Some of them didn't even have guns and the hunting-clothes and boots they wore had been on a store shelf yesterday" (215). Whatever sanctity the hunt may have had fades with the arrival of the outsiders; the hunt as spectacle, presented for those who are not even hunters themselves, undermines Ike's idea that he "[has] been found worthy to be a part of it too or even just to see it too" (217).

The scene of Old Ben's death becomes a moment of dramatic disillusionment for the reader seduced by Ike's perspective. Rather than enacting a scripted ending to some cosmic play, as Ike has imagined it, the scene is singularly awkward and ugly. Old Ben, removed from the mythic space at the heart of the swamp where Ike perceived him as a mystical "apotheosis," proves to be only a larger-than-average bear, capable of enormous violence but eminently mortal. The manner of Old Ben's death—essentially caught in a trap between Lion's mechanistic worrying of his throat and Boon, the one that Ike claimed could never be the one to bring Old Ben down, driving his knife into his back—can fit no poetic design or grand narrative. Our final tableau of the hunt presents a dead bear, an eviscerated Lion, a blood-smeared Boon, and Sam Fathers, Ike's spiritual mentor, "lying motionless on his face in the trampled mud" (231).

Old Ben's death is, in essence, a distillation of the moment Baudrillard describes when he claims that "it is dangerous to unmask images, since they dissimulate the fact that there is nothing behind them." The inevitable end of the great pageant, in its antimythic ugliness, undermines the conception of the wilderness that Ike and Sam Fathers have so earnestly constructed. No codes or proprieties govern Old Ben's death—no divine spirit of the wilderness governs his passing. From this point on, *Go Down, Moses* resolves itself in a series of disillusionments, deconstructing Ike's philosophy after revealing the emptiness of the *truth*, to echo Evans's characterization of what Ike ultimately seeks in the wilderness, upon which it is based.

Taken alone, as an autonomous short story without the troublesome fourth section, "The Bear" might still be read as a tragic paean to the vanishing wild wetlands—the degradation of the final hunt as evidence not of the falsity of Ike's mythic conception but of its inevitable demise alongside the wilderness that produced it. Section 5, in particular, seems to underscore this idea, as Ike witnesses the wasteland of the denuded woodlands and confronts the final, cruelly parodic degradation of the hunt—Boon's ranting at the foot of a single tree, full of squirrels with no place to go, and insisting as he pounds his broken gun that they are his. The physical destruction of the wilderness, clearly influenced by Faulkner's observation of the timber industry's "deswamping" of the South over the preceding decades, certainly figures prominently in *Go Down, Moses* and lends some credence to those who perceive the novel to be protoecological.

However, the presence of the fourth section of "The Bear," and of "The Old People" and "Delta Autumn" as the bookends of *Go Down, Moses*'s central "romance," serves primarily to problematize Ike's governing perspective, returning the focus from "the biotic community" to the realities of Southern culture. We have seen that the description in "The Old People" of Sam Fathers's "cage"—the tainted blood that renders him his own battleground, in McCaslin Edmonds's words—troubles the blood baptism that he imparts to Ike in initiating his wilderness novitiate. Section 4 of "The Bear" and the events of "Delta Autumn" further reveal the problems inherent in Ike's understanding and shift the focus of the tragedy from the slow demise of the physical wilderness to the revelation of the empty core of his philosophy. Further, they underscore Faulkner's deconstruction of the elemental purity and power of the swamp as a space removed from cultural influence and as a space of potential escape from the realities of blood lineage and social structure. Vileisis has pointed out that wetlands, since America's inception, have always presented problems to traditional concepts of land ownership: "Traditionally, land has been considered as private property and water as public property—because wetlands are not only land but land *and* water, regarding them simply as real property with no other consideration has been a fundamental error in paradigm" (5–6). In turning to the bottomlands as a refuge from his own rejected birthright, Ike attempts to replace one lineage with another, to distance himself from the original sin of claiming the land as something that could be owned, relying on the land's fundamental resistance to concepts of ownership—however, Faulkner reveals his efforts as heroic failures and, in so doing, belies the remaining subversive power and potential of the Southern swamp.

Section 4 of "The Bear" presents problems for readers for a number of reasons—its complex language, nonlinear progression, and intermittent partial revelations of Ike's family history foremost among them. The most significant and telling difficulty in reading the section, though, comes from the confused inconsistency of Ike's defense of his decision to renounce his patrimony. Ike mounts a defense based on a jumble of biblical references and self-contradictory assertions in an effort to escape the clearer textual facts of the ledgers, which tell him of his inherited guilt, of incest and suicide: "He would never need look at the ledgers again nor did he; the yellowed pages in their fading and implacable succession were as much a part of his consciousness and would remain so forever, as the fact of his own nativity" (269). The confusion of Ike's attempted spiritual and textual defense for his repudiation of what those ledgers have made an inextricable part of his identity becomes evident as McCaslin Edmonds leads Ike to reverse his initial claim that no one may own the land in the first place:

> *"You said how on that instant when Ikkemotubbe realised that he could sell the land to Grandfather, it ceased forever to have been his. All right; go on; Then it belonged to Sam Fathers, old Ikkemotubbe's son. And who inherited it from Sam Fathers, if not you?"*
>
> *"Yes. Sam Fathers set me free." (286)*

Ike's inscrutable response reveals two things: first, that the patrimony he accepts is Sam Fathers's rather than his own father's, and second, that his ideas are based around a central contradiction—the land he has inherited from Sam Fathers sets him free from the corrupt system of land inheritance. Of course, Sam Fathers, the embodiment and source of Ike's freedom, is himself trapped by his patrimony, and Ike's acceptance of McCaslin Edmonds's characterization of his legacy as inheritance of the land reveals his renunciation as essentially semantic. Whether passed through pure or impure lineage, the land, Ike concedes, still belongs to him—and it is that ownership that, he claims, gives him freedom from ownership itself.

Ike's and McCaslin Edmonds's brief discussion of Keats's "Ode on a Grecian Urn" reveals another flaw in Ike's conception of the hunt as untainted by artifice or human influence. When McCaslin Edmonds explains to a puzzled Ike that "he was talking about truth. Truth is one. It doesn't change. It covers all things which touch the heart—honor and pride and pity and justice and courage and love" (283), Ike is ambivalent: "He didn't know. Somehow it had seemed simpler than that, simpler than somebody talking in a book about a young man and a girl he would never need to grieve over. . . . He had heard about an old bear and finally got big enough to hunt it and he hunted it four years and at last met it with a gun in his hands and he didn't shoot" (284). Confronted with a literary construction that embodies his unarticulated emotional conception of the hunt—a poetic invocation of the truth he hoped to find in a space removed from cultural artifice—Ike responds with confusion and uncertainty. The authoritative narration of "The Bear" is suddenly problematized by its poetic precursor and kindred literary sentiment.

The uncertainty introduced in section 4 of "The Bear" is heavily and tragically compounded in "Delta Autumn." Here, a much older Ike reflects back on the blood baptism that was his wilderness initiation: "That day and himself and McCaslin juxtaposed not against the wilderness but against the tamed land, the old wrong and shame itself, in repudiation and denial at least of the land and the wrong and the shame even if he couldn't cure the wrong and eradicate the shame, who at fourteen when he learned of it had believed he could do both when he became competent and when at twenty-one he became competent he knew that he could do neither but at least he could repudiate the wrong and shame, at least in principle, and at least the land itself in fact, for his son at least: and did, thought he had" (334). Ike acknowledges here the troubled nature of his gesture, its slow decline from an attempt to right ancestral wrongs to a repudiation in principle whose limited success even now is an uncertainty. Ike's once vital belief in the purity and regenerative capability of the wilderness—the classic American wilderness myth—has retreated now to a matter of principle, disconnected from the physical and empirical world. And yet "Delta Autumn" reveals the fundamental failure of even that diminished survival of his original intent. Perhaps the greatest condemnation of Ike's efforts comes when the granddaughter of Tennie's Jim blames Ike for the younger Edmonds's moral failings: "I would have made a man of him. He's not a man yet. You spoiled him. You, and Uncle Lucas and Aunt Mollie. But mostly you . . . when you gave to his grandfather that land which didn't belong to him, not even half of it by will or even law" (343). Ike's renunciation of his heritage leads not to the repudiation of shame and guilt for himself and for his nonexistent son but to a compounding of that same guilt for his de facto heir and the suffering of still another woman of color and product of guilty miscegenation. Their parting underscores Ike's realization of the emptiness of his efforts to cling to the alternative lineage of the wilderness as an ameliorative to hereditary guilt. As the woman leaves, Ike reaches out to touch her hand: "He didn't grasp it, he merely touched it—the gnarled, bloodless, bone-light bone-dry old man's fingers touching for a second the smooth young flesh where the strong old blood ran after its long lost journey back to home" (345). Ike's failure is clear in this strange legacy by proxy, as he passes on money that is not his to the child that is not his, bearing blame for her dilemma precisely *because* of his efforts to escape guilt and now, in defeat, deserted by the empty baptism in the blood of the wilderness—"bloodless," touching but not grasping the flesh that bears the blood that should have been his. Had he retained his patrimony, he could have offered her practical help—as it is, he can only give her his hunting horn, the last empty ornament of the heredity he has adopted in place of his birthright.

The meaningless gift of the horn becomes the final stage in the diminution of the sacred hunt—a clear reduction, to echo Baudrillard, of the sacred to the "signs that constitute faith" (5).

I do not mean to suggest, by this reading, that Faulkner is wholly dismissive of Ike's efforts, or that the romanticization of nature and sympathy for its passing that run so strongly throughout *Go Down, Moses* serve merely to underscore Ike's misguided foolishness. Certainly, a writer who has become as synonymous with twentieth-century Southern fiction as Faulkner shows some sympathy for noble, doomed endeavors. Faulkner claimed to read *Don Quixote* every year (*Faulkner in the University* 50)—his sympathy for the deluded idealist is clear in *Go Down, Moses*. Faulkner's novel, rather, provides a sad realization that, with the physical destruction of the wilderness and of the swamp, which was, for the South, the most stubborn survival of the purely wild, comes the revelation that the attendant myths of the wilderness's immortality were not just no longer true but were never true. Where Kennedy, Lanier, and Cable posited the swamp as forever beyond the reach of social construct, with varying judgments of what that status meant, *Go Down, Moses* sounds a death knell for the Southern swamp as a legitimate contender with the forces of Southern culture. The Baudrillardian moment of Old Ben's death, when the mask is stripped away to reveal that it hid only an empty illusion, reveals a postmodern conception of the limits of imagination in constituting meaning, or in finding truth.

Faulkner's affinities with Baudrillard, particularly in his understanding of the fate of the Southern swamp, go beyond *Go Down, Moses*: in *Faulkner in the University*, he describes the fate of Ikkemotubbe's descendants, the remaining people who lived beyond white conceptions of land ownership: "There are a few of them still in Mississippi, but they are a good deal like animals in a zoo: they have no place in the culture, in the economy, unless they become white men, and they have in some cases mixed with white people and their own conditions have vanished, or they have mized with Negroes and they have descended into the Negroes' condition of semi-peonage" (43). Like Baudrillard's Tasaday, doomed to destruction by the encroachment of ethnology, the remaining swamp dwellers are doomed to destruction by the first touch of white culture.

Hurston, Smith, and Faulkner all attest to the ephemerality of purity in the modern Southern swamp. Hurston, emphatically removed from white culture, can envision that purity as a necessary casualty of progress, of the advancement of African Americans, as a tragic loss in the progression toward a greater gain.

Smith and Faulkner, though, depict a final victory for Southern culture in the war begun with William Byrd II's attempts to mark a dividing line through the Great Dismal Swamp: even if it is modernization that destroys the physical swamps, it is the flawed, guilty, but still entrenched specter of white Southern cultural tradition that triumphs over the false myth of the surviving swamp as a space for redemption.

Chapter Four

THE SWAMP IN THE POSTMODERN SOUTH
CONSERVATION, SIMULATION, AND
COMMODIFICATION

In light of the prominent trend in Southern literary modernism of reevaluating the swamp in a more favorable light, one might assume a general shift in attitudes toward swamps in the nation as a whole. Unfortunately, the pattern that has emerged in the previous chapter of representing the swamp as a space for potential escape from both flawed Southern past and encroaching future can be conceived as its own tragic story. The perspectives echoed in the Southern writers' conceptions of the swamp's regenerative possibilities—however pessimistic their conclusions—were originally strictly those of Northerners (with the notable exception of Sidney Lanier). Thoreau's and Bartram's conceptions of the swamps as distillations of an idealized wilderness rather than the impure, threatening spaces represented by antebellum Southern writers are the clearest antecedents of the newly emerging Southern visions of the swamp. Though ecological attitudes toward wetlands in general certainly underwent dramatic changes in the middle part of the twentieth century, the swamps largely retained their negative tropes. Ironically, even as Southern writers recast Bartram's and Thoreau's perspectives in the tragic context of a stifling South, outside representations—particularly in Hollywood films—persisted in reviving the superstitious, viscerally menacing swamps of Southern convention, which proved, of course, much more marketable than images of fragile wilderness.

It is also ironic that, even as H. L. Mencken and W. J. Cash were blasting Souths old and new in their influential writings, Hollywood was busily romanticizing, sanitizing, and sanctifying the plantation South for popular consumption. The 1939 release of *Gone with the Wind*, perhaps the most influential representation of the American South in the twentieth century, and its legion of less-noted precursors and ubiquitous imitators largely redefined the nation's conception of the antebellum South. Edward D. C. Campbell, in his 1981 study *The Celluloid South: Hollywood and the Southern Myth*, explains that in the late 1930s and early 1940s "plantation stories were good business, attracting Academy Awards and, most importantly, customers" (23). Campbell explains the power and impact that film representations of an imagined South have exerted over popular understanding: "Throughout most of their history, the movies presented the mythology of a culture of economic and social units of at least a hundred blacks, an overseer, grand surroundings, and a life of ease. . . . The South was a section more oriented to dirt farming and land clearing with the help of only the immediate family. The impact of a film mythology accepted by several generations which so completely alters that fact has been enormous" (28). As Hollywood aggrandized the plantation South's physical and economic conditions, it de-emphasized social inequalities and slavery. Until the birth of the civil rights movement in the late 1950s, Campbell explains, "film versions of the slave South functioned far more as agents of reinforcement than as agents for change. . . . Although there were subtle hints . . . that the mythology of the happy slave was at least wearing thin, overall the movies still succumbed to romanticism's clichés" (20). In embracing of an idealized simulacrum of plantation tradition that downplayed its history of racial and social injustice, Hollywood, in a sense, accomplished what antebellum Southern apologists had failed to do—it re-created the defeated Old South as an idealized, chivalric, prosperous place, peopled with dashing gentlemen and demure ladies, maintained by amiable and grateful slaves.

As they recreated the myths underpinning an idealized plantation South, studios proved equally true to Southern aristocratic convention in reviving the image of the Southern swamp as breeding ground for natural and supernatural horrors. Even as Hurston and Faulkner reimagined the swamps in a positive, regenerative light, Hollywood bombarded the public with films about swamp monsters (*Curse of the Swamp Creature* [1966] is a typical example of the B-movie swamp craze, as is 1959's *Attack of the Giant Leeches*), lurid depictions of criminals escaping into hellish, steamy swamps (*Swamp Women* [1955], a

Roger Corman effort, stands out in this genre, as do better-regarded films such as *I Am a Fugitive from a Chain Gang* [1932]), and images of riverboat captains wrestling alligators in forbidding swamp landscapes (1956's *Swamp Fire*, starring Johnny Weissmuller, best known for his portrayals of Tarzan, is a dubious but notable entry in this category). Even after the vogue for romanticized visions of the plantation South passed after World War II, to be replaced by far less flattering depictions of "a postwar South populated by pitifully poor farmers, unrepentant bigots, sadistic rednecks, sex objects, and greedy, ambitious members of a corrupt upper class" (Campbell 143), the swamp retained its vilified status. A new wave of films depicted the swamp-ridden South as its own forbidding hell for the hapless outsider—*Swamp Country* (1966), for example, tells the tale of a California man wrongly accused of murder in a sleepy Southern town who flees a lynch mob into the Okefenokee, where he battles a gamut of serpents and alligators before making his escape. Hollywood, particularly in B movies, perpetuated horrific visions of the Southern swamps, undoing the regenerative work of the Southern novelists discussed in the preceding chapter in spectacularly stereotyped fashion.

While most of the films of the "evil swamp" genre merit only passing notice as part of a larger trend, one in particular bears closer examination: Jean Renoir's *Swamp Water* (1941), adapted from Tennessee writer Vereen Bell's 1940 novel, provides a telling early case study in Hollywood's transformation of the Southern swamp from the sanctified space that it had become in Southern literature to a den of Hollywood horrors.

Bell's novel represents the Okefenokee swamp in a way that essentially echoes the perspective of Ike McCaslin, without Faulkner's mediating skepticism and disillusionment. As Vereen Bell, Jr., claims in his foreword to the 1981 edition, "it is squarely in the mainstream of American fiction that runs through *Huckleberry Finn*, for instance, as far back as the novels of James Fenimore Cooper. . . . In the case of *Swamp Water* the variation is a frank celebration of wildness, both inside and outside human nature, and of the excitement and mystery of contending with it" (xi). The novel tells the story of Ben Ragan, a young man disowned by his father for venturing into the swamp to trap furs. Ben is drawn to the swamp in spite of the folklore that demonizes it: "They said Okefenokee held danger and unspeakable terrors; and yet for Ben it was a place of weird fascination" (6). Searching the swamp for his lost dog, Ben meets the fugitive Tom Keefer, wrongly accused of murdering his wife, who becomes a spiritual mentor similar in many ways to Sam Fathers.

Although the novel does not engage issues of race in any meaningful way, Keefer does claim that his time in the swamps has transformed him, in a kind of essentialist racial osmosis, into an Indian: "Living out here, and messing around in they mounds, I got to where I'm nearly-bout Indian myself" (90). Further, Keefer introduces Ben to a new philosophy, underscoring a kind of blood-deep connection with all living things, removing humanity from the center of existence. He explains his conception of the afterlife to Ben: "They say a dog is dead when he dies, but human folks ain't. I don't see how come that should be. You take that coon yonder, trying to slip off with your cow horn. Ain't he got life in him, just like you? . . . If you got a soul, how come he ain't got one too? . . . How come his life's goan end when I get fed up with his devilment and kill him, if your life ain't goan end when you die?" (106). Keefer's alternative, spiritual vision of the wilderness and of life awakens Ben to civilization's moral failings. Bell contrasts a dramatic scene in which Keefer catches a buck in a bare-handed embrace, only to release it, explaining, "When I don't need the meat, just seems like it's hard to do. Every time I grab one like that, and hold him tight up to me, and feel the life pounding and fighting in him, I just ain't got the heart" (96), with a later scene in which the Dorson brothers, ignorant of Keefer's view of nature, use egrets' concern for their young to kill them: "Suddenly an empty sickness ran through him. The young birds would starve; and there were hundreds of them in the other nests. The adult egrets had forgotten their shyness to return to protect their nests— and meet death" (128). Disgusted with the Dorsons' methods, Ben refuses any of the money that the hunt will bring; Keefer's swamp-born ethics become superior to those of the underhanded but socially accepted Dorsons.

As the novel progresses, Ben finds the swamp increasingly preferable to civilization. At a town festival, Ben finds himself "puzzling over the peace he felt when in the swamp and the strange loneliness that held him now in the midst of the gaiety" (128). Further, he comes to accept Keefer more and more explicitly as his spiritual guide and rejects the judgmental and alienating church. Concerned about the idea of sin, Ben is intimidated at the thought of asking the stern preacher, but "Tom Keefer, now, he had done a sight of thinking about such things, maybe he would know. Ben resolved to ask him, next time he went to the swamp" (132).

True to the American masculinist, wilderness tradition, the swamp's purity becomes pitted against the controlling nature and inherent duplicity of the women in the novel, rendering it a more emphatically masculine realm than do even the all-male hunts of *Go Down, Moses*. Throughout, women react to the swamp with jealousy, fear, and resentment. Hannah, Ben's stepmother, chides her husband for his swamp hunts, threatening that "[s]omeday another . . . I'll pizen them hounds" (12). While Thursday, Ben's father, hunts in the swamp, Hannah begins an affair with the local reprobate Jesse Wick. Mabel, Ben's erstwhile girlfriend, who regards him "possessively" and "acts purely bossified" (18), warns him against the swamp and regards the place with jealousy—that Ben regards the swamp as an escape, in part, from her is clear as he muses on returning from his first long stay in the Okefenokee that he has not thought of her "in days" (47). Further, Tom Keefer owes his fugitive status to a lie told by Katie Wick, Tom's sister and the wife of the man he has killed; although Keefer kills Josiah Wick for abusing Katie, she betrays him, claiming that "Josiah, her husband, had caught Tom stealing a hog, and that Tom had shot him. . . . Tom was her own brother; there had been no call to doubt her word" (216). The novel reaches its misogynist peak, though, as Mabel betrays Ben in a moment of jealousy and tells the townspeople that Ben has been meeting Keefer in the swamp: "Ben watched her with an emotion that was too deep for anger; she had gone out of her way to be treacherous, to break her word. That was the woman in her" (178). The swamp, for Bell, is a space of masculine escape and owes its purity in no small part to its distance from the world of women.

The novel ends, as do most modern treatments of the swamp as escape, tragically: as Keefer attempts to return to civilization and clear his name, the Dorson brothers, whose livestock thefts have been blamed conveniently on the swamp-dwelling fugitive, murder him. Keefer's death sounds the demise of Ben's wilderness-born innocence, and he can react only by running from the scene, directionless.

Considerably less complex and ambivalent than the swamp-centered works of Hurston, Smith, and Faulkner, *Swamp Water* can be considered an archetypal modern reclamation of the Southern swamp: it posits the swamp as a pure space, communion with which renders one ethically superior to the mores of a woman-dominated Southern society, and a space for transcendent connection with all life. The novel's straightforward romanticization of the swamp renders its film adaptation all the more striking in its wholesale revisioning of Bell's central themes.

The creation of the film *Swamp Water* can best be understood as a clash of four perspectives and ideologies, resolved in strictly hierarchical fashion. The conflicting perspectives were those of Bell; Dudley Nichols, the screenwriter, who had previously scripted *Stagecoach*, among other widely respected films; Jean Renoir, the director; and Daryl Zanuck, the producer. These men had widely divergent conceptions of how the film should be made, as Alexander Sesonke points out in his 1982 article "Jean Renoir in Georgia: *Swamp Water*"—the most detailed study of the film's creation. Nichols was the first to recast the story in writing a first draft of the script. Bell had been vague about the time period of his story but wrote to Nichols that he had intended that the story take place in the early 1890s. As Sesonke explains, "Nichols [was] much more concerned about the commercial success of the film than the integrity of the novel" (26). Nichols, believing that "a contemporary story is much more saleable than one set in the past" (qtd. in Sesonke 26), set the film in the present. Thus, the film version began by eliding a half-century of Southern history, feeding into the conception that however grand the plantation South may have been, the contemporary South was culturally stagnant, its society and landscape virtually unchanged in fifty years.

Nichols made a number of other changes, all of which "brought the script more into conformity with the Hollywood formulas of the day" (Sesonke 26), and many of which drastically compromised essential ideas and themes in Bell's novel. Nichols, dedicated to "establishing the menace of the swamp, as a dreaded and avoided background to the human life in the area" (27), opens his screenplay with an eerie and factually shaky invocation, appearing as a written introduction in the film, of the very dangers that Bell so pointedly downplays: "The locale of this story is the Okefenokee swamp in the State of Georgia. Not so many years ago, its seven hundred miles of marsh and cypress were an unknown wilderness to the people who lived around its edges. They knew that its sluggish waters were filled with alligators and that its boggy forests harbored the deadly cottonmouth snake. They feared these creatures, but much more they feared the unexplored vastness in which a man might disappear, never to be seen again." Nichols visualized *Swamp Water* as a vehicle for trope-laden representations of an endless, mysterious swamp, populated by venomous and terrible beasts. His conception of the swamp as such would transform the entire novel, so that the finished product bears little resemblance to Bell's original work.

In keeping with his demonization of the swamp, Nichols introduced a central redemptive character to attest to the values of family and domesticity, and to blunt the novel's antiwoman edge. Nichols created Julie Keefer, Tom's daughter, who becomes the reason that Keefer remains in the hellish swamp rather than trying to escape—the pull of the domestic, rather than the shelter of the swamp, keeps him in Okefenokee. Julie becomes Ben's chief romantic interest, contrasted starkly with the manipulative Mabel: while Mabel uses the threat of infidelity in an attempt to curtail Ben's swamp visits, Julie, despite her initial barefoot, disheveled appearance, becomes a domestic ideal, offering to clean Ben's cabin for him after he tells her of her father's safety and remaining loyal to him throughout. Julie's civilizing influence on Ben is clear: Nichols emphasizes the romance plot, and uses it to foreground positive changes in Ben's behavior. An increasingly domesticated Ben tells Julie at one point, "I never in my life asked for no kiss. I always just took 'em. But dogged it I ain't askin' you now, Julie. Do you mind?" By introducing Julie Keefer, Nichols makes the story of *Swamp Water* as much about Ben's domestication as it is about the sensationalized, menacing swamp. Publicity for the film reflected its distance from Bell's novel: one print ad read, "SWAMP GIRL: For love of her two men braved 700 miles of nameless terror in the strangest, wildest story the screen has ever told" (qtd. in Sesonke 59).

The transformation of *Swamp Water* for the screen owes at least as much to the influence of producer Daryl Zanuck as it does to Nichols's rewrites. Director Jean Renoir, chosen after the first draft of the script was completed, initially saw the film as an opportunity to see "real America." On the eve of his trip to Georgia to research the setting of *Swamp Water*, he wrote to a friend of his in France that "I am going to try to see something besides California, which is a sort of desert, artificially irrigated" (qtd. in Sesonke 28). Upon his arrival, Renoir was struck by the beauty of the swamp, and much impressed with Georgia, which he saw as "primitive" but appealing—"a land where nature is at the same time soft and hostile" (qtd. in Sesonke 30). However, upon visiting the Okefenokee itself, "he found that it had become a National Wild Life Refuge. . . . [H]e saw little resemblance to the dreaded area described in Nichols' script" (Sesonke 31). He wrote to Zanuck to explain that "Okefenokee is now completely explored. Very practical maps have been made of it. . . . In the heart of the swamp I saw a child of ten years fishing all alone, quite peacefully—and this in a place reputed to be the haunt of the very biggest alligators" (qtd. in Sesonke 31). Zanuck's response exemplifies his attitude toward the South and toward concerns about authenticity: "The people who live down in Georgia and know the swamp, which is one out of every five million who will see the picture, will automatically think that the story is laid in a period somewhere about 1895. The general public, who know nothing about Georgia except that it is a land of swamp, will believe that the story takes place in a more or less modern period. I don't think any writing should be changed or details altered because of this" (qtd. in Sesonke 31). Renoir's drive for authenticity met powerful resistance from Zanuck, as Sesonke recounts: "[T]he idea of Renoir actually shooting some scenes in the swamp was met with incredulity. . . . He was told that a perfectly fine swamp would be built in the studio" (31). The studio swamp, augmented with footage of trained alligators rented by Zanuck, serves as the setting for most of *Swamp Water*'s swamp sequences.

Renoir eventually did a small amount of location shooting in the Okefenokee but was accompanied only by Dana Andrews and the dog who played Trouble. Renoir was able to leave some mark on the film, departing from the limited script conceptions of swamp shots to present a series of deep focus shots that created an illusion of endless depth, transforming the environs into a surreal landscape in which Ben Ragan could plausibly become lost. His artistic manipulation of illusion, however, was a great deal removed from his initial hopes of rendering an authentic, sympathetic portrait of the people and landscape of Georgia. Renoir eventually claimed that his work on the film "presents no artistic interest at all," and later wrote to Nichols that "I would rather sell peanuts in Mexico than make films at Fox" (qtd. in Sesonke 54). Renoir was left out of the final editing process, and the film's ending was shot by another director by Zanuck's close instructions.

The product of these various revisions and ideological clashes is fascinating in its strange mix of corn-pone convention and stock horror sensibility, with bits of Bell's novel peeking through at odd and infrequent intervals. The film's opening, after the somber written introduction already quoted above, presents an image of a human skull on a weathered cross protruding from the brackish waters of the swamp. Upon discovering the remains, Eugene Pallette's sheriff character, another Nichols creation, cries out, "Ki-yippety-yi! They was gator-et!" Throughout the film, the swamp is introduced by ominous, threatening music and is surreal and menacing, overgrown and unnavigable except by Walter Brennan's Tom Keefer. Some elements of Bell's Keefer survive in truncated form: he expounds briefly on his ideas of life and afterlife and has a natural resistance to snake bites and other swamp dangers. Still, Keefer's relationship with the swamp is fundamentally different in the film than in the novel—he claims mournfully that "[l]ivin' alone in this swamp's just like livin' on another star" and pines for his lost daughter. When Ben tells him he may be exonerated and allowed to return to society, Tom proclaims jubilantly that "[i]t's like being dead all these years, and now you're telling me to come back to life again." Keefer's quasi-animistic philosophy, so central to Bell's novel, is utterly upended here—the swamp is death; civilization, life.

The film's focus on civilization, without any direct or sustained critique, is also remarkable. The swamp does not appear at all for a forty minute stretch in the middle of the ninety minute film, as Ben's family troubles and his blossoming romance with Julie become the film's chief subject. While individual characters are despicable, the duality of pure swamp and tainted society vanishes, and the film ends with a restoration of family and order.

The ending, in fact, is the most dramatic departure from Bell's work and contains the film's most shameless evocation of menacing, hellish swamp tropes. Almost entirely Zanuck's creation, the ending was shot by Henri Pichel in Renoir's absence. Instead of ending with Keefer's murder on the verge of his return to civilization, the film depicts the swamp's awful vengeance on the villainous Dorson brothers, who have come hunting Keefer and Ben. In a drawn-out and hideous scene, one Dorson brother sinks into a pool of quicksand, devoured by the swamp itself. After disarming the other, Keefer effects the film's most bizarre reversal of the original novel's themes: he literally damns him to existence as a fugitive in a swamp that he now figures as a kind of hell: "That's where you're headin' right now, Tim. If you can learn to live with cottonmouths and gators and panthers and places where there ain't a solid bit of ground to stand on, well, I reckon you're welcome to your life. Now get goin'!" No place of morally pure escape, the swamp becomes a nightmare world of exile and damnation in a remarkable reinscription of antebellum tropes. The film ends by reaffirming the values of community and society, with a tearful Keefer watching Ben and Julie dance together at a town celebration.

In undoing the novel's central tragedy and reasserting nineteenth-century clichés about the swamp and Southern society, the film *Swamp Water* reflects, in a sense, its own tragedy. The movement in Southern literature to reclaim the swamp as the lamentably fading locus of an alternative Southern culture was virtually undone as Hollywood bombarded the public with images of a stagnant South, oddly outside of history, where the old representations of civilized society and uncharted, menacing swamp were still true and relevant.

In de-emphasizing the social critique at the core of the most prominent swamp-focused literary works to present a simulacral, romanticized plantation South, Hollywood also blunted the protoenvironmentalist sentiments informing the works of writers such as Faulkner and Bell. General attitudes about the swamps were slow to change: several decades of irreversible damage would pass

before the conservation movement would make any serious strides towards preserving the vanishing Southern wetlands.

The current climate of ecological awareness, and its attendant valuation of
wetlands as both natural and cultural resources, developed slowly and hesitantly.
The drive to conserve wetlands began as early as the first decade of the twentieth
century, and parts of some Southern swamps—notably the Okefenokee, whose
northern tip became a National Wildlife Refuge in 1936—were converted to
national parks and wildlife preserves even before writers such as Faulkner and
Bell redeemed the swamps in literature. The ideology of the gentleman's dominance over nature so strong in Southern culture long mitigated against ecological consciousness. From its early origins in the works of Emerson and Thoreau,
the environmental movement has been philosophically at odds with the
Cavalier underpinnings of traditional Southern agrarian philosophy. In *Silent
Spring* (1962), a book exposing the dangers of pesticides to humans and plant
life, Rachel Carson wrote that "[t]he 'control of nature' is a phrase conceived in
arrogance, born of the Neanderthal age of biology and philosophy, when it was
supposed that nature exists for the convenience of man" (297). In 1875, pioneer-
ing ecologist John Muir identified a similar problem in advancing ecological
awareness: "No dogma taught by the present civilization seems to form so insu-
perable an obstacle in a way of a right understanding of the relations which culture sustains as to wilderness, as that which declares that the world was made
especially for the uses of men."

Despite the prevalence of these beliefs in the South, there were some ecological stirrings in the mid-twentieth century. The early Southern conservation
movement was acutely tied to the preservation of elements of Southern culture
threatened by wetland development. Sportsmen, hunters, and fishermen, often
politically conservative in other respects, banded together to protect the land
that enabled their activities. Like Faulkner, these activists were considerably less
concerned with what Judith Wittenberg calls "the biotic community" in her
article "*Go Down, Moses* and the Discourse of Environmentalism" than they
were with the perpetuation of a wildlife-centered culture. Even now, the environmental movement in the South is made up of what might seem strange bed-
fellows: more traditional ecologists, academics, and conservationists as well as
throngs of hunters and fishermen—a group that has claimed the tongue-
in-cheek designation "Bubba Environmentalists." Parke Puterbaugh, in his
1997 book *Southeastern Wetlands*, describes the late 1960s movement to thwart
the channelization of the Alcovy river greenway, a place where 30 miles from

Atlanta "a pristine river flows through a peaceful backcountry of swamps and bottomlands," as typical of the odd mix of Southern advocates for wetland preservation: "State agencies like the Game and Fish Commission, environmental groups like the Georgia Wildlife Federation and Ducks Unlimited, and citizens who had grown up fishing, hunting, and combing the Alcovy river and its associated swamps and bottomlands raised a hue and cry" (20), forcing the Army Corps of Engineers to abandon the project in 1974. The Georgia Wildlife Federation represents one of the most active and enduring organizations founded by these cultural environmentalists: as their website proclaims, "GWF began as a sportsman's organization in 1936 and since then we've grown to become Georgia's oldest and largest conservation organization. Today, our members include bird watchers, hunters, anglers, educators, gardeners, hikers—a diverse group of individuals united by our concern and compassion for the environment." The drive for wetland preservation in the South has thus been characterized by a different set of core values than one might stereotypically associate with environmentalism—that is, preservation of wilderness free from human or cultural interference. On the contrary, Southern environmentalism is as much about cultural preservation as it is about maintenance of biotic communities.

The voices of the Bubba Environmentalists would carry comparatively little weight until their conservationist agenda could be implemented on a national level. Government programs to preserve wetlands began in fits and starts around midcentury; the first major steps came with the programs of the New Deal; however, as Ann Vileisis points out, government programs and agendas often worked at cross purposes, funding initiatives both to conserve and to drain wetlands: "Without federal assistance, any wetlands would have remained only partially drained or entirely undrained. . . . Yet without federal assistance, continental waterfowl populations might have dropped irreversibly, and there would be fewer refuges, fewer wildlife biologists, and no Everglades National Park. By lending its authority to both drainage and conservation, the federal government legitimized both contradictory policies" (193). Though government action did curtail some of the assault on wetlands, its programs, along with scientific advances in understanding the wetlands and their role in cleaning water, nurturing wildlife populations, and buffering shorelines to provide flood protection, had little effect: as Vileisis points out, "rampant development following World War II resulted in a blitz of wetlands destruction. All in all, between the mid 1950s and the mid 1970s, 11 million wetland acres were converted to shopping centers, airports, farms, suburbs, and other uses" (7). Donald Hey and Nancy Philippi describe the extent of the damage that had occurred by the time of the general environmentalist "awakening" of the 1970s: "By the time the nation moved to curb the pollution of the surface waters, in the environmental decade of the 1970s, more than half of the wetlands that had once filtered out so many sediments, nutrients, and other pollutants had been destroyed" (2).

Not until the late 1970s did there emerge a unified system of legislation that united government agencies formerly at odds with regard to wetland conservation: the Fish and Wildlife Service, the USDA, the Army Corps of Engineers, and the Environmental Protection Agency (EPA). The key piece of legislation in the new environmental agenda was Jimmy Carter's Executive Order 11990, passed on May 24, 1977, which stipulated that "each agency shall provide leadership and shall take action to minimize the destruction, loss or degradation of wetlands, and to preserve and enhance the natural and beneficial value of wetlands" (President). Executive Order 11990 provided organization, funds, and legitimacy to conservation efforts and, in finally mandating protection of endangered wetlands, began in earnest the transformation of the Southern swamp into an entirely new phenomenon.

The contemporary Southern swamps are now, for the most part, protected; many have been designated as wildlife preserves, protected from drainage, deforestation, and contamination. No longer sheltered from progress by impenetrability and myth, the swamps are now shielded by federal mandate. These swamps' physical survival is somewhat secure; their contemporary signification, though, remains an intriguing and complex question.

Maintaining swamp protections, though, requires a degree of marketing to the American public. A close look at *Southeastern Wetlands: A Guide to Selected Sites in Georgia, North Carolina, South Carolina, Tennessee, and Kentucky* (1997), a fairly representative guide to the Southern swamps published by the EPA and the Tennessee Valley Authority, provides compelling insights into the swamps' place in the contemporary South. Author Parke Puterbaugh sums up the book's central aim as "invit[ing] and inspir[ing] readers to visit wetlands," while describing in some scientific detail the flora and fauna one might expect to find within. Throughout, Puterbaugh's book presents an odd mix of testaments to the swamps' untouched beauty and distance from civilization with exhortations to tourists to visit them, to experience the absence of human influence in droves. Puterbaugh claims that "I've attempted to dispel some of the popular myths surrounding wetlands—namely that they are foul-smelling and forbidding places whose murky depths harbor disease and diabolical creatures. Nothing could be further from the truth. A healthy wetland teems with life, has some of the purest water found anywhere, and carries a light floral scent, if it smells at all" (12). In fact, in a later discussion of the Okefenokee swamp, Puterbaugh brings to light an intriguing misconception about its atmosphere: "Travelers heading along I-95 assume that the sickly 'rotten egg' odor permeating the air originates inside this massive, 600-square-mile swamp. . . . Contrary to popular belief, the foul aroma that causes travelers to grimace is not the Okefenokee . . . but the paper mills and chemical plants of Brunswick, Woodbine, and St. Mary's, Georgia" (46). Puterbaugh aesthetically sanitizes the swamps, replacing mythic miasma with a light perfume. Such marketing must be expected from a book essentially aimed at garnering support for the EPA's protection of wetlands that, if not for preventative legislation, would no doubt now be suburbs of Atlanta or subsumed into similar urban sprawl. Still, the essential paradox at the heart of marketing the swamp on the basis of its pristine distance from human adulteration makes for some bizarre moments in Puterbaugh's appeal: "Wetlands are precious and irreplaceable. They represent some of the last wild places where one can encounter nature in the raw, essentially untouched by civilization. . . . In the great spirit of the outdoors, lace up your sneakers, hiking boots, waders, or whatever footwear seems appropriate and explore some of our beautiful Southeastern wetlands" (13). Puterbaugh's work presents an ironic mix of ideas that is largely representative of contemporary attitudes toward the wetlands: he encourages a new, informed consciousness of the wetlands' real and beneficial functions and dispels the old myths that rendered the swamps diabolical, replacing them with visions of natural purity. But even as he extols the wetlands' removal from civilization, he encourages tourism and promotes the "broad spectrum of recreational activities" that they offer (13).

The wetlands have become not only national parks but theme parks—a kind of simulacral "Natureworld" built on paradox. Puterbaugh claims that to visit the Alcovy River Greenway's swamps "is to explore a world that is relatively untouched by civilization, considering the river's proximity to Atlanta" but then closes his section with a list of particulars, including "When It's Open," as well as a list of convenient hotels. The Green Swamp Preserve in southern North Carolina—"no wetland is more impenetrable. . . . It perseveres almost as an act of defiance" (79)—embodies the idea of swamp as theme park: forbidding, impenetrable wildness with convenient interstate access. Perhaps the crowning irony comes in Puterbaugh's discussion of the Altamaha River Bioreserve in central Georgia, as he encourages visitors to "be sure to visit the extensive salt marshes that inspired poet Sidney Lanier to compose the celebrated poem of tribute 'The Marshes of Glynn' while sitting beneath an oak tree viewing his beloved 'Golden Isles'" (35). Lanier, who so railed against the superficialities of swamp tourism and sought in the marshes a spiritual regeneration beyond culture, now becomes his own attraction in the postmodern swamp.

My purpose here is not to deride Puterbaugh for his complicity in the paradoxical status of contemporary swamps. Marketing is an irrefutably necessary element in contemporary conservation. I simply want to underscore the remarkable transformation of the Southern swamps since the antebellum era. The wetlands as theme parks, as "swamps under glass," represent the strange completion of an arc that began with Southern colonists' practical frustration with the swamps' intractability, and the resultant superstitious demonization, and culminates with the current trend of marketing preserved swamps as accessible examples of pristine impenetrability. Baudrillard's epitaph for the Tasaday, killed by ethnography, can be transferred meaningfully to characterize the remaining Southern swamps: "frozen, cryogenized, sterilized, protected to *death*, they have become referential simulacra, and science itself has become pure simulation" (8).

The remnants of Southern swamps have spawned a surprisingly vigorous industry, particularly in southern Louisiana. If the official preserves "market" the swamps on the basis of their freedom from human adulteration and their pristine, natural beauty, the Louisiana swamp-tour industry balances ecological appeal with promises of "extreme" encounters with primordial wildlife, appeals to myth and superstition, and carefully constructed claims of cultural authenticity. While the government may preserve the physical land, the business of swamp tourism thrives in part on the persistence of the myths and tropes of old, repackaged to appeal to contemporary sensibilities. Such a move seems an inevitable symptom of the postmodern condition: swamp tours, and their sensational repackaging of the swamp landscape for consumption, provide what Fredric Jameson has described as "a commodity rush, our 'representations' of things tending to arouse an enthusiasm and a mood swing not necessarily inspired by the things themselves" (x).

A study of a few representative Louisiana swamp tours reveals a trend of combining the three chief "selling points" of the surviving swamps—unadulterated wilderness experience, carefully framed cultural authenticity, and supernatural terror—into a strange and uneasy coexistence.

A web search for "swamp tours" returns over fifty-two hundred results, an overwhelming majority of which are hosted by Louisiana businesses. The Louisiana concentration makes sense; after the Civil War, Louisiana was one of the only Southern states in which a significant number of the residents turned to the swamps for their livelihood in the face of agricultural decline and poverty. As Carl Brasseaux points out in his 1992 book *Acadian to Cajun*, although a majority of Acadians before the Civil War who lived among the south Louisiana swamps essentially shunned them in favor of more "aristocratic," planterly pursuits, the widespread poverty in the wake of Southern defeat forced great numbers of Acadians into the swamps, "to seek their livelihoods first as cypress lumberjacks, later as fishermen and trappers in the Atchafalaya Basin and in the coastal marshes" (151). Acadian culture, then, stands as the only thriving Southern subculture that became increasingly connected to the swamps at the dawn of the twentieth century, as swamps in general were experiencing widespread destruction. Though the Louisiana swamps remain as threatened as those in other parts of the South, and are certainly no longer as central to contemporary Cajun culture as they were a half century ago, the swamps are a considerably more positive element in Cajun cultural identity than they are for the South in general.

Most swamp-tour companies combine the central irony of swamp preservation, the promise of easy access to unsullied nature in the confines of an artificial preserve, with the kind of "extreme wildlife" showmanship mandatory for commercial success in the era of the "Crocodile Hunter." Munson's Swamp Tours, for example, boasts on its website that it is "the most 'authentic' swamp tour in the state of Louisiana bar none! . . . We are the only swamp tour in South Louisiana that operates on totally private property. . . . You will be in a wildlife environment that has not changed in hundreds of years, nature at it's [*sic*] most primitive level." The paradox of a swamp whose pristine nature is guarded through the mechanism of private ownership compounds the irony of the site's claim to present nature free of human interference: alongside the promise of undisturbed and primal nature is an extreme close-up photograph of an alligator's head held between two hands. The website for Cajun Pride Swamp Tours opens with a flash animation of an alligator leaping from the water to take a piece of meat from an outstretched arm, all within view of a tour boat. The site claims that "swamp creatures, seeing our boats daily, recognize them as part of their normal environment. Unafraid and responsive to their boat captain's call, they peak [*sic*] out from underbrush and between moss-draped trees and shrubs frequently coming directly to the boat." Even the most ecologically and environmentally oriented business I found, Dr. Paul Wagner's Honey Island Swamp Tours, balances its claim that the tour presents "one of the least-altered river swamps in the country . . . almost a pristine wilderness" with the promise that the guide will attract alligators with special calls and that "almost as if on cue, alligators glide toward him for their reward—a few marshmellows [*sic*]." Swamp tours balance the promise of the primeval with assurances that the primitive reptiles tourists want to see will perform on cue, selling both pristine swamp and wildlife circus.

Similar ironies come with the tours' promises of cultural authenticity. Most swamp tours market their guides as vigorously as the swamps themselves, trading on their legitimacy as exemplars of swamp culture. Gator Swamp Tours' "Captain Danny" stands as the foremost example of cultural marketing. The biography page on Captain Danny attests that "[h]e spent almost all of his life hunting, fishing, and learning about life in the southeast Louisiana swamps and waterways. From trapping to shrimping, from oyster fisherman to eco-landscaping his expert knowledge of the local wildlife, flora and fauna makes him a respected horticultural and wildlife authority." And yet, the true testament to Captain Danny's authenticity comes from his television appearances on the History Channel and the Discovery Channel and the fact that he "has provided swamp location expertise, countless times, for music videos and major feature-length films." The site even includes a titillating promise: "[H]e is very well known among entertainers and celebrities worldwide. . . . In fact, it is not that unusual for a 'very familiar' face of music, movie or television fame, to be seated, right there with the regular tourists, taking in nature's sights and sounds, on one of Gator's daily tours!" Captain Danny's true credibility is measured by his role in shaping simulacral swamps for television and film; the references offered are not trappers or fishermen but entertainment personalities.

Tour guides are not the only locus of cultural marketing in the swamp tour business. Though they generally take exotic views of cultural history—most tend to emphasize pirates and voodoo queens—some tours claim to offer glimpses into Cajun culture. Cajun Pride Swamp Tours offers the opportunity for tourists to "view a trapper's cabin as your captain/guide teaches you about Cajuns—who they were, their origins, habits, lifestyle and other interesting historical facts." The capitulatory past tense in which the ironically named Cajun Pride Swamp Tours refers to the Cajuns underscores the Baudrillardian overtones that characterize the swamp tour phenomenon: though a great number of south Louisiana residents still emphatically identify as Cajuns, the "authentic" Cajun culture promised on the tour is relegated to the past. Swamp-dwelling Cajuns have become the stuff of "interesting historical fact"; their culture, like the primitive splendor of the marshmallow-grabbing alligator, is represented and marketed as tourist entertainment.

Balancing claims of cultural authenticity are promises of supernatural terror. Collapsing the actual and tropic dimensions of the swamp, many companies augment the allure of the physical and factual swamp with veiled promises of swamp horrors, again to be viewed from the comfort and safety of Coast Guard–approved vessels. (The Gator Swamp Tours homepage includes the reassuring promise "We never sell a *one-way ticket* from our village dock!") Cajun Pride Swamp Tours offers the most fright-intensive feature in the form of the "Haunted Nite Swamp Tour": "Dare you venture into the night with us deep into the heart of the Manchac Swamp? The very swamp that after being cursed by voodoo queen Julie Brown was totally destroyed by the 1915 hurricane & whose residents are buried in unmarked graves on the property. . . . An adventure filled with nocturnal creatures, spirits, mystical blue lights & glowing red eyes that watch your every move. . . . Fact and legend collide in this tour for a night of intrigue, mystery, history, folklore & nature's surprises." Like a frame superimposed over the natural swamp, the swamp of myth, folklore, trope and superstition becomes part of the draw for tours that simultaneously market themselves as unadulterated access to nature. Cajun Pride is not alone in playing to quaint superstition: even Dr. Wagner's tour, generally more ecologically focused and scientifically oriented than most, with a great deal of information about swamp flora and fauna, lures customers with the possibility of viewing the Honey Island Swamp Monster, a creature alternately called a Bigfoot or a "Wookie," purported to resemble a seven-foot orangutan. While the site underscores that "those touring the swamp are more entranced by its natural beauty, and the sights and sounds of wildlife in this pristine wilderness" than by promises of monsters, Dr. Wagner rather reluctantly adds some credence to the legend; in response to a question about mysterious swamp sounds and the Wookie, Wagner responds, "It could be. . . . Actually, I was fishing near a canebrake one night and I heard some footsteps. Whatever it was, it sounded big. . . . Maybe it was Wookie, but I sure didn't hang around to find out!"

The old tropic swamp demons, their roots older than the American colonies and now powerfully reinforced by Hollywood imagery, still haunt contemporary representations of Southern wooded wetlands—even among those who preserve them and whose livelihood depends on their maintenance. The Honey Island "Wookie," the dark, wild, simian creature whose very name, a derivation from the film *Star Wars*, can be seen as a kind of simulacral heir to the dreaded swamp Maroons of the nineteenth century, stripped of the cultural context of race and slavery that gave birth to the image even as its threat is stripped of its human face. The specters of chaos that initially freighted the swamps with fear and menace have become faint evocations of movie monsters, the stuff of tongue-in-cheek entertainment and savvy marketing.

The contemporary Southern swamp has taken on a new set of paradoxes and contradictions, superseding the old contradictions of water and land, purity and pollution. It has become an embodiment of Baudrillardian postmodernity, an image that has replaced and effaced its referent, a space kept pure of human artifice by artifice itself. In an era when Southern identity must now be considered in terms of the urban, thriving, vital, and increasingly multicultural New South, the swamps have become odd embodiments of a vanished identity, repositories of faded fears, forgotten cultural history, and compromised purity. At last thoroughly subjugated to human will, the swamps seem to have become as much a product of postmodernity as the celluloid images that blend fact and fiction, culture and cliché to present the technicolor "history" of the Hollywood South.

Amid the dissonance of countless varying definitions, one seemingly inevitable commonality of most postmodern thought is the conceptual disappearance of nature. The natural world, and the empirical factuality of scientific disciplines, have been as much casualties of postmodern thought as other seemingly objective truths and master narratives. To this point, this entire study has charted representations of the swamp: either efforts to construct it in ways that support the dominant mythology of the South, reappropriations of it to give voice to those excluded from the master narrative, or, often, seeming capitulations to the swamp's status outside narrative control. The postmodern era presents its own set of challenges to swamp representation. Jameson posits the postmodern as displacing and replacing nature: "Postmodernism is what you have when the modernization process is complete and nature is gone for good. It is a more fully human world than the older one, but one in which 'culture' has become a veritable 'second nature'" (ix). Nature joins the litany of extinction that characterizes much of postmodern thought. As Jameson puts it, "The last few years have been marked by an inverted millenarianism in which premonitions of the future, catastrophic or redemptive, have been replaced by senses of the end of this or that. . . . [T]aken together, all of these perhaps constitute what is increasingly called postmodernism" (1).

Must we, then, herald "the end of the swamp" as natural site and subversive space? My urge, as conservationist and cultural critic, is to resist such an apocalyptic view. And yet, as Linda Hutcheon points out, such an impulse may itself signify consciousness of a depth of loss—even clinging to ideas of authentic, inviolate natural spaces may itself capitulate to the loss of such possibilities, carrying us into nostalgia: "Nostalgia, in fact, may depend precisely on the irrecoverable nature of the past for its emotional impact and appeal. . . . This is rarely the past as actually experienced, of course; it is the past as imagined, as idealized through memory and desire. . . . The aesthetics of nostalgia might, therefore, be less a matter of simple memory than of complex projection; the invocation of a partial, idealized history merges with a dissatisfaction with the present." Wistful nostalgia may aptly characterize mainstream Southern responses to fading swamps—for the dominant voices, and for most Southerners today, they were more often appreciated as places of recreation than anything else and now tend to represent carefully preserved reminders of idealized times gone by.

Such a total concession of the natural world to the vagaries of human will, though, is a dangerous, limited, and potentially irresponsible move. If the natural no longer exists, is entirely a product of human imagination, then what stands in the way of practical ecological catastrophe, pollution, deforestation, and a host of other potential and current disasters? In recent years, the discourse of ecocriticism has emerged in answer to precisely this problem. Theorizing nature out of existence, ecocritics argue, can only support the forces that threaten it physically.

Ecocriticism, or "green studies," is similar to postmodernism in that it seems to be in a constant state of definition and redefinition. Its central tenets, though, are relatively clear. Lawrence Coupe sums up the central conflict between ecocriticism and much of postmodern theory in his introduction to *The Green Studies Reader* (2000): "To declare that there is 'no such thing as nature' has become almost obligatory within literary and cultural studies. The great fear has been to be discovered committing what might be called 'the referential fallacy'" (2). This way of thinking, however, has "encouraged a heavy-handed culturalism, whereby suspicion of 'truth' has entailed a denial of non-textual existence" (2). Ecocriticism, while not rejecting postmodern theory out of hand, clears a space for the natural as well as the human in understanding the world: "Green studies does not challenge the notion that human beings make sense of the world through language, but rather the self-serving inference that nature is nothing more than a linguistic construct" (3). In *Practical Ecocriticism* (2003), Glen Love states the central crisis that ecocriticism addresses: "In a real world of increasing ecological crisis and political decision making, to exclude nature except for its cultural determination or linguistic construction is also to accept the continuing degradation of a natural world that is most in need of active human recognition and engagement" (8). Kate Soper, in her 1995 book *What is Nature?* states the issue more urgently: "In short, it is not language which has a hole in the ozone layer; and the real thing continues to be polluted and degraded even as we refine our deconstructive insights at the level of the signifier" (151). Essentially, as Love puts it, "Ecocriticism, unlike all other forms of literary inquiry, encompasses nonhuman as well as human contexts and considerations. On this claim, ecocriticism bases its challenge to much postmodern critical discourse as well as to the critical systems of the past" (1).

It is important to note that ecocriticism does not posit the natural as utterly independent of the human but as coexisting with, rather than wholly created by, ideology and imagination: thus, it works alongside, rather than in opposition to, cultural studies. As I have claimed throughout this book, the swamps signified, and continue to signify, differently for various cultures that experience them, and various constructions of the swamps have been influenced by technology and science as well as by ideology and culture. While the mainstream contemporary South, however one defines it, may regard the swamps with nostalgia and idealization, cultures that lived, and continue to live, in the swamps themselves respond differently. For surviving swamp-identified cultures, natural and cultural degradation and destruction are inextricably linked. Two recent novels, *The Next Step in the Dance* (1998), by Acadian author Tim Gautreaux, and *Power* (1998), by Native American poet and novelist Linda Hogan, engage the interrelationship of fading physical swamp landscapes and threatened cultures in a way that combines an ecocritical perspective with a pronounced cultural focus. While both works posit a purer vision of the natural world as a vehicle of cultural salvation, neither falls into the trap of positioning nature itself as a savior—a position which landscape theorist Krista Comer calls "surely . . . one of the most heavy-handed signs of human projection available in western discourse" (12). Both, instead, represent human relations to, and constructions of, landscape as potentially redemptive *cultural* expressions—cultural survival comes not from nature itself but through the persistence of cultural relationships with the natural world.

In *The Next Step in the Dance*, Gautreaux considers both the cultural and ecological impact of postmodern society on the fictitious Louisiana coastal swamp community of Tiger Island. Gautreaux, a Louisiana native, critiques what he regards as the toxic forces of postmodernity from a perspective more modern than postmodern: in a 1998 interview, he describes himself as a Catholic writer in the tradition of Walker Percy and claims that "it's impossible to write about South Louisiana culture without writing about the Catholic Church, because it permeates everything from wedding ceremonies to industrial fishing to the sugarcane industry to the way people think about eating on Friday." Further, Gautreaux professes his belief that "each of us has a type of ingrained, almost instinctual interest in a theme, whether it's pollution or child abuse or alienation or depression. . . . It's almost inevitable that a writer can [*sic*] escape the themes that are in his soul" ("Novel" 3). Gautreaux's religious principles inform his view of Acadian culture; his work centers on personal and cultural values and the possibility of redemption.

The Next Step in the Dance directly engages the clash between postmodern, consumerist values and traditional Cajun culture. Alongside the conflict between his central protagonists, Paul and Colette Thibodeaux, is a deeper conflict between what Gautreaux sees as the markers of postmodern society—aimless, unquenchable desire, superficiality, and artificiality—and a powerful but threatened sense of cultural authenticity. Gautreaux's Tiger Island is a dying place, polluted and economically depressed, with an aging population and little, on the surface, to recommend it to the young and ambitious: "Tiger Island was the most knuckle-knocked of the river towns: The only theater was the Silver Bayou Drive-In; the largest building was a metal shed where oil-field equipment was sandblasted. . . . [S]omething about Tiger Island was slightly out of balance, a little too littered, sun-tortured, and mildewed" (16). Colette, the "prettiest girl on Tiger Island," is profoundly dissatisfied with her life there. Her seemingly shiftless and irresponsible husband is only part of the problem. Colette, who has "read *Cosmopolitan* and *Woman's World* and [has] begun to think that Tiger Island [is] a small, muddy pond" (2), grows disgusted with her stagnant job at the bank, her machinist husband's perceived philandering (he actually only dances with other women), and the increasing oppressive ugliness of the decaying Cajun community where she has lived her entire life. She leaves her uncomprehending husband and takes off for California in search of fulfillment.

California becomes, for Gautreaux, the embodiment of postmodern consumerist excess and artificiality. Colette takes a job at a bank and is immediately
stigmatized for her cultural identity: "She did not fit in with her fellow workers,
who thought she talked funny, the way she flattened her *a*'s. The people she
longed to be like made jokes about her, called her 'the swamp queen.' The ones
who were friendly were friendly in a way she did not understand, unlike the
people in Tiger Island" (75). California immediately, and somewhat predictably, falls somewhat short of her expectations: "Most people she'd met were
into exercising, collecting, or recreational sex, and as much as she tried to forget
it, at heart Colette was still a food-loving, nonmaterialistic Roman Catholic.
The air was cool and dry, but poisonous; the highways were smooth and fast,
but long; the people were good to look at, healthy and smart, but restless, never
satisfied. Most people she had met and spoken with seemed to be waiting for
something to happen to them" (79). Colette, driven to California by a vague
desire to meet "people who sparkle" (23), finds herself mimicking the restless
desires of those she meets: "She looked around and wondered what she had
begun waiting for" (79). She buys a Mercedes—"She needed the car the way she
needed painkiller for a storming headache" (102)—and maintains it obsessively,
"since it and glittering things like it were what she had come to California for"
(105). She develops an insatiable appetite for something indefinable, consuming commodities and landscape alike without satisfaction: "She had driven the
length of California, from the Oregon border to Tijuana, and knew that she
had been too greedy with the landscape, had eaten it up too quickly" (119). In
California, Colette lives out a postmodern consumerist obsession—a constant
desire for more that can never truly be satisfied, always waiting for something
that will never arrive.

Paul stands as a pure contrast to Colette, manifesting what is, to her, a stulti-
fying lack of ambition. Gautreaux has claimed that a lack of ambition characterizes Cajun culture in general. He claims, in fact, that his own lack of writerly
ambition is "one thing that marks me as a Louisiana native" ("Novel" 32). As the
novel progresses, however, we see that Paul's seeming lack of ambition stems
primarily from a philosophical difference with Colette: "Was that ambition, to
want to own a machine shop? Two machine shops? A chain of machine shops
strung out along the Chieftain River like franchise hamburger stands? Colette
would like that, MacLeBlanc's, over one billion crankshafts repaired" (54). Paul
is not, in fact, without ambition—his ambitions simply center on labor rather
than acquisition. In many ways, removed by his Louisiana swamp setting from

the moral problem of slavery at its root, Paul embodies the Agrarian ideal of a proper relationship to labor—work for its own sake, rather than for acquisition. He is a master craftsman with old machines and approaches his work with a rare passion: as he fixes an engine at work, Gatlin, a co-worker from North Louisiana, remarks, "Damn . . . I never seen nobody have sex with a engine before" (52). In contrast to Colette's unquenchable need for an ill-defined "more," Paul finds satisfaction in his work itself. It is exactly this, Gautreaux suggests, that drives Colette to leave him: as her father puts it, "You left him because he was happy" (150). Colette, in the early chapters, simply cannot understand the modified Agrarian philosophy that characterizes most of Tiger Island: she says of an old woman who works all day in her garden that "it was stupid for a ninety-year-old woman to kill herself in a garden for vegetables she could walk to the store and buy" (65). Paul, however, maintains his commitment to this philosophy throughout the novel: he can succeed in Los Angeles, and is even offered a job servicing machinery in Baudrillard's ultimate embodiment of simulacral postmodernity, Disneyland, but he never embraces the troubled ideology of ambition he encounters there.

Paul also remains staunchly resistant to the artificiality he perceives in California. In one telling scene, he goes to a Cajun restaurant in Los Angeles. Approaching it hopefully, he is greeted by "a dim, crowded dining room under a drooping net that held a few dried starfish, animals he had seen only in pictures" (80). The menu, which features such dubious dishes as Escargot de Lafayette and blackened swordfish, is far removed from anything in Paul's experience: "I never seen a swordfish in my whole life" (80). The waiter superciliously informs Paul that "[i]t takes time to develop a true Cajun palate," to which Paul responds, "Let me tell you, it sure don't take much time to ruin one" (81). Paul's disaffection with the inauthenticity that surrounds him extends beyond the false evocations of his home culture to California in general. As he regards the Forest Lawn cemetery, he muses, "In Tiger Island, a cemetery was the ultimate reality, where all the bullshit of life was put away in the face of a final fact, and a name of one's bloodline on a cross formed not celebrity, but a remembrance of either love or nothing, heaven or hell. . . . Not so in the City of Angels. A cemetery was a tourist attraction, the ultimate amusement park, a Disneyland of the Dead" (82).

Eventually, both Paul and Colette are driven to return to Louisiana by moral corruption that accompanies the artificiality they encounter in California: Paul refuses to allow faulty machinery to pass inspection and is fired, and Colette is blatantly sexually harassed by her boss, who behaves as if he learned all his moves "in an old cowboy film" (106). Gautreaux blends his discourse of authenticity versus superficiality with a strikingly moralistic element: as ugly and polluted as Tiger Island may be, its ethics and virtues are categorically removed from the, admittedly clichéd, sparkling moral morass of California.

After establishing the cultural and moral distance between the postmodern wasteland of California and the modified Agrarianism of Tiger Island, Gautreaux extends his cultural critique to consider landscape and ecology. Bucky Tyler, Paul's chief rival for Colette and the purest villain of the novel, exudes an aura of menace that blends threats both to the culture of Tiger Island and to the ecosystems he pollutes. From his first appearance, Tyler is clearly an outsider: when Colette suggests to Paul that she may go on a date with him, he asks, "Who the hell's that? That guy from Texas? The cowboy?" When Colette replies that "[h]e's got money and style," Paul counters by calling him "a worm for Texaco. He screws old people out of their mineral rights" (39). An air of inauthenticity accompanies Tyler at every appearance: when Paul first meets him face to face, Tyler, wearing his signature cowboy hat, "a cheap white straw thing bought in a feed store," "[smiles] like a movie star" before succinctly insulting Paul's cultural heritage and expressing a disrespect for women that immediately casts doubt on his relationship with Colette: "Hey, coon-ass, where can a man get laid around here?" (57). When Colette returns from California and begins a relationship with Tyler, his inauthenticity remains palpable in Gautreaux's imagery. Tyler takes Colette to Lafayette to eat in a fancy restaurant: "Next to them on a room divider was a giant stuffed alligator purporting to creep through a patch of plastic swamp growth. . . . He told Cajun jokes while she looked out the window. . . . [T]hey got up and moved through a two-step to the geriatric house band's music. She decided she liked his cowboy version well enough, though he had a little too much hop in his step" (146). As they discuss Colette's relationship with Paul, Tyler brings up the subject of her Catholicism. When Colette says that neither she nor Paul can remarry until the other dies, Tyler responds, "That'd be a good revenge. . . . Live a long life, gal, and keep the poor bastard horny till the day he dies" (147). Colette responds, "I don't think you understand religion" (147). Tyler's sensibilities are utterly alien to those of the Tiger Island Cajun community, and his very presence threatens Colette's ability to maintain her cultural values.

Significantly, Tyler represents an ecological as well as a cultural threat. He runs a "stink plant" in the swamp, taking in toxic chemical waste from all over the world and dumping it into the ground. Colette, taking a job with Tyler out of desperation, notes early on that "the business was strange: An occasional bargeload of liquid would come in from Ghana or Italy, and sometimes the whole region smelled like toilet-bowl cleaner for two days" (149). Eventually, as Paul is driven by the pervasive economic depression that blights Tiger Island to work for him as well, it becomes clear that Bucky Tyler embodies the worst aspects of ambition, poisoning the Louisiana wetlands for his own profit: "Instead of being satisfied with his modest though profitable recycling business, Bucky sought out more and more dangerous items to deal with, some of which he had no idea how to process. Paul watched as a small tank farm sprang up, soon to be filled with insecticide from Italy, orange oil from Arizona" (159). Bucky Tyler, economic opportunist, wholesale polluter, and eventually, as he rigs an accident to kill Paul so that Colette will be his, attempted murderer, embodies all the ills that threaten the swamp community of Tiger Island.

Colette, fittingly, purges those ills as she takes revenge for what Tyler has done to Paul. As she turns Tyler in to the federal authorities for illegally disposing of toxic materials, she turns a personal corner even as she vindicates her natural surroundings. Out of work by virtue of getting her employer arrested, she turns to the swamps to make money for herself, her unborn baby, and for Paul. Taking up the rifle she used as a child, Colette becomes a trapper, assuming one of the oldest traditional Acadian professions, and hunts nutria in the swamps. Taking guidance from Grand-père Abadie, who becomes a signifier of cultural tradition and guide for both Paul and Colette as they rediscover their cultural roots, she rides out into the heart of the swamps and kills the great rats to sell to a dog food company. Gautreaux carefully does not romanticize the endeavor—it becomes the antithesis of Colette's glamorous California life, as she rides through snake- and spider-infested swamps to pile rats into her skiff—but her trapping, and eventually fishing, bring Colette into contact with a culture she had once sought to repudiate. While early passages in the novel seem to repudiate "women's magazine feminism" as superficial and empty, Colette becomes, in later chapters, a kind of intracultural feminist: she does remain in her small swamp community and surrenders her ambitions to go elsewhere, but she becomes an accomplished trapper, fisher, and sharpshooter, even winning a shooting contest against all male opponents. Colette eventually finds herself, and reconciles with Paul, as she claims her cultural heritage—she makes her way as her ancestors did, by harvesting the bounty of the swamps and coastal waters.

Ultimately, at the novel's climax, Gautreaux provides his final hard-won cultural validation. Paul and his friends are lost in a storm at sea, as he risks his life to make a big enough haul to win Colette back. Colette searches desperately, helped by unquestioning friends and family in a show of community. Ultimately, though, it is Abadie, the embodiment of tradition, who rejects weather reports because he feels that "the government made the weather on TV" (332), who seeks out Paul and Etienne in the coastal marsh, "trusting perhaps the map of feeling in his head" (329). Abadie, who has served as a kind of savant and spiritual guide to the young couple throughout the various stages of their relationship, brings them together at the novel's close. Paul, Colette, and their new child come to represent hope for Tiger Island, the only images of youth and new life in a community that has primarily been rendered through images of death and decay. Like the stained glass window of the Tiger Island Catholic Church, showing Adam and Eve against a red sky, Paul and Colette become symbols of hope for the troubled community. Gautreaux leaves the reader with an image of qualified hope as Colette looks out over the roofs of Tiger Island: "[S]ome were storm-worn and bent, some eroded and rusty, porous as a ruined soul, and some were scraped clean and gleaming with new silver paint" (340).

Gautreaux's novel is particularly suited to an ecocritical reading in that it poses an inextricable relationship between the natural swamp and coastal marsh environments of Tiger Island and the culture that survives there, both of which are under attack by various outside forces. While his is a narrative of environmental and cultural pollution and salvation, nature is not a savior but an enabler and constituent of a waning but still vital culture outside the mainstream of both Southern and American culture. As the swamps go, so goes Acadian culture—and Paul and Colette become potential symbolic redeemers of both cultural tradition and ecological purity.

Linda Hogan's complex and lyrical 1998 novel *Power* similarly engages the central issues of culture and nature in a vanishing swamp community in southern Florida. She, like Gautreaux, engages the relationship of ecology and marginalized cultures; also like Gautreaux, she expresses measured hope for both natural and cultural survival. As Michael Hardin puts it in "Standing Naked before the Storm: Linda Hogan's *Power* and the Critique of Apocalyptic Narrative" (2003), "Hogan is an environmentalist—one who reads the environment in terms of conquest, colonialism, and survival—but not an apocalypticist. . . . The world is changing, the ancient is confronting the modern; but instead of abandoning one for the other, Ama and Omishto [her central characters] seek the space between the two, the space that is neither, or the space that encompasses both" (151). Hogan's novel, like so many swamp discourses of the twentieth century, uses the swamp landscape and the fiction-alized culture it sustains to intervene in larger issues, standing against the homo-genizing forces of postmodern society. In this sense, the ecological and cultural issues faced by a tiny group of Florida Indians take on significance beyond the local and regional.

Hogan's narrator is Omishto, a teenaged girl whose name means "The One who Watches." Omishto is caught between cultures—she is Taiga by heritage, but her mother has left the Taiga behind and converted to Christian-ity. Omishto idolizes Ama, her "aunt," who adheres to, and believes in, the traditions of the Taiga, but Omishto herself is skeptical in the beginning: "I don't give superstition even an ounce of weight" (22). Nevertheless, she feels a deep and intuitive connection to the natural world around her that comes from her Taiga heritage: "I have a strong wind inside me, is what Grandma said. . . . I feel lives and spirits in the woods, and I see the growing things" (4). Omishto, her name and intuitive connection with nature notwithstanding, stops short of projecting her cultural ideas onto the swamps and forests that surround her. Taiga mythology inverts the typical postmodern conception of reality, that it is constructed by those who perceive it: "Aunt Ama says what you look at is what you become, so I don't look into the trees. I don't want to become like the shadows hiding in the eyes of animals, harboring insects and lizards or runaways" (3).

It is important in reading Hogan's work from an ecocritical perspective to note the inaccessibility of nature even to those who live closest to it. As Eric Gary Anderson points out, Hogan's novel is not a simple paean to natural purity as an antidote to postmodern pollution and waste; he claims that "Hogan's insistence on, and enactment of, a complex notion of inaccessibility helps distinguish her work from that of various nature writers" (178). This step, in part, defends Hogan's work from claims that she merely does away with one construction of the natural to replace it with another. Omishto, the observer, achieves a kind of understanding as the novel progresses, but much of what she comes to understand is the inherent mystery of nature itself. She does not lie heir to an intuitive "map" of the wild swamps that doubles as a blueprint for cultural survival—instead, she comes to embrace an alternative ontology, an antimodern conception of her and her culture's place in a nature that she cannot—and should not—hope to understand completely.

Hogan's Taiga Indians are a marginalized people, seemingly bound for cultural extinction: "Some say we, too, are fallen. We are Taiga Indians and no one has heard of us. We are a small tribe and we are swamp people. . . . We, my family, clan, and me, are one-third of the number of Taiga Indians still in this world" (85). The Taiga, self-identified "swamp people," are linked powerfully to the natural landscape throughout the novel. Hogan's South Florida swamps are clearly besieged by both physical and ideological forces; as the swamps have been cleared and polluted, "we, us Taiga people, haven't run. Instead, silent and nearly invisible, most of us have been pushed up against the wild places, backed against them. And some of them are still there, like a dark corner in the minds of the intruders" (8). While the Taiga land, "still wet and fertile," remains a pristine space within a degraded natural landscape, "all other land is poison now, like the pestilence of Mama's Bible that entered the houses as if to claim the firstborn sons" (90). Despite the resistance of the Taiga lands, Hogan suggests early in the novel that the possibility of renewal, at least by European paradigms, is slim at best. Near the Taiga land is the spring that the Spanish believed was the fountain of youth—"And that's another joke because now it's polluted like all this land and you can't even drink a cupful of that thin trickle of bad water" (5). Hogan clearly links the pollution of the swamps—home to both the Taiga and to Sisa, the panther who becomes central to her narrative—to the degradation of life, not just for the Taiga but for all humanity: "The world has grown small where Sisa lives. It has lost its power and given way to highways and streets of towns where once there were woods and fens and bodies of water. . . . Because of this, humans have lost the chance to be whole and joyous, reverent and alive. . . . What they've forgotten is large and immense, and what they remember is only a small, narrow hopelessness" (191). The clearance and development of the natural landscape clashes directly with the beliefs of the Taiga elders, like Janie Soto, who believes that "we do not have the right to live in any way we desire; our way was made for us out of clay by the adept fingers of creation, the leafbed of its mud, from air and what lives in it" (184). Further, any hope for cultural survival for the Taiga has become linked with ecological "salvation": the elders have "seen all of it, the drained swamps, the rushing cars, the near destruction of their world, all of it mixed in right next to the old, dark-leafed world they cling to as if it will save them, and maybe it will" (158).

Alongside the physical and spiritual degradation that comes with polluting and clearing the swamps is a simulacral appropriation of the panther itself, which has been adopted as mascot by Omishto's high school: "Panther, our high school mascot. The idea of the panther is loved while the animal itself is hated, unwanted" (105). The gulf between the actual and imaginary, the genuine and simulacral, that ecocritical discourses seek to close becomes powerfully clear as Hogan sets the stage for her tale of troubled redemption.

The ideological battle enacted in *Power* is not limited to Native American spirituality against the impersonal forces of contemporary society. The traditions of the Taiga are also pitted against Omishto's mother's Christianity, to which Omishto feels drawn in spite of herself: "The preacher thinks different from the Taiga way of thinking. . . . [H]e doesn't believe in what's on earth or birds; he says it's all an illusion, this life on earth, a dream, a miserable place we will one day escape into the golden streets of heaven. I would like to think this way" (40). To Hogan, Christianity also interposes between humans and nature; further, it drives a wedge between Omishto's mother and her cultural heritage: "She doesn't love herself, I know this, because she believes what they tell her in church, that it was our fate to be destroyed by those who were stronger and righter. She believes evil and ignorance are the natural state of humans, swamps, and animals, and we must save ourselves from it" (187).

Ama, the self-sacrificing hero of Hogan's novel, exists between the old world and the new. Hogan aligns her powerfully with nature and tradition but marks her with a kind of restlessness: "She never seems quite at home in anything, not shoes or clothing, not houses, not even her own muscles, just in the wild swamps and grasses and trees" (9). While she "lives in a natural way at the outside edges of our lives, and . . . 'keeps up relations,' as she says, with nature and the spirit world" (17), she is set apart from the Taiga elders by a knowledge of the contemporary world: "Ama said the old ways are not enough to get us through this time and she was called to something else. To living halfway between the modern world and the ancient one" (23). This knowledge leads Ama to her quest in the swamp, to her killing of the weak, pitiful panther she tracks into the heart of the wilderness; she disposes of the panther's body so that they will not see how weak and sickly it had become, which would shake their faith to its core. Ama becomes a savior for the Taiga, sacrificing herself to save their world, even facing the ultimate penalty of banishment because of her unwillingness to produce the cat's body, or to explain her reasons for doing so. For a people as powerfully linked to place as the Taiga, "the word for 'banish' and the word for 'kill' is the same word; it's the same because in traditional belief, banishment is equal to death. It is death to be split from your own people, your self, to go away from the place you so love" (172).

In banishment, Ama, in Omishto's mind, returns to the swamps that seemed her only true home: "Maybe she laid herself down on the ground and reached into clay . . . knelt down and laid her knees and palms in it . . . until she sank into the mud and earth and closed her eyes in the shining clay and stopped her own breath until there would be another time four years from now, when once again she could surface. I think she could do that, become earth in that way, and I would rather know this than believe she was in a city, walking down the street with a newspaper in her hand. Ama has always been what is hidden" (227). Significantly, Ama is here linked, however fancifully, not only to nature but also to the unknown—what is hidden. Ama's character remains a cipher throughout the novel, filtered through Omishto's perceptions, always at least partially beyond the girl's ability to understand. While she enacts a redemption myth, an unquestionable human projection onto nature, the basis of the myth lies in the unknown, the mysteries beyond human conceptual or physical dominance.

The implicit validity of myth is, in large part, what sets *Power* apart from similar tales of natural redemption. As others have observed, Ama's hunt in many ways recalls Faulkner's "The Bear": the spiritual guide leads the young initiate into the heart of the wilderness, led by a quasi-mystical animal who seems "every so often to lead [them] forward, as if it knows what it is doing" (64). It is also similar in that the culmination of the hunt seems degraded and anticlimactic, and the mystical animal proves sickly and pathetic when cornered. However, the overall logic of the novel redeems the hunt—it proves, after all, to be an almost literal reenactment of the panther legend and leads, indirectly, to the seeming redemption of the Taiga. While Ike McCaslin's claim that "Sam Fathers set me free" ultimately rings tragically false, Ama emerges in Omishto's eyes as a genuine savior: "I look at her and see that she is the kind of person who would kill herself to set the world straight again. Even if it breaks her own personal world apart. . . . [S]omeone had to find a way to renew the world, and no one else would do it" (125). The final chapter, entitled "What I Have Left," sounds an unmistakable note of hope, as Omishto returns to the Taiga after a personal awakening: "Ama is saving a world. But I am saving myself being here, and in all these savings, the path of things is changed forever" (224). The Taiga, persisting in the "little patch of land behind the swamp," live on, "[remembering] the stories that are the force of living, how Panther woman went into the black trees and returned, finally, with magic words which she withheld until the time when the world teetered on the rib of death and she spoke them" (231). The novel's close even brings us a vision of another panther, this one strong and regal, redeemed, implicitly, by Ama's ritual and sacrifice. The final image in the novel is of Omishto dancing with her people while "someone sings the song that says the world will go on living" (235).

For all the hopefulness of the novel's ending, its implications remain complex and potentially troubling. As Anderson points out, "The ending of *Power* appears to be more positive and hopeful than the conclusion of 'The Bear,' but perhaps at a cost, since Hogan's ending can be understood as both a needed return to traditional ways and a self-progenitive retreat from multicultural engagement" (175). For all the precarious mythological balancing of individual action and global salvation, the implications of Ama's act and Omishto's return to her people for the impersonal world that presumably will continue to threaten them are unclear. Hogan's quasi-mystical connection of local and global, while potentially working to transcend the constraints of specific "place" as opposed to a more malleable and plastic sense of "space," as Comer urges, cannot help but leave us with a sense of how small and isolated her fictitious Taiga seem to be.

Both Hogan and Gautreaux present stories of cultural salvation borne on the shoulders of individual, youthful representatives who return to ways of life that center on inextricably linked ideas of tradition and the natural swamp landscape. Both also, inevitably, leave us with a powerful sense of the fragility of their reassuring endings. Anderson describes *Power* as "less a novel about recovering the old ways and returning to the old roots than . . . a novel about how these old ways are one teenaged Indian girl away from being not only relinquished but also extinguished" (167). That very discomfort, the limited and qualified nature of the redemption created in both novels, makes them particularly significant from an ecocritical perspective. The swamps remain, beleaguered but still powerful, in each case: but in each case, we are reminded that whether we reject them or idealize them, they remain at imminent practical risk. The stylized panther on the high school banner may remain, but the actual panther still faces extinction. In both novels, local action, personal commitment, redeems the powerfully linked elements of culture and landscape, but both novels also serve as ecocritical interventions into practical action, reminding us of the greater consequences of destroying and polluting the natural world—and of the powerful interrelationship between physical nature and personal and cultural identity.

BIBLIOGRAPHY

Adams, Stephen. *The Best and Worst Country in the World: Perspectives on the Early Virginia Landscape*. Charlottesville: University Press of Virginia, 2001.

Agassiz, Louis. *Contributions to a Natural History of the United States of America*. Boston: Little, Brown and Company, 1857–62.

———. *A Journey in Brazil*. 1868. Introduction by A. C. Wilgus. New York: Praeger, 1969.

Allmendinger, David. *Ruffin: Family and Reform in the Old South*. New York: Oxford University Press, 1990.

Anderson, Eric Gary. "Native American Literature, Ecocriticism, and the South: The Inaccessible Worlds of Linda Hogan's *Power*." *South to a New Place: Region, Literature, Culture*. Ed. Suzanne W. Jones and Sharon Monteith. Baton Rouge: Louisiana State University Press, 2002. 165–83.

Andrews, Eliza. *The War-Time Journal of a Georgia Girl, 1864–1865*. 1908. Ed. Jean Berlin. Lincoln: University of Nebraska Press, 1997.

Baker, Houston A., Jr., and Dana D. Nelson. "Violence, the Body and 'The South.'" *American Literature* 73 (2001): 231–44.

Baker, Vaughn. "In and out of the Mainstream: The Acadians in Antebellum Louisiana." *The Cajuns: Essays on their History and Culture*. Ed. Glen Conrad. Lafayette: University of Southwestern Louisiana Press, 1983. 95–112.

Bartram, William. *Travels through North and South Carolina, Georgia, East and West Florida, the Cherokee Country, the Extensive Territories of the Muscogulges, or Creek Confederacy, and the Country of the Choctaws; Containing an Account of the Soil and Natural Productions of These Regions, Together with Observations on the Manners of the Indians*. 1792. Ed. Francis Harper. Athens: University of Georgia Press, 1998.

Baudrillard, Jean. *Simulacra and Simulation*. Trans. Sheila Faria Glaser. Ann Arbor: University of Michigan Press, 1994.

Bell, Vereen. *Swamp Water*. 1940. Athens: University of Georgia Press, 1981.

Bell, Vereen, Jr. Introduction. V. Bell v–xvii.

Berlin, Jean. Introduction. Andrews i–xii.

Berman, Marshall. *All That Is Solid Melts into Air: The Experience of Modernity.* New York: Penguin Books, 1988.

Biles, Roger. *The South and the New Deal.* Lexington: University Press of Kentucky, 1994.

Blake, Nelson Manfred. *Land into Water, Water into Land: A History of Water Management in Florida.* Tallahassee: University Presses of Florida, 1980.

Brantley, Will. *Feminine Sense in Southern Memoir.* Jackson: University Press of Mississippi, 1993.

Brasseaux, Carl A. *Acadian to Cajun: Transformation of a People, 1803–1877.* Jackson: University Press of Mississippi, 1992.

Brooks, Cleanth. "Faulkner and the Fugitive Agrarians." *Faulkner and the Southern Renaissance.* Ed. Doreen Fowler and Ann J. Abadie. Jackson: University Press of Mississippi, 1981. 22–39.

Brown, Alan. " 'De Beast' Within: The Role of Nature in *Jonah's Gourd Vine." Zora in Florida.* Ed. Steve Glassman and Kathryn Lee Seidel. Orlando: University of Central Florida Press, 1991. 76–86.

Bryan, Violet Harrington. *The Myth of New Orleans in Literature.* Knoxville: University of Tennessee Press, 1993.

Buell, Lawrence. "Faulkner and the Claims of the Natural World." *Faulkner and the Natural World: Faulkner and Yoknapatawpha, 1996.* Ed. Donald R. Kartiganer and Ann J. Abadie. Jackson: University Press of Mississippi, 1999. 1–18.

Bunyan, John. *The Pilgrim's Progress from This World to That Which Is to Come.* Ed. James Blanton Wharey and Roger Sharrock. Oxford: Oxford University Press, 1967.

Byrd, William, II. *History of the Dividing Line: A Journey to the Land of Eden and Other Papers.* New York: Macy-Masius, 1928.

Cable, George Washington. *Dr. Sevier.* Boston: J. R. Osgood, 1885.

———. *The Grandissimes.* 1880. Athens: University of Georgia Press, 1988.

———. *Old Creole Days.* 1879. New York: Charles Scribner's Sons, 1921.

Cajun Pride Swamp Tours. 9 Jan. 2002. <http://www.cajunprideswamptours.com>.

Campbell, Edward D. C. *The Celluloid South: Hollywood and the Southern Myth.* Knoxville: University of Tennessee Press, 1981.

Carson, Rachel. *Silent Spring.* Boston: Houghton Mifflin, 1962.

Cash, W. J. *The Mind of the South.* New York: Alfred A. Knopf, 1941.

Cherry, Wynn. "William Faulkner and Lillian Smith: Two Distinct Journeys." *Southern Quarterly* 35.4 (1997): 23–30.

Chesnut, Mary Boykin. *A Diary from Dixie.* New York, 1905. *Documenting the American South: The Southern Experience in Nineteenth-Century America.* Ed. Ji-Hae Yoon and Natalia Smith. 1997. Academic Affairs Lib., U of North Carolina, Chapel Hill. 11 Jan. 2005 <http://docsouth.unc.edu/chesnut/maryches.html>.

Clark, Thomas D. *The Greening of the South: The Recovery of Land and Forest.* Lexington: University Press of Kentucky, 1984.

Clark, William Bedford. "The Serpent of Lust in the Southern Garden." *Interracialism: Black-White Intermarriage in American History, Literature, and Law.* Ed. Werner Sollors. New York: Oxford University Press, 2000. 291–304.

Clifford, James. *The Predicament of Culture: Twentieth-Century Ethnography, Literature, and Art*. Cambridge: Harvard University Press, 1988.

―――. "Introduction: Partial Truths." *Writing Culture: The Poetics and Politics of Ethnography*. Berkeley: University of California Press, 1986. 1–26.

Comer, Krista. *Landscapes of the New West: Gender and Geography in Contemporary Women's Writing*. Chapel Hill: University of North Carolina Press, 1999.

Commager, Henry Steele. *Fifty Basic Civil War Documents*. Malabar: R. E. Krieger, 1965.

Conkin, Paul. "The South in Southern Agrarianism." *The Evolution of Southern Culture*. Ed. Norman V. Bartley. Athens: University of Georgia Press, 1988. 133–68.

Coupe, Lawrence. Introduction. *The Green Studies Reader: From Romanticism to Ecocriticism*. London: Routledge, 2001. 1–12.

Cowan, Tynes. "The Slave in the Swamp: Affects of Uncultivated Regions on Plantation Life." *Keep Your Head to the Sky: Interpreting African American Home Ground*. Ed. Grey Gundaker. Charlottesville: University Press of Virginia, 1998. 193–207.

Cowdrey, Albert E. *This Land, This South: An Environmental History*. Lexington: University Press of Kentucky, 1983.

Crapanzano, Vincent. "Hermes' Dilemma: The Masking of Subversion in Ethnographic Description." *Writing Culture: The Poetics and Politics of Ethnography*. Ed. James Clifford and George E. Marcus. Berkeley: University of California Press, 1986. 51–76.

Daniel, John W. *Robert E. Lee: An Oration*. Savannah, 1883.

Daniel, Pete. *Deep'n as It Come: The 1927 Mississippi River Flood*. New York: Oxford University Press, 1977.

Davis, Donald W. "Historical Perspective on Crevasses, Levees, and the Mississippi River." *Transforming New Orleans and Its Environs: Centuries of Change*. Ed. Craig E. Colten. Pittsburgh: University of Pittsburgh Press, 2000. 84–106.

Dennis, John V. *The Great Cypress Swamps*. Baton Rouge: Louisiana State University Press, 1988.

Dixon, Thomas. *The Leopard's Spots: A Romance of the White Man's Burden—1865–1900*. New York: Doubleday, Page, 1902.

Douglas, Mary. *Purity and Danger: An Analysis of Concepts of Pollution and Taboo*. New York: Frederick A. Praeger, 1966.

Drake, W. Magruder. Introduction. King i–xlviii.

DuBois, W. E. B. *The Souls of Black Folk*. Millwood: Kraus-Thomson Organization Limited, 1973.

Dunbar-Nelson, Alice Moore. "People of Color in Louisiana." 1916. *Creole: The History and Legacy of Louisiana's Free People of Color*. Baton Rouge: Louisiana State University Press, 2000. 3–9.

Dupré, Louis J. *Fagots from the Campfire*. Washington, DC, 1881. *Documenting the American South: The Southern Experience in Nineteenth-Century America*. Ed. Heather Bumbalough, Jill Kuhn, and Natalia Smith. 1998. Academic Affairs Lib., U of North Carolina, Chapel Hill. 11 Jan. 2005 <http://docsouth.unc.edu/dupre.html>.

Edel, Leon. Introduction. *The American Scene*. By Henry James. Bloomington: Indiana University Press, 1968. i–xiv.

Evans, David. "'The Bear' and the Incarnation of America." *Faulkner and the Natural World: Faulkner and Yoknapatawpha, 1996.* Ed. Donald R. Kartiganer and Ann J. Abadie. Jackson: University Press of Mississippi, 1999. 179–97.

Faulkner, William. *Faulkner in the University: Class Conferences at the University of Virginia, 1957–1958.* Ed. Frederick L. Gwynn and Joseph L. Blotner. New York: Vintage Books, 1959.

———. *Go Down, Moses.* New York: Vintage Books, 1990.

Fiedler, Leslie. *Love and Death in the American Novel.* 1960. New York: Stein and Day, 1966.

Floyd, Samuel A., Jr. *The Power of Black Music.* New York: Oxford University Press, 1995.

Fox, Richard. *Recapturing Anthropology: Working in the Present.* Santa Fe: School of American Research Press, 1991.

Gabin, Jean S. *A Living Minstrelsy: The Poetry and Music of Sidney Lanier.* Macon: Mercer University Press, 1985.

Garmon, Gerald M. "Roderick Usher: Portrait of the Madman as an Artist." *Poe Studies* 1 (1972): 11–14.

Gator Swamp Tours. 2002. 9 Jan. 2002 <http://www.gatorswamptours.com>.

Gautreaux, Tim. *The Next Step in the Dance.* New York: Picador, 1998.

———. "Novel Approach: Tim Gautreaux Takes 'The Next Step.'" *New Orleans Magazine* Mar. 1998: 31.

Gay, Peter. *Freud, Jews, and Other Germans: Masters and Victims in Modernist Culture.* New York: Oxford University Press, 1978.

Georgia Wildlife Federation. 1996. 7 Jan. 2002 <http://www.gwf.org/aboutus.htm>.

Giblett, Rod. *Postmodern Wetlands: Culture, History, Ecology.* Edinburgh: Edinburgh University Press, 1996.

Gladney, Margaret Rose. Introduction. *Killers of the Dream.* By Lillian Smith. New York: W. W. Norton, 1994. 1–10.

Gomez, Gay M. "Perspective, Power, and Priorities: New Orleans and the Mississippi River Flood of 1927." *Transforming New Orleans and Its Environs: Centuries of Change.* Ed. Craig E. Colten. Pittsburgh: University of Pittsburgh Press, 2000. 109–20.

Gordon, John Brown. *Reminiscences of the Civil War.* Atlanta, 1904. *Documenting the American South: The Southern Experience in Nineteenth-Century America.* Ed. Jennifer Kellerman, Jill Kuhn, and Natalia Smith. 1999. Academic Affairs Lib., U of North Carolina, Chapel Hill. 11 Jan. 2005 <http://docsouth.unc.edu/gordon/gordon.html>.

Grammer, John. *Pastoral and Politics in the Old South.* Baton Rouge: Louisiana State University Press, 1997.

Grant, Ulysses S. *Memoirs and Selected Letters.* New York: Library of America, 1990.

Gray, Richard. *Writing the South: Ideas of an American Region.* Baton Rouge: Louisiana State University Press, 1997.

Greenberg, Kenneth. *Honor and Slavery.* Princeton: Princeton University Press, 1996.

Guilds, John Caldwell. *Simms: A Literary Life.* Fayetteville: University of Arkansas Press, 1992.

Hanger, Kimberly S. "Coping in a Complex World: Free Black Women in Colonial New Orleans." *The Devil's Lane: Sex and Race in the Early South.* Ed. Catherine Clinton and Michelle Gillespie. New York: Oxford University Press, 1997. 218–31.

Hardin, Michael. "Standing Naked before the Storm: Linda Hogan's *Power* and the Critique of Apocalyptic Narrative." *From the Center of Tradition: Critical Perspectives on Linda Hogan.* Ed. Barbara J. Cook. Boulder: University Press of Colorado, 2003. 135–56.

Harper, Francis. Introduction. Bartram xvii–xxxvi.

Harrison, Beth. "Lillian Smith as Author and Activist." *Southern Quarterly* 35 (1997): 17–22.

Hemenway, Robert. *Zora Neale Hurston: A Literary Biography.* Chicago: University of Illinois Press, 1980.

Hey, Donald, and Nancy Philippi. *A Case for Wetland Restoration.* New York: Wiley, 1999.

Hobson, Fred. *Tell about the South: The Southern Rage to Explain.* Baton Rouge: Louisiana State University Press, 1983.

Hogan, Linda. *Power.* New York: W. W. Norton, 1998.

Honey Island Swamp Tours. 2002. 9 Jan. 2003 <http://www.honeyislandswamp.com>.

Hopkins, Charles F. "Hell and the Survivor." *American Heritage* Oct.–Nov. 1982: 78–93.

Humphreys, Margaret. *Yellow Fever and the South.* New Brunswick: Rutgers University Press, 1992.

Hurston, Zora Neale. *Dust Tracks on a Road.* 1942. New York: Harper-Perennial, 1991.

———. *Jonah's Gourd Vine.* 1934. New York: Harper-Perennial, 1990.

———. *The Sanctified Church.* Foreword by Toni Cade Bambara. Berkeley: Turtle Island, 1983.

Hutcheon, Linda. *Irony, Nostalgia, and the Postmodern.* 1997. *University of Toronto English Library.* Ed. Marc Plamondon and Ian Lancashire. University of Toronto. 11 Jan. 2005 <http://www.library.utoronto.ca/utel/criticism/hutchinp.html>.

Jackson, Camilla. Interview. *Born in Slavery: Slave Narratives from the Federal Writers Project, 1936–1938.* 23 May 2001. *American Memory.* Manuscript Division, Library of Congress. 8 June 2004 <http://memory.loc.gov/ammem/snhtml>.

Jackson, Kenneth T. *The Ku Klux Klan in the City, 1915–1930.* New York: Oxford University Press, 1967.

Jacobs, Harriet. *Incidents in the Life of a Slave Girl.* 1901. Introduction Valerie Smith. New York: Oxford University Press, 1988.

James, Henry. *The American Scene.* 1907. Bloomington: Indiana University Press, 1968.

Jameson, Fredric. *Postmodernism: Or, The Cultural Logic of Late Capitalism.* Durham: Duke University Press, 1992.

Jefferson, Thomas. *Notes on the State of Virginia.* 1787. New York: Penguin Classics, 1999.

Johnson, Kendall. " 'Dark Spot' in the Picturesque: The Aesthetics of Polygenism and Henry James's 'A Landscape Painter.' " *American Literature* 74 (2002): 59–87.

Jones, Anne Goodwyn. *Tomorrow Is Another Day: The Woman Writer in the South, 1859–1936.* Baton Rouge: Louisiana State University Press, 1981.

Jones, Suzanne. Introduction. Cable, *The Grandissimes* i–xv.

Kartiganer, Donald M. Introduction. *Faulkner and the Natural World: Faulkner and Yoknapatawpha, 1996.* Ed. Kartiganer and Ann J. Abadie. Jackson: University Press of Mississippi, 1999. vii–xx.

Kemble, Frances A. *Journal of a Residence on a Georgia Plantation. Principles and Privilege: Two Women's Lives on a Georgia Plantation.* Ed. Dana Nelson. Ann Arbor: University of Michigan Press, 1995. 1–337.

Kennedy, John Pendleton. *Swallow Barn: Or, A Sojourn in Old Dominion*. 1854. Introd. Lucinda MacKethan. Baton Rouge: Louisiana State University Press, 1986.

Kennedy, Richard. *Literary New Orleans: Essays and Meditations*. Baton Rouge: Louisiana State University Press, 1992.

———. *Literary New Orleans in the Modern World*. Baton Rouge: Louisiana State University Press, 1998.

King, Edward. *The Great South*. 1875. Baton Rouge: Louisiana State University Press, 1972.

Kirby, Jack. *Poquosin: A Study of Rural Landscape and Society*. Chapel Hill: University of North Carolina Press, 1995.

Kolodny, Annette. *The Land before Her: Fantasy and the Experience of the American Frontiers, 1630–1880*. Chapel Hill: University of North Carolina Press, 1984.

Kreyling, Michael. *Inventing Southern Literature*. Jackson: University Press of Mississippi, 1998.

Kristeva, Julia. *The Powers of Horror: An Essay on Abjection*. Trans. Louis Roudiez. New York: Columbia University Press, 1982.

Ladd, Barbara. *Nationalism and the Color Line in George W. Cable, Mark Twain, and William Faulkner*. Baton Rouge: Louisiana State University Press, 1996.

Lanier, Sidney. *Florida: Its Scenery, Climate, and History*. 1875. Gainesville: University of Florida Press, 1973.

———. *The Marshes of Glynn*. 1878. St. Petersburg: St. Petersburg Printing, 1971.

———. "The New South." *The Centennial Edition of the Works of Sidney Lanier*. Vol. 5. Baltimore: Johns Hopkins University Press, 1945. 334–38.

———. *Poems and Letters*. Ed. Charles R. Anderson. Baltimore: Johns Hopkins University Press, 1969.

LeConte, Joseph. *The Autobiography of Joseph LeConte*. Ed. William Dallam Armes. New York: D. Appleton, 1903.

Leopold, Aldo. *A Sand County Almanac*. 1948. New York: Ballantine, 1966.

Lewis, Henry Clay. *Odd Leaves from the Life of a Louisiana Swamp Doctor*. Baton Rouge: Louisiana State University Press, 1997.

Lewis, R. W. B. *The American Adam: Innocence, Tragedy, and Tradition in the Nineteenth Century*. Chicago: University of Chicago Press, 1955.

Lockridge, Kenneth A. *The Diary and Life of William Byrd II of Virginia, 1674–1744*. Chapel Hill: University of North Carolina Press, 1987.

"Louis Agassiz." *The National Academies Website*. 5 May 2002 <www.nationalacademies.org/history/members/agassiz.html>.

Love, Glen. *Practical Ecocriticism*. Charlottesville: University Press of Virginia, 2003.

Loveland, Anne C. *Lillian Smith: A Southerner Confronting the South*. Baton Rouge: Louisiana State University Press, 1986.

Lowe, John. *Jump at the Sun: Zora Neale Hurston's Cosmic Comedy*. Urbana: University of Illinois Press, 1997.

Lurie, Edward. Introduction. *Essay on Classification*. By Louis Agassiz. Cambridge: Belknap Press of Harvard University, 1962.

MacKethan, Lucinda. *The Dream of Arcady: Place and Time in Southern Literature*. Baton Rouge: Louisiana State University Press, 1980.

Mallard, Robert Q. *Plantation Life before Emancipation*. Richmond: Whittet and Shepperson, 1892.

Mann, Thomas. *Fighting with the Eighteenth Massachusetts: The Civil War Memoir of Thomas H. Mann*. Ed. John J. Hennessy. Baton Rouge: Louisiana State University Press, 2000.

Martin, Matthew. "The Two-Faced New South: The Plantation Tales of Thomas Nelson Page and Charles W. Chesnutt." *Southern Literary Journal* 30.2 (1998): 17–36.

Marx, Karl. "Speech at the Anniversary of the *People's Paper*." *The Marx-Engels Reader*. Ed. Robert C. Tucker. 2nd ed. New York: W. W. Norton, 1978. 577–78.

Marx, Leo. *The Machine in the Garden: Technology and the Pastoral Ideal in America*. New York: Oxford University Press, 1964.

Mathew, William. *Edmund Ruffin and the Crisis of Slavery in the Old South: The Failure of Agricultural Reform*. Athens: University of Georgia Press, 1988.

Matthews, John T. *The Play of Faulkner's Language*. Ithaca: Cornell University Press, 1982.

McGinnis, Adelaide. "Charles Bon: The New Orleans Myth Made Flesh." *Critical Essays on William Faulkner: The Sutpen Family*. Ed. Arthur F. Kinney. New York: G. K. Hall, 1996. 221–26.

Miller, David C. *Dark Eden: The Swamp in Nineteenth-Century American Culture*. New York: Cambridge University Press, 1989.

Mitchell, W. G. T. Introduction. *Landscape and Power*. Chicago: University of Chicago Press, 2002. 1–4.

Morris, Ann R., and Margaret M. Dunn. "Flora and Fauna in Hurston's Florida Novels." *Zora in Florida*. Ed. Steve Glassman and Kathryn Lee Seidel. Orlando: U of Central Florida, 1991. 1–12.

Muir, John. "Wild Wool." 1875. *Wildernet*. Ed. Thomas Thurston. 11 Jan. 2005 <http://pantheon.cis.yale.edu/~thomast/texts/wool.html>.

Munson Swamp Tours. 9 Jan. 2002 <http://www.munsonswamptours.com>.

Myers, Jeffrey. "Other Nature: Resistance to Ecological Hegemony in Charles W. Chesnutt's *The Conjure Woman*." *African American Review* 37 (2003): 5–20.

Nelson, Dana. Introduction. *Principles and Privilege: Two Women's Lives on a Georgia Plantation*. Ann Arbor: University of Michigan Press, 1995. xxi–li.

Nicholls, Peter. *Modernisms: A Literary Guide*. Basingstoke: Macmillan, 1995.

Olmsted, Frederick Law. *A Journey in the Seaboard Slave States in the Years 1853–1854, with Remarks on Their Economy*. 2 vols. New York: G. P. Putnam's Sons, 1904.

Orso, Ethelyn G. "Paradise Lost: Louisiana as Microcosm for the South in Fictional and Documentary Films." *Images of the South: Constructing a Regional Culture on Film and Video*. Ed. Karl G. Heider. Athens: University of Georgia Press, 1993. 9–23.

Page, Thomas Nelson. *In Ole Virginia, or "Marse Chan" and Other Stories*. 1895. Introd. Clyde Wilson. Nashville: J. S. Sanders, 1991.

Payne, J. P. "Lillian Smith's *Strange Fruit*." *Southern Quarterly*. 35 (1997): 9–15.

Person, H. S. *Little Waters: Their Use and Relations to the Land*. Washington, DC: Soil and Conservation Service, Resettlement Administration, and Rural Electrification Administration, 1936.

Peterkin, Julia. *Scarlet Sister Mary*. Indianapolis: Bobbs-Merrill, 1928.

Petry, Alice Hall. "Native Outsider: George Washington Cable." *Literary New Orleans: Essays and Meditations*. Ed. Richard S. Kennedy. Baton Rouge: Louisiana State University Press, 1992. 1–7.

Phagan, Patricia, ed. *The American Scene and the South: Paintings and Works on Paper, 1930–1946*. Athens: Georgian Museum of Art, University of Georgia. 1996.

Pilkington, John. "Nature's Legacy to William Faulkner." *The South and Faulkner's Yoknapatawpha: The Actual and the Apocryphal*. Ed. Evans Harrington and Ann J. Abadie. Jackson: University Press of Mississippi, 1977. 104–27.

Poe, Edgar Allan. "The Facts in the Case of M. Valdemar." 1845. *Great Short Works of Edgar Allan Poe*. New York: Harper & Row, 1970. 479–89.

———. "The Fall of the House of Usher." 1839. *Great Short Works of Edgar Allan Poe*. New York: Harper & Row, 1970. 216–37.

———. Rev. of *The Partisan*, by William Gilmore Simms. *Southern Literary Messenger* Jan. 1836. Rpt. in *Edgar Allan Poe: Essays and Reviews*. New York: Literary Classics of the United States, 1984. 897.

Porte-Crayon. "The Dismal Swamp." *Harper's New Monthly Magazine* Sept. 1856: 452–53.

Poser, Charles M., and George W. Bruyn. *An Illustrated History of Malaria*. New York: Parthenon, 1999.

President. Executive Order 11990. "Protection of Wetlands." *Federal Register* 42 (24 May 1977). 10 June. 2003 <http://www.epa.gov/owow/wetlands/regs/eo11990.html>.

Puterbaugh, Parke. *Southeastern Wetlands: A Guide to Selected Sites in Georgia, North Carolina, South Carolina, Tennessee, and Kentucky*. Alexandria: U.S. Environmental Protection Agency and the Tennessee Valley Authority, 1997.

Quinn, Arthur Hobson. *Edgar Allan Poe: A Critical Biography*. Baltimore: Johns Hopkins University Press, 1998.

Rinehart, Floyd, and Marion Rinehart. *Victorian Florida: America's Last Frontier*. Atlanta: Peachtree, 1986.

Rogers, Raymond A. *Nature and the Crisis of Modernity*. New York: Black Rose Books, 1994.

Rosenberger, Francis Coleman, Ed. *Virginia Reader: A Treasury of Writings, from the First Voyages to the Present*. New York: E. P. Dutton, 1948.

Royster, Charles. *The Fabulous History of the Dismal Swamp Company: A Story of George Washington's Times*. New York: Alfred A. Knopf, 1999.

Rubin, Louis D. "The Division of the Heart: George Washington Cable's *The Grandissimes*." *The Southern Literary Journal* 1.2 (1969): 27–47.

———. *The Edge of the Swamp: A Study in the Literature and Society of the Old South*. Baton Rouge: Louisiana State University Press, 1989.

———. "The Other Side of Slavery: Thomas Nelson Page's 'No Haid Pawn.'" *Studies in the Literary Imagination* 7 (1974): 95–99.

Ruffin, Edmund. *Agricultural, Geological, and Descriptive Sketches of Lower North Carolina and the Similar Adjacent Lands*. Raleigh: Institution for the Deaf and Dumb and the Blind, 1861.

———. *Agriculture, Geology, and Society in Antebellum South Carolina: The Private Diary of Edmund Ruffin, 1843*. Ed. William M. Mathew. Athens: University of Georgia Press, 1992.

———. "Observations Made during an Excursion to the Dismal Swamp." *Farmer's Register* 4 Jan. 1837: 514–30.

———. "Southern Agricultural Exhaustion and its Remedy." *DeBow's Review* 14.1 (1853): 34–46.

Schama, Simon. *Landscape and Memory.* New York: Vintage Books, 1996.

Schmid, James A. "Wetlands as Conserved Landscapes in the U.S." *Cultural Encounters with the Environment: Enduring and Evolving Geographic Themes.* Ed. Alexander B. Murphy and Douglas L. Johnson, with the assistance of Viola Haarmann. Lanham: Rowman and Littlefield, 2000. 133–56.

Schneider, Stephen H., and Lynne Morton. *The Primordial Bond.* New York: Plenum Press, 1981.

Sesonke, Alexander. "Jean Renoir in Georgia: *Swamp Water.*" *Georgia Review* 36 (1982): 24–66.

Shuffleton, Frank. Introduction. *Notes on the State of Virginia.* By Thomas Jefferson. New York: Penguin Classics, 1999. vii–xxxii.

Simms, William Gilmore. *The Life of Francis Marion.* Freeport: Books for Libraries Press, 1971.

———. Rev. of *Odd Leaves from the Life of a Louisiana Swamp Doctor,* by Henry Clay Lewis. *Southern Quarterly Review* 17 (1850): 537.

———. *The Partisan: A Romance of the Revolution.* 1835. Chicago: Donohue Henneberry, 1890.

———. *Woodcraft.* 1854. New York: W. W. Norton, 1961.

Simpson, Lewis. *The Brazen Face of History.* Baton Rouge: Louisiana State University Press, 1980.

———. *The Dispossessed Garden: Pastoral and History in Southern Literature.* Athens: University of Georgia Press, 1975.

———. *The Fable of the Southern Writer.* Baton Rouge: Louisiana State University Press, 1987.

———. "New Orleans as Literary Center: Some Problems." *Literary New Orleans: Essays and Meditations.* Ed. Richard Kennedy. Baton Rouge: Louisiana State University Press, 1992. 76–88.

Singal, Daniel. *The War Within: From Victorian to Modernist Thought in the South, 1919–1945.* Chapel Hill: University of North Carolina Press, 1982.

Smith, Lillian. *Killers of the Dream.* 1949. New York: W.W. Norton, 1994.

———. *Strange Fruit.* New York: Reynal and Hitchcock, 1944.

———. *The Winner Names the Age: A Collection of Writings by Lillian Smith.* New York: W. W. Norton, 1978.

Soper, Kate. *What Is Nature?* Oxford: Blackwell, 1995.

Spivey, Ted. *Revival: Southern Writers and the Modern City.* Gainesville: University of Florida Press, 1986.

Stowe, Harriet Beecher. *Dred: A Tale of the Great Dismal Swamp.* Ed. Judie Newman. Halifax: Ryburn, 1992.

Sundquist, Eric J. *The Hammers of Creation: Folk Culture in Modern African-American Fiction.* Athens: University of Georgia Press, 1993.

"Swamp." *Oxford English Dictionary.* 2005 <http://dictionary.OED.com>.

Swamp Water. Screenplay by Dudley Nichols. Dir. Jean Renoir and Henri Pichel. Prod. Daryl Zanuck. Perf. Walter Brennan, Walter Huston, Anne Baxter, Dana Andrews, and Eugene Pallette. 20th Century Fox, 1941.

Toomer, Jean. *Cane.* Ed. Darwin Turner. New York: W. W. Norton, 1988.

————. *The Wayward and the Seeking: A Collection of Writings by Jean Toomer*. Ed. Darwin Turner. Washington, DC: Howard University Press, 1980.

Vileisis, Ann. *Discovering the Unknown Landscape: A History of America's Wetlands*. Washington, DC: Island Press, 1997.

Viosca, Percy. "Louisiana Wetlands and the Value of their Wildlife and Fishery Resource." *Ecology* 9 (1928): 216–29.

Wall, Cheryl A. *Women of the Harlem Renaissance*. Bloomington: Indiana University Press, 1995.

The War for States' Rights. Ed. Kevin Eisert. 2 May 2002 <http://civilwar.bluegrass.net/battles-campaigns/1863/630120-22.html>.

Waselkov, Gregory, and Kathryn Braund, eds. *William Bartram on the Southeastern Indians*. Lincoln: University of Nebraska Press, 1995.

Watson, Ritchie. " 'The Difference of Race': Antebellum Race Mythology and the Development of Southern Nationalism." *Southern Literary Journal* 35.1 (2002): 1–13.

Waud, A. R. "On Picket Duty in the Swamps of Louisiana." *Harper's Weekly* 9 May 1863: 302.

Whitman, Walt. *Leaves of Grass and Other Writings*. Ed. Michael Moon. New York: W. W. Norton, 2002.

Wilds, John, Charles Dufour, and Walter Cowan. *Louisiana: Yesterday and Today*. Baton Rouge: Louisiana State University Press, 1996.

Williams, Susan Millar. *A Devil and a Good Woman, Too: The Lives of Julia Peterkin*. Athens: University of Georgia Press, 1997.

Williamson, Joel. *New People: Miscegenation and Mulattoes in the United States*. New York: Macmillan, 1980.

Wilson, Clyde. Introduction. *In Ole Virginia, or "Marse Chan" and Other Stories*. By Thomas Nelson Page. Nashville: J. S. Sanders, 1991.

Wittenberg, Judith Bryant. "*Go Down, Moses* and the Discourse of Environmentalism." *New Essays on Go Down, Moses*. Ed. Linda Wagner-Martin. New York: Cambridge University Press, 1996. 49–72.

Woodward, Comer Vann. *The Burden of Southern History*. Baton Rouge: Louisiana State University Press, 1968.

Wyatt-Brown, Bertram. *Southern Honor: Ethics and Behavior in the Old South*. New York: Oxford University Press, 1982.

INDEX

Abolitionists, xii, 79; in "No Haid
  Pawn," 83
Acadians (Cajuns), xvi, xviii, xxiv, 10,
  66–67, 177, 179. *See also* Gautreaux, Tim
Agriculture, 41–46, 100, 108, 109
Andersonville Prison Camp, xx, 64
Andrews, Dana, 170
Andrews, Eliza, xxi; *War-Time Journal of a
  Georgia Girl*, 69–74
Army Corps of Engineers, 111, 173, 174
Atchafalaya Basin, 107, 109
Attack of the Giant Leeches (film), 164

Barthes, Roland, 136
Bartram, William, xix, 14, 31, 33–36, 40, 44,
  77, 163
Baudrillard, Jean, xxiv, 153, 176, 179, 180,
  185; *Simulacra and Simulation*, 153, 161
Bell, Vereen, xxiv; *Swamp Water*, xxiv,
  165–68, 170–72
Benning, Henry, 41
Brennan, Walter, 170
Bryant, William Cullen (*Picturesque
  America*), 75
Buffon, George-Louis Leclerc, Comte de, 8
Bunyan, John, xiv
Burnside, Ambrose, 63
Byrd, William, II, xvii, xix, xx, 14, 26–33,
  34, 35, 37, 42, 43, 44, 48, 68, 77, 162;

A History of the Dividing Line, 28–33, 48,
  53, 62

Cable, George Washington, xxii, 62, 84–98,
  101, 110, 161; "The Convict Lease System
  in the Southern States," 88; "The
  Freedman's Case in Equity," 88; *The
  Grandissimes*, xxii, 87–98; "Jean-Ah
  Poquelin," xxii, 90–93; *Old Creole Days*,
  87–88, 90–93
Carson, Rachel (*Silent Spring*), 172
Carter, Jimmy, 115, 174
Cash, W. J., 5, 15, 42, 73, 164
Cavalier Ideology, xvii, xx, 3–7, 14–17, 24,
  26, 41, 47–51, 56, 74, 77, 82, 172
Chesnut, Mary Boykin (*Diary from
  Dixie*), 69
Chesnutt, Charles, 125
Civil War, xxi, 62–70
Clifford, James, 28–29
Confessions of Nat Turner, The, 11
Conservation, 112–14, 176; Agricultural
  Conservation Program (1944), 115;
  Civilian Conservation Corps (CCC), 114;
  Executive Order 11990, 115, 174. *See also*
  Environmentalist Movement
Cooke, Morris, 114
Corman, Roger, 165
Curse of the Swamp Creature (film), 164

Dante Alighieri, xiv
Darrow, Clarence, 117
Davis, Jefferson, 6
Disston, Hamilton, 108, 109
"Dixie Highway," 109
Dixon, Thomas, 78, 116; *The Clansman*, 79;
    The Leopard's Spots, 79, 116
Douglas, Mary, xviii, xx, 9–10, 33, 61, 93,
    120, 149
DuBois, W. E. B., xxiii, 138; *Souls of Black
    Folk*, 125–27, 130
Ducks Unlimited, 173
Dupré, Louis, 65

Eatonville, Fla., 130, 138
Ecocriticism, xi, xxv, 181–82, 188
Emerson, Ralph Waldo, 172
Environmental Protection Agency, 174
Environmentalist Movement, xv, xxiv,
    112–13, 123, 153, 163, 171–74; "Bubba
    Environmentalists," 172–73
Ethnography, 28–29
Everglades, 108, 109, 112, 173

Faulkner, William, xxiii, xxiv, 121, 123, 162,
    164; *Go Down, Moses*, xxiv, 124, 138,
    149–61, 165, 167, 171, 172, 192, 193
Fiedler, Leslie, 4
Fish and Wildlife Service, 174
Fitzhugh, George, 74, 98
Fugitive Agrarians, xxii, xxiii, 118–21, 133,
    139, 140; Davidson, Donald, 118; *I'll Take
    My Stand*, 100, 118–19; Ransom, John
    Crowe, 118–20; Warren, Robert Penn, 118

Game and Fish Commission, 173
Gautreaux, Tim, xxiv; *The Next Step in the
    Dance*, 182–88, 193
Georgia Wildlife Federation, 173
Gone with the Wind (film), 164
Gordon, John Brown, 65–66
Grant, Ulysses S., 63–64
Great Depression, 115, 123

Great Dismal Swamp, xiii, xix, 7, 14, 26,
    37–40, 162. *See also* Byrd, William, II;
    Great Dismal Swamp Company;
    Washington, George
Great Dismal Swamp Company, xiii, xix,
    26, 37–40, 55, 107
Greenberg, Clement, 136
Griffith, D. W. (*Birth of a Nation*), 116

Harlem Renaissance, xxiii, 103, 120, 123–25,
    129
Harrison, William H., *How to Get Rich in
    the South*, 107
Hogan, Linda, xxiv; *Power*, 182, 188–93
Honor, 4, 5. *See also* Cavalier Ideology
Hopkins, Charles F., 64–65
Hughes, Langston, 125
Hurston, Zora Neale, xxiii, 121, 123, 124,
    129–38, 149, 150, 152, 161, 164; *Dust Tracks
    on a Road*, 130; *Jonah's Gourd Vine*, xxiii,
    129–38; *The Sanctified Church*, 127

I Am a Fugitive from a Chain Gang (film),
    165

Jacobs, Harriet, xviii, 11–12
Jamestown, 25
Jefferson, Thomas, 7–8; *Notes on the State
    of Virginia*, 7–8
Jones, Ann Goodwyn, 17–18

Kemble, Frances (Fanny), xviii, 20–24
Kennedy, John Pendleton, xix, xx, 15, 51–55,
    57–61, 62, 161; *Swallow Barn*, 52–55,
    58–61, 62, 80, 84, 126, 138
King, Edward, *The Great South*, 75–78, 85,
    88, 89, 101, 104, 107
Ku Klux Klan, xxii, 115–17, 121, 122

L'Abadieville, Battle of, 67
Lanier, Sidney, xxii, 31, 63, 84, 98–103, 161,
    163, 176; "Corn," 100; *Florida: Its Scenery,
    Climate, and History*, 99–100; "The

Marshes of Glynn," 101–2; "The New South," 101
Laveran, Alphonse, 31
LeConte, Joseph, *Autobiography of Joseph LeConte*, 67–69
Lee, Robert E., 63
Leopold, Aldo, 150, 151
Lewis, Henry Clay, xix, 15–17
Locke, Alain, *The New Negro*, 125, 130
Louisiana Meadows Investment Company, 108

Malaria, xii, 31, 46, 49, 59–60, 64, 69
Mallard, Robert Q., *Plantation Life Before Emancipation*, 68
Mallarmé, Stéphane, 153
Mann, Thomas (Union Soldier), 64
Marion, Francis, 41, 44, 46, 48–50, 66
Maroons, xviii, 12–13, 180
Marx, Karl, 134
Meecker, Joseph Rusling, 75
Mencken, H. L., 73, 117, 145, 164; "The Sahara of the Bozart," 117
Miasma, xii, 9–10, 31, 46, 58, 59, 66, 69, 105
Milton, John, xiv, 18
Mississippi River Flood of 1927, 110–11
Modernism, 121–23, 136, 152, 163
Muir, John, 172

Native Americans, xv, xvi, xviii, xix, 10, 14; in Bartram, 33–36; in Byrd II, 32–34; in DuBois, 126; in Faulkner, 161; in Simms, 49. *See also* Hogan, Linda, *Power*
New Deal, 114, 173
New Orleans, La., xxi, 84–98, 110–12; drainage systems, 86, 111. *See also* Mississippi River Flood of 1927
Newman, Randy, 112
Nichols, Dudley, 167, 169, 170
Night Riders' War, 113

Okefenokee Swamp, 165, 169, 172, 175
Olmsted, Frederick Law, 12–14, 30

Page, Thomas Nelson, xxi, 78–79; *In Ole Virginia, or "Marse Chan" and Other Stories*, 79; "No Haid Pawn," 79–84
Pallette, Eugene, 170
"Pastoral republicanism" (John Grammer), 57
Percy, Walker, 183
Person, H. S., *Little Waters: Their Use and Relations to the Land*, 114
Peterkin, Julia, *Scarlet Sister Mary*, 144–46
Pichel, Henri, 171
Poe, Edgar Allan, xx, 48, 51–52, 55–61, 77; "The Facts in the Case of M. Valdemar," 56–57; "The Fall of the House of Usher," 57–61, 62, 80, 82; "The System of Dr. Tarr and Professor Fether," 57–58
Porte-Crayon, 12
Postmodernism, 180–81
Puritans, xiv, xv, 7

Quakerism, 33

Redeemer Governments, 117
Renoir, Jean, *Swamp Water*, 165, 168–71
Romanticism, 34
Ruffin, Edmund, xii, xix, 26, 41–46, 47, 55, 60, 61, 68, 98

Schama, Simon, xi, xix, 3, 40
Scopes Trial, 115, 117–18
Sigourney, Lydia, 18
Simms, William Gilmore, xix, xx, 14, 15, 26, 41, 42, 46–51, 58, 61, 62, 66, 69, 70; *Biography of Francis Marion*, 41, 46–50; *The Partisan*, 41, 46, 52; *Woodcraft*, 50–51
Simpson, O. H., 111
Slaves: as swamp laborers, xii, 38–40, 107; escaping into swamps, xvi, xviii, 10, 12–13. *See also* Maroons
Smith, Lillian, xxiii, xxiv, 121, 123, 138–48, 150, 161, 162, 167; "Humans in Bondage," 139; *Killers of the Dream*, 139–41, 148; *Strange Fruit*, xxiii, 124, 138, 140–48

Stowe, Harriet Beecher, xix, 11, 18–19, 40; *Dred: A Tale of the Great Dismal Swamp*, 11, 18–19, 24, 31, 40, 132; *Palmetto Leaves*, 74; *Uncle Tom's Cabin*, 116
Strachey, William, 25–26
Swamp: definitions of, xiii–xv; demographics, xvi; distinctions from other wetlands, xiii–xiv; distribution of, xiii; drainage, 105, 109, 110–15; environmental benefits of, xxiv, 113–14; field guides to, 175–76; in film, 163–65; flooding, 105, 110, 113–14; tourism, xxi, xxiv, 74, 75, 99, 176–80; in Union and Southern rhetoric, 40–41; "Vogue," 75, 108, 109
Swamp Country (film), 165
Swamp Fire (film), 165
Swamp Land Acts, 105–6, 108, 113, 114; and fraud, 106
Swamp Water (film), xxiv, 165, 167–71
Swamp Women (film), 164
Symbolists, 152

Talmadge, Eugene, 138
Thoreau, Henry David, xv, xxii, 3, 34, 98, 101, 150, 151, 163, 172

Timber Industry, 104–13, 122. *See also* Great Dismal Swamp Company
Toombs, Robert, 40
Toomer, Jean, xxiii, 138; *Cane*, 126–29, 133
Travel guides, 74, 75, 104
Twain, Mark, 88

United States Department of Agriculture (USDA), 115, 174

Viosca, Percy, 114
Virginia Colony, 7–8, 25
Virginia Company of London, 25

Washington, George, xii, xix, 37–40, 62. *See also* Great Dismal Swamp Company
Waud, A. R., 75
Webster, Daniel, 40
Wetland Reclamation. *See* Swamp Drainage
Whitman, Walt, xv

Yellow Fever, 105

Zanuck, Daryl, xxiv, 168–71